I0360878

# Tune My Heart to Sing

## Devotions for Church Choirs Based on the Revised Common Lectionary

**Wayne L. Wold**

Augsburg Fortress
Minneapolis

Tune My Heart To Sing
*Devotions for Church Choirs Based on the Revised Common Lectionary*
Wayne L. Wold

Copyright © 1997 Augsburg Fortress. All rights reserved. Except for brief quotations in critical articles or reviews, no part of this book may be reproduced in any manner without the prior written permission from the publisher or from the other copyright holders. Write to: Permissions, Augsburg Fortress, Box 1209, Minneapolis, MN 55440-1209.

Scripture quotations, unless otherwise noted, are from the New Revised Standard Version Bible © 1989 Division of Christian Education of the National Council of the Churches of Christ in the U.S.A. Used by permission.

*Revised Common Lectionary* copyright © 1992 Consultation on Common Texts (CCT), 1522 K Street NE, Suite 1000, Washington, D.C. 20005-1202. All rights reserved.

*God Is Praised in Music* by Wayne L. Wold, copyright © 1996 Abingdon Press. Used by permission.
Prayer for Church Musicians and Artists from *Lutheran Book of Worship,* copyright © 1978 Augsburg Fortress.

Prayers: Martin A. Seltz
Editors: Carol Carver, Lani Willis
Interior design: Lani Willis
Cover design: Lecy Design

Library of Congress Cataloging-in-Publication Data
Wold, Wayne L., 1954-
   Tune my heart to sing: devotions for church choirs based on the Revised Common Lectionary/Wayne L. Wold.
   p. cm.
  ISBN 0-8066-3613-0 (alk. paper)
   1. Choirs (Music)--Prayer-books and devotions--English.  2. Bible. N.T. Gospels--Meditations. I. Title.
BV4596.c48W65 1997
242'.69--dc21                                                       97-15984
                                                                                 CIP

The paper used in this publication meets the minimum requirements of American National Standard for Information Sciences—Permanence of Paper for Printed Library Materials, ANSI Z329.48-1984. ∞ ™

Printed in the U.S.A                      ISBN 0-8066-3613-0                       10-36130

02   01   00   99   98   97   1   2   3   4   5   6   7   8   9   0

# Table of Contents

# *Preface*

Choirs are found in parishes of most Christian denominations. Though each has its own unique character (and unique characters!), they do have some common characteristics.

- ❧ Choirs are made up largely of volunteers who have made a commitment to a time-intensive, often under-appreciated activity.

- ❧ Though the presence of choirs in worship is usually assumed, defining their role by pastors, choir directors, and even the singers themselves is difficult and often divisive.

- ❧ Because of the routine and vagueness of purpose that sometimes accompanies choir membership, keeping morale high and focus sharp can be challenging.

- ❧ A choir is an important arena for ministry. It shares in the ministry of worship, it has its own specialized means of ministering, and, at its best, it serves as a support group for its own members.

These devotions grew out of these realizations as I served parishes as a music director. I started the practice of opening each rehearsal with a brief meditation to center our thoughts and set the stage for what we would be preparing that evening. In my striving to make the meditations appropriate to specific seasons and festivals, I began to write them myself. Positive feedback from choir members at three different congregations kept me writing new ones and reworking old ones, using them even when we knew that every minute was crucial for working on upcoming music. Yes, rehearsal time is precious, but so are we, individually and collectively. I believe that focusing, learning, and praying together is time well spent. The following are principles that guided the formation of these devotions:

- ❧ They are short, requiring about two minutes to be read aloud (a little less in the Midwest, a little more in the South).

- ❧ They are based on the gospels of the three-year Revised Common Lectionary, used by most Christian denominations. The reading is briefly summarized or quoted in the body of the meditation, making it unnecessary to read aloud the entire gospel at the rehearsal, and saving its specialness for Sunday worship.

- ❧ They are conversational in style. As brief commentaries for a specific audience and occasion, they attempt to be more reflective and meditative than theological or exegetical.

- ❧ They quote hymns that relate to the day. Emphasis is given to hymns used across denominational lines, across the ages, and across the globe. These may or may not be the exact hymns your choir will sing the next Sunday, but they still communicate as devotional poetry, and they pattern the partnership between what is spoken and what is sung.

- ❧ They emphasize the choir's role in worship. While trying to avoid taking a specific denominational point of view, my convictions about the choir as worship leaders, the centrality of worship to all aspects of congregational and personal life, the balance between objectivity and subjectivity in worship and music, music as rich metaphor, and the necessity of high standards do, I hope, shine through in helpful ways.

These devotions are, as noted earlier, intended for use at the beginning of choir rehearsals. Who should be the reader/leader will be for you to decide. Many directors will want to take that pastoral role themselves. Some choirs may have a designated "chaplain." Or, members may wish to take turns in this role. When using these myself, I always concluded with the proper prayer of the day (collect). The salutation and response—"The Lord be with you," "And also with you"—would be an appropriate way to move from devotion to closing prayer. Others may wish to offer a different prayer, create their own, or omit one altogether. A collection of seasonal prayers, composed by Martin Seltz, is included in this resource.

I offer *Tune My Heart to Sing* to the glory of God and for the enrichment of God's singing people everywhere.

Wayne L. Wold
Hagerstown, Maryland
Second Sunday of Easter, 1997

"O Sons and Daughters, Let Us Sing!"

# CYCLE A

# First Sunday in Advent

Happy New Year! We live in many "years"—fiscal years, calendar years, school and program years. The beginning of the church year goes little noticed compared to the others, even to many Christians. And maybe that is all right in one sense. Our weekly choir rehearsals and weekly worship services go on uninterrupted; we come out of habit. For many of us, church has become so automatic that it would take more of a conscious effort to stay away than it does to come.

This Sunday we will hear Jesus tell his disciples, "Keep awake, therefore, for you do not know on what day your Lord is coming." Many choir directors would like the phrase "keep awake, therefore" to be the unwavering motto of every choir member. We all know the consequences of not staying alert. We might make weak entrances or sloppy cut-offs, jumbling the message we had hoped to convey. We might not notice if we are asked to sing softer, or louder, or smoother, or more accented, or to speed up, or to slow down—making our message less convincing than it could be. Not being awake and aware, we miss the opportunity to do something spontaneously, a gift and sign of the Spirit's presence.

So it is with much of life. We probably miss opportunities daily because we are not ready or able to see the obvious signs around us. These missed opportunities are unfortunate, but they are nothing compared to the "biggie"—watching for Christ to come in the end time. Philipp Nicolai, in what is known as the "King of Chorales," advises:

> The bridegroom comes! Awake;
> Your lamps with gladness take! Alleluia!
> Prepare yourselves to meet the Lord,
> Whose light has stirred the waiting guard.
>
> "Wake, Awake, for Night Is Flying"

The quest to be ready has been undertaken in many ways: Some sit idly by, not becoming involved in any activity that might distract them from "watching;" some search for signs to try get some inside information on the time and place of Christ's return. Are these the best ways to respond to the call? Perhaps we better look at what follows the command to "keep awake." It concludes, ". . . for you do not know on what day your Lord is coming." What a twist! Christ tells us even he does not know the time. That should help us focus on more appropriate and faithful ways to be ready.

We are most ready when being ready becomes a habit. We are ready not by avoiding busyness but by being busy for the kingdom; not by being preoccupied with ourselves but by taking our eyes off our own interests for the sake of being Christ for others; not by being "so heavenly minded that we are no earthly good." Rather, we live and work in this world, watching and worshipping, singing and praying, knowing there are tasks to be done until the time heaven comes to us.

# Second Sunday in Advent

*For the herald's voice is crying*
*In the desert far and near,*
*Calling us to true repentance,*
*Since the Kingdom now is here.*

"Comfort, Comfort Now My People"

So we sing in Johann Olearius' great Advent hymn, which considers the life and ministry of John the Baptist. In the opening lines of this Sunday's gospel we hear his preaching once again. We simultaneously love and hate to hear his admonition, "Repent, for the kingdom of heaven has come near." He calls the Pharisees and Sadducees a "brood of vipers." He tells of the coming one who will clear the threshing floor, gathering the wheat but burning the chaff. His masterful preaching at once attracts and cuts through us, causing both anticipation and anguish. As some have remarked, "It comforts the afflicted and afflicts the comfortable."

Christians place high expectations on preaching, knowing that proclamation needs the precision of well-chosen, well-delivered words to convey the subtleties of the gospel message. Preaching at its best is not merely a religious lecture or an emotional soliloquy—it is a powerful means of grace.

But before we heap any more superlatives on preaching we should consider John's other activities. Even his nickname reminds us that he was a "baptizer." His words engaged the mind, his actions blessed the body, and both transformed the soul. This partnership of words and actions made for an irresistible call to experience the grace of God. Different traditions in different times and places have experimented with, fought over, and even caused schisms over the relationship between speech and action in worship. It is with this same partnership and balance of word and sacrament that the contemporary church often still struggles.

Where does music fit into all this? Choirs do not deliver sermons or preside at baptisms or eucharists. But music can be an effective partner in both preaching and presiding. Preaching, sacraments, and music are each potent enough to minister on their own. But, when combined in non-competitive partnership, they enrich and magnify each other. They are parables in themselves on how we are to live—drawing our greatest fulfillment by giving ourselves to each other and by committing to a partnership for the sake of something greater than our individual selves.

May this Advent find us in true partnership with each other as we join with preachers, presiders, and baptizers to prepare the way of the Lord.

# Third Sunday in Advent

In the continuing proclamation of the Advent message, we shall hear more this Sunday of John the Baptist. This time, he is in prison, the place where he will soon experience death. Hearing of the deeds of Jesus, he sends his disciples to ask, "Are you the one who is to come, or are we to wait for another?"

Jesus answers, "Go and tell John what you hear and see: the blind receive their sight, the lame walk, the lepers are cleansed, the deaf hear, the dead are raised, and the poor have good news brought to them." Swedish hymnwriter Frans Mikael Franzén interprets these works of Jesus:

> *His is no earthly kingdom;*
> *It comes from heaven above.*
> *His rule is peace and freedom*
> *And justice, truth, and love.*
>
> "Prepare the Royal Highway"

It looks as though both Jesus and John are dealing with evidence. John sends the questioning messengers because he has heard of Jesus' deeds but still wants assurance. Jesus answers the question by telling the messengers to go and tell John what they themselves have seen and heard. Jesus expects that his words and deeds will speak for themselves.

Ours is an age of skepticism. There are actually organizations made up of members who doubt that the world is round, or do not believe that astronauts have actually set foot on the moon, or even refuse to believe that the Holocaust happened, all because they themselves have no first-hand evidence as proof. The truths of biblical witness and the reliability of church teachings have always been ripe for skeptics from inside and outside the church. The principle seems to be, "If I have not experienced it, and if I cannot trust the witness of others, then it must not be true or worth my trust."

Christ does call us at times to a blind faith—believing in that which is removed from our experience or even opposite of our rational thought. But thank God for those times when the object of our faith is made known in clear, believable ways.

Did the first Christians have an easier time believing because they could see and hear Jesus and his works among them? Perhaps, but we have a different advantage over them; we know a bigger portion of salvation's story. We know how it turns out, so in our observations of the world around us, our vision can be even more panoramic. We, too, can see the healing brought to the sick, the good news being brought to the poor, the lives changed by the Spirit.

In our music and worship leadership, we are a part of the command to "go and tell" of the Christ. It will be heard by ears that need to hear it and seen by eyes that long to see it—possibly even our very own!

# Fourth Sunday in Advent

Have you ever tried to formulate a definition of the word "music?" Avid amateurs and degreed professionals alike would surely struggle when trying to define something so ubiquitous, yet so nebulous. "You have to experience it to understand it," we might say, "and even then words will fail us when we try to define it." Perhaps that is the greatest sign of the power of music—what it conveys cannot be expressed by words; it speaks a different, often deeper language.

Joseph might have been equally hard-pressed to explain his actions as described in this Sunday's gospel. We will hear recounted his willingness to remain engaged to the pregnant Mary, his decision to marry her, and his naming the baby boy "Jesus." What influenced him to take such remarkable actions? He got his direction from an angel who appeared to him in a dream! Dreams and angels served Joseph well, for they would later warn him of Herod's murderous plan, and then, when all was safe, signal that it was time to return from Egypt. If we could ask Joseph what these dreams were like and how he could have placed so much faith in them, his answer would probably be similar to our attempts at defining music. "You have to experience it yourself to understand," he might say.

We usually describe as "experiential" those faith traditions which place all or most emphasis on feelings, experiences, and an inner personal communication with God. At the opposite pole are the "creedal" traditions, those with carefully worked-out theologies, striving for universal truths that transcend the individual. Often there are tensions between the objective and subjective camps that can be found between and within denominations, congregations, and even choirs.

Does Joseph fit the category of an experientialist because he placed so much importance on his dreams and his feelings about them? Probably not; he was surely well-grounded in the Jewish scriptures and traditions. Joseph represents for us one who kept both the mind and the heart engaged in a healthy tension, checking and informing each other.

Worship benefits from a similar balance. Music and liturgies that are well-crafted and rendered with reverence still need that spark of the Spirit; but the Spirit surely works wonders through our theologies, lectionaries, and liturgies of grace-filled actions, words, and music.

May our minds and hearts be fully engaged as the season of Advent comes to a close and as we enter even more fully into the mysteries of the incarnation. Martin Luther's hymn, based on St. Ambrose, sings:

> *Savior of the nations, come;*
> *Show the glory of the Son!*
> *Every people, stand in awe;*
> *Praise the perfect Son of God.*
>
> "Savior of the Nations, Come"

# The Nativity of Our Lord

*Silent night, holy night!*
*All is calm, all is bright*

"Silent Night, Holy Night!"

It is rather ironic that this hymn has become one of the most popular Christmas songs of all time. We hear it in churches, on television specials, and piped into the mall. It is everywhere! Yes, it does have a worthy text and a pleasant tune, and they do complement each other. The ironic part lies in its description of the night. We have a hard enough time picturing a Christmas night that is holy and bright, much less one that is calm. And silent? That hymn must be for those who lived in ages past, not for our modern, noisy days. Or maybe it still speaks to the "worship consumers," those folks in our congregation who just show up for a Christmas worship experience. Pastors, musicians, and other worship leaders are not meant to understand a silent, holy night, where all is calm and bright.

We have worked hard in our preparations for leading Christmas worship. We do it out of commitment and contracts, out of heart and habit. We give it as a gift to our God, to our congregation, and to ourselves. Celebrating and proclaiming the incarnation of our God is worth all we can give and so much more. We would probably feel guilty if we did experience a calm, restful, stress-free Christmas.

If that is the type of Christmas we think we want, we should think again. What was so calm about being in a strange town at the time a baby is to be born? What is so stress-free about trying to find a room in a sold-out town? What is so silent about animals? And, if the child Jesus was resting so quietly, why does so much of our Christmas music keep telling him to hush up and go to sleep?

The calm, the silence, the peace of Christmas is so noticeable because it is the exception; it stands in stark contrast to its surroundings, as much now as it did then. Peace is present, not in absence of its competition, but amidst it.

Joseph Mohr did not author "Silent Night, Holy Night" because he had nothing else to do or because he was so inspired by the sense of calm and peace around him. He created it frantically, on the very day it was needed, upon finding that the church's organ was broken and the scheduled music could not be used. The organist, Franz Gruber, was probably not thrilled when his pastor showed up with the news of the organ's condition and asked for a new tune on the spot. Christmas Eve was not the time to discuss job descriptions, unreasonable expectations, or staff relations. All was probably not calm nor bright as they rushed to write, prepare, and perform their new work that very evening. But, we hope that they were able to experience at least a small amount of the heavenly peace their creation has brought to the world. May our music be such a generous gift to all we will touch.

# First Sunday after Christmas

The dreamer is back. In this Sunday's gospel we will hear of the flight of Joseph, Mary, and the young Jesus to Egypt. They go to escape the murderous Herod, who has ordered that all children under the age of two are to be killed. Once Herod has died, the holy family begins to return to Judea, but they detour and instead end up in Nazareth. At each important juncture of this remarkable journey, Joseph, as before, gets his life-saving directions from an angel who appears to him in a dream.

Joseph and Mary must have felt like puppets at times. Besides the announcements and instructions from the angels, they had prophecy to deal with. The flight to Egypt was for safety, but Matthew comments that it was also to fulfill the prophet's words, "Out of Egypt I have called my son." They change their return destination after discovering that Herod's son was now ruling in Judea. For safety they divert to Galilee. But Matthew again asserts that this was to fulfill the prophet's declaration, "He will be called a Nazarene." With fate seeming to control so much of their lives, Mary and Joseph must have wondered about their own destinies. How much of this was scripted, and how much up to them?

God found in Mary and Joseph the qualities that would allow God to not so much control them as to work through them. They were caring and nurturing parents, giving protection and freedom when necessary. They honored God's covenant with Israel, observing the rites of the temple and the synagogue. They walked with God, keeping an open relationship with the almighty power who had so drastically affected their lives. They had faith, trusting that the one who kept all promises was guiding them throughout this awesome adventure. And they were flexible; their motto could well have been "plans subject to change at any time." They probably disliked big sudden changes as much as we do, but all was secondary to answering God's call to bear the Word-made-flesh. A Hispanic folk song captures the bittersweet emotions of Jesus' parents:

> Oh, sleep now, holy baby, with your head against my breast;
> meanwhile the pangs of my sorrow are soothed and put to rest.
>
> "Oh, Sleep Now, Holy Baby"

Even so early in the Christmas season we are confronted with Herod. Must we give up the peace and beauty to dwell on the evil and ugly? Must the consonance of our Christmas Eve lullabies and pastorales give way for dissonance?

Just as dissonance and consonance interact to give music energy and vitality, playing the chords of sin and salvation side by side proclaim a life redeemed by God. Such a dramatic redemption God has planned for us, and so we journey forth in faith.

# Second Sunday after Christmas

Some folks say they are in the home building or home improvement business, but what they really mean is that they work on houses. Calling them homes makes it more pleasant and warm because of what the title conveys. We might recall Guest's poem "It takes a heap of living to make a house a home."

An author writes hundreds of pages of a story with great action and suspense, but the editor says the main character does not seem real. "Put some flesh and blood on him," the editor advises.

A politician tries to run a campaign using only signs and media ads. Her advisor tells her she better get out, meet folks, and "press some flesh" if she hopes to gain a following.

In choir we say we have to keep track of our music, but what we are referring to are pieces of paper printed with words and symbols. With them we plan to make music.

Rather than bother with a real instrument or work with a real accompanist, a church opts for pre-recorded soundtracks. The notes are perfect, the technology impressive, but the final product lacks a sense of presence. It's hard to take seriously a musical offering created at another time, at another place, and by anonymous musicians.

What is missing from an empty house, a dry novel, a distant politician, a piece of paper with symbols, or canned music? The human touch, the genuine article.

Such is the world described by St. John in the opening paragraphs of his Gospel. The world came into being through the Word, but the world knew him not. What was the Father to do? In the words of a Bohemian carol:

> *Into flesh is made the Word. Hallelujah!*
> *He, our refuge and our Lord. Hallelujah!*
> *On this day God gave us*
> *Christ, his Son, to save us.*
>
> "Let Our Gladness Have No End"

In the incarnation of Christ, God made the ultimate leap. The Word made Flesh makes all of human life the realm of God's presence. The divine has entered humanity's house and has made it a home.

# The Epiphany of Our Lord

A central symbol of the festival and season of Epiphany is the star. The vision of the Bethlehem star thrills those of every age. On this festival of Epiphany we will again hear of that brilliant glow which captured the attention of the Magi from the East. They came a long distance, from a foreign culture, not knowing exactly where they were going, but having enough trust in the holy sign to keep following it. That star did not disappoint them—it faithfully led them to the very doorway of the Christ they sought to worship and honor with precious gifts.

Stars are truly amazing things. From earliest history they have inspired astronomers and astrologers, navigators and nomads, poets and painters. To our eyes, stars are never static; they sparkle, change colors, and move with the passing of time and seasons. They seem alive. Science has taught us even more amazing things about stars. Those whose light we see now may not even be in existence anymore. Just like the saints, their legacy lives on. The imagery of stars enters into the church's hymnody, as well. The great Danish hymnwriter Nikolai Gruntvig wrote:

> As a star, God's holy Word
> Leads us to our King and Lord;
>> "Bright and Glorious Is the Sky"

German hymnwriter/composer Philipp Nicolai addresses Jesus:

> O Morning Star, how fair and bright!
> You shine with God's own truth and light,
> Aglow with grace and mercy!
>> "O Morning Star, How Fair and Bright!"

Contemporary American hymnwriter Kathleen Thomerson professes:

> God set the stars to give light to the world.
> The star of my life is Jesus.
>> "I Want to Walk as a Child of the Light"

Stars indeed are metaphors for Christ, for the gospel, for creation, and for our calling as Christians to let our lights shine in a dark world. The season when it is easy and even fashionable to shine has just passed. Many folks pack away their shine along with the tinsel and electric lights until next Christmas. But now, exactly when the rest of the world has hidden it all away, is the most important time for Christians to keep shining. Just how can we keep up our sparkle? We cannot do it on our own, for our light is not of our own making. Rather, we stay close to Christ, the true "star" of Christmas, for he is that life-giving presence which the world so desperately needs. And we stay close to each other in this church community, called to shine in work, worship, praise, song, and prayer to Christ, our light.

# The Baptism of Our Lord
## First Sunday after the Epiphany

Many of us can recall the decade-long news stories about the struggles of the working people in Poland. Their leaders' names became household words, and the name of their union gave new meaning to the word "solidarity." That word still brings to mind images of struggling, standing firm, banding together, working for just causes, and identifying with each other. The people came to trust in the union and join its cause not so much because of its name, as good as it was, but because of its actions. The people heard with their ears and saw with their eyes that this union was of them and for them.

This Sunday we will hear of an even greater pledge of solidarity. Once again we will proclaim and celebrate the beginning of Jesus' public ministry as he is baptized by John in the Jordan River. The Spirit descends like a dove, and a voice from heaven proclaims, "This is my Son, the Beloved, with whom I am well pleased." Jesus' baptism is the great sign that God is in solidarity with him.

Though he is God's beloved Son, Jesus still comes to be baptized. Who would have thought that Jesus would need to be baptized? Surely not John, who felt himself unworthy to even untie the thong of his sandal. Surely we would not have guessed it—we who are baptized for the forgiveness of sins and into the death and resurrection of this very Jesus. F. Pratt Green explores this paradox in a hymn:

> When Jesus came to Jordan to be baptized by John,
> He did not come for pardon but as the Sinless One.
> He came to share repentance with all who mourn their sins,
> To speak the vital sentence with which good news begins.

"When Jesus Came to Jordan"

Jesus' baptism is an example of what we are called to do. His and our baptisms are the source and sustenance of our ministries on this earth. His and our baptisms are the proclamation of God's solidarity with us in this life, in our deaths, and in the life to come. In our baptisms, God is well pleased; it is the assurance that God's promises are true. And that is a pledge of solidarity worth singing about!

Matthew 3:13-17

# Second Sunday after the Epiphany

So much of the church's liturgy comes from the Bible. The "Gloria in Excelsis" finds its roots in the song of the angels over Bethlehem. "Worthy Is Christ" draws images from the Book of Revelation. The "Sanctus," or "Holy, Holy, Holy Lord" comes from Isaiah's vision in the temple. The list could go on with many more examples of how our worship grows from and is rooted in Holy Scripture.

In this Sunday's gospel we will hear the basis for an especially beloved portion of the church's liturgy—the "Agnus Dei." As John the Baptist sees Jesus coming toward him, he calls out, "Here is the Lamb of God who takes away the sin of the world!" Again the next day, as he is speaking with two of his disciples, he sees Jesus and exclaims, "Look, here is the Lamb of God!"

John was one of the first to know the true identity of Jesus. He had long proclaimed him, yet he was still awe-struck in his presence. His first response indicates his own deep emotions at seeing the Messiah. His second response is noteworthy in that it begins with the imperative "Look!" It is as if the first encounter was personally transforming; but by the second time he was ready to share the excitement. "Look, here is the Lamb of God!"

Just whom was John telling to look? First of all he told two of his own disciples. According to the biblical record, the two then became followers of Jesus, and they went with him for the rest of the day. The gospel-writer tells us that one of the two was Andrew, who soon found his brother Simon Peter and said to him, "We have found the Messiah!" John's call to "behold the Lamb of God" soon saw great fruits as his own disciples joined the growing crowd who followed Jesus.

Who else was John telling to look? Every generation since his own has beheld and embraced Christ as the Lamb of God. Just as John was moved by the Spirit to tell others, the pattern continues, and it shows no signs of letting up.

As Christians we have the opportunity and responsibility to see and know this Lamb of God and to call the world to come and see. By singing "Lamb of God" as we receive Holy Communion, we are reminded that in this meal Christ promises to make himself known to us. Through the proclamation of the word and the celebration of the sacraments, through our commitment to worship and music ministry, and through our witnessing and living, we too say, "Look, here is the Lamb of God!" With hymnwriter Elizabeth Cruciger's help, we can pray:

> *Awaken, Lord, our spirit to know and love you more.*
> *In faith to stand unshaken, in spirit to adore.*
> "The Only Son from Heaven"

# Third Sunday after the Epiphany

The day-to-day ministries of Jesus as he lived on this earth are often summarized as three activities. The gospels for the Epiphany season contain these descriptions often, and this Sunday we shall hear the reading conclude, "Jesus went throughout Galilee, teaching in their synagogues and proclaiming the good news of the kingdom and curing every disease and every sickness among the people." Teaching, proclaiming, and curing—also known as teaching, preaching, and healing—are the three action verbs used to describe Jesus' work. We might want to call them "high-action" verbs, considering all they represent.

Teaching has been and remains a high priority for Christians. Through education minds are developed, ideas are grown, worldviews are expanded, life is enhanced, and skills are honed for the good of God's Kingdom. By his teaching, Jesus gave us an example to follow and placed his noble blessing on our ministry of teaching.

Preaching is a treasured means of grace in the church. Artful preaching gives inspiration and direction, focus and fortitude. By his preaching, Jesus gave us an example to follow and placed his noble blessing on our ministry of preaching.

What about healing? Our feelings today are often affected by those who exploit the miracle or take a showbiz approach. Many ignore the issue entirely rather than attempt to tread in such a sensitive area. Yet, by ignoring healing, a major portion of Jesus' earthly ministry is overlooked. Jesus' work is surely present in those who embody the healing presence of Christ. Some congregations offer the Service of the Word for Healing as a sign of God's care for the whole person—mind, body, and spirit. By his healing, Jesus gave us an example to follow and placed his noble blessing on our ministry of healing.

How can we be a part of these basic components of Jesus' ministry? Many opportunities exist in all three areas, but we should not overlook the fact that, in music ministry, we are involved in all three. We teach by example in our worship leadership and by bringing to the people the great words and music of the church. We preach the gospel when we conduct ourselves in a manner that shows us to be servants of God, of the worshipping community, and of each other. And we heal. We give of ourselves knowing that well-crafted, well-delivered music has the power to lift hearts to God and mend broken relationships. Music expresses the ecstasy that is too high and the sigh that is too deep for words. With the words of hymnwriter Martin Franzmann we pray that we may more fully take part in Christ's ministry:

> Give us lips to sing thy glory,
> Tongues thy mercy to proclaim,
> Throats that shout the hope that fills us,
> Mouths to speak thy holy name.
>> "Thy Strong Word"

Matthew 4:12-23

# Fourth Sunday after the Epiphany

As church musicians we don't do our work for the sake of getting compliments, as appreciated as they are when they do come our way. But have you ever received a compliment that seemed to have a touch of something besides good will? "You played better than usual today," or "The choir sounds almost as good as when the last director was here," are rather easy to label as "backhanded compliments."

How about, "The piece of music you did today sounded really hard." That one may take a while to sort out because it points out a primary paradox of the arts. No matter how hard it was to create, learn, or perform a piece of music, in the end it communicates best when it is rendered with ease. If it sounds hard, they probably detect the struggle and may have missed the message.

We need not resent paradox, for it is a common denominator of many great truths. In this Sunday's gospel we will hear paradox after paradox as Jesus delivers his famous "beatitudes." He says it is the poor who have the kingdom, it is the meek who will inherit the earth, it is the persecuted who should rejoice, and that, in countless other situations, things are not what they seem.

The arts have long been an effective means for expressing paradox. In the church's hymnody we find, for example, the poetry of Frank Mason North:

> *Where cross the crowded ways of life,*
> *Where sound the cries of race and clan,*
> *Above the noise of selfish strife,*
> *We hear your voice, O Son of Man.*
>
> "Where Cross the Crowded Ways of Life"

The single voice, heard over the struggling noise of humanity, is surely grace expressed in paradox.

More paradoxical truths can be found in the simple texture of chant: Diverse voices can sing different melodies and still somehow proclaim unity. Some traditions express faith within the restrictions of a pentatonic musical language. We look to the past and find new sounds; the rich look to the poor for new voices of the gospel. All these and more are paradoxes in the music with which we deal every day. They proclaim a God who became human, who died to give life, who departed this world in order to come again, yet is present whenever two or three are gathered in his name.

And so we gather again this week, still struggling to fathom and understand a God of such paradoxes, but finding here the blessing of God to be a blessing to each other.

# Fifth Sunday after the Epiphany

In our language classes we learned the difference between two figures of speech called simile and metaphor. Do you remember that a simile is when a comparison is made between two things using the words "as" or "like?" An example might be "The choir's singing sounded like a bulldozer." A metaphor boldly states that something is something else, such as, "The choir is a band of glorious angels." Such figures of speech add interest, of course, but they also make statements stronger and they highlight facets otherwise missed.

Jesus uses two metaphors in this Sunday's gospel. "You are the salt of the earth . . . You are the light of the world," he declares to his followers.

Salt is one of the most plenteous substances in the world. Using salt as a flavor enhancer and food preserver is something we share with people from ancient times.

And what about light? There are many celestial bodies and substances in nature that glow. And with the harnessing of electricity we can light up our buildings, parking lots, stadiums, vehicles, and even handbags. Light brings comfort and security whether in the blazing lights that surround a prison wall or a three-watt nightlight. Light makes us know and realize things otherwise left in the dark.

Salt and light—not many other commodities in this world are more plentiful or as simple. Hymnwriter Cesareo Gabarain includes even more of Jesus' metaphors in a song that begins:

> You are the seed that will grow a new sprout;
> you're a star that will shine in the night;
> you are the yeast and a small grain of salt,
> a beacon to glow in the dark.

"You Are the Seed/Sois la Semilla"

To be salt and light is the baptismal call for all Christians, and it is no less applicable to those who participate in the ministry of music. There is a lot of saltless music out there, and quite a few bland faces and lethargic voices could use some flavoring. There are many dimly lit choir lofts and organ benches that need a good jolt of energy. Well-constructed, well-performed music is salt and light to us and to those we lead in worship. To lose our saltiness or to hide our light under a bushel is to deny God rightful worship and to deny ourselves the joy of spreading the good news.

Nobody was saltier or more light-giving than Jesus. Left to our own devices our salt will lose its flavor and our lights will dim and finally go out. As usual, Jesus provides to us what he commands of us. In him, our shakers are constantly being filled and our batteries are charged and ever ready. Thanks be to God for the energizing means of grace!

# Sixth Sunday after the Epiphany
## Proper 1

There is a picture of God and the church that the media and the cynics love. It is of a God who hands out a list of "thou shalt nots," who sits in scorn of those who cannot live up to the list, and whose followers are either bland puppets or self-righteous hypocrites. Sadly, that is the view of many even inside the church.

"We are left with many gray areas," we argue. "Not everything is spelled out as succinctly as 'Thou shalt' or 'Thou shalt not.'" We find Christians on both sides of many issues, and each may claim to be based on Jesus' teachings. There are times when we wish that Jesus had been more precise on specific moral issues. Or, do we?

This Sunday's gospel gives us such a list, and in a manner quite unlike what we hear from Jesus' lips elsewhere in the scriptures. In seventeen verses Jesus condemns those who are angry or insulting, those who even think adulterous thoughts, those who divorce, and those who swear oaths. Do we feel any better knowing what some of God's standards are? We may wish we hadn't asked, after all.

God's expectations are high, and we need to know them so we realize what is good and can measure by how far we miss the mark. Once we realize we have no leg to stand on, our only course of action is to seek the mercy of God. We may flounder with hymn-writer Isaac Watts when he wrote:

> Oh, that the Lord would guide my ways
> To keep his statutes still!
> Oh, that my God would grant me grace
> To know and do his will!
>
> "Oh, that the Lord Would Guide My Ways"

Christ confirms that he has not come to relax or abolish the law, but to fulfill it. His own perfect life, sacrificed, has brought his imperfect followers the gift of God's perfect righteousness. In response to God's grace and mercy, we live our lives and sing our songs in praise, gratitude, and service.

# Seventh Sunday after the Epiphany
## Proper 2

Let us imagine that we are viewing a newly-decorated room. We notice that the colors match and the furnishings are well-balanced, and we can tell that the decorators obviously knew their charts and formulas for successful results. Yet, the room fails to really charm us; it is easy to leave and forget.

Or, perhaps we are at a concert. We notice that there is not a note out of place, attacks and releases are precise, the singer's diction is text-book correct, and every tempo and dynamic marking from the score has been followed. Yet, once it is over, we politely applaud and wonder why we feel disappointed.

Or, we are at worship. The service is well-ordered, the hymns and all musical portions are appropriate to the liturgy, the leaders know their roles and carry them out correctly and reverently. Yet, when it is all over, we have a hard time identifying or remembering anything special about this service.

What was missing in each of these situations? The room, the concert, and the liturgy each lacked something rather hard to define, but perhaps "inspiration" comes close. They fulfilled the first mile as far as following the rules, but they did not go that second mile which would have captured the spirit of those rules and made it all worthwhile.

Following the rules of decorating, music, and liturgy puts us on the right track and forms the environment for creativity to blossom. A first mile is necessary for there to be a second mile, but the second mile is the reason for the first mile to exist. The second mile is that part of the journey where we encounter the magic, the passion, the profound.

Jesus teaches us about the second mile in this Sunday's gospel, a continuation of his Sermon on the Mount. He tells us to offer the second cheek to those who strike one, to throw in our cloak when someone takes our coat, and to walk two miles with those who force us to go one. Furthermore, we are to love our enemies and pray for our persecutors, not just for those who are easy to love and pray for.

"Be perfect, therefore, as your heavenly Father is perfect," he says. That is his hope and promise for us. In response, we strive for that second mile of life which gives meaning to our existence and glorifies the one who meets and assists us there. We plead with the hymn of Bernard of Clairvaux:

> O Jesus, ever with us stay!
> Make all our moments fair and bright!
> Oh, chase the night of sin away!
> Shed o'er the world your holy light.
> "O Jesus, Joy of Loving Hearts"

Matthew 5:38-48

# Eighth Sunday after the Epiphany
## Proper 3

Have you ever had someone say to you, "Oh, you sing in a church choir? That must be fun. I wish I had extra time to do things like that." After the urge to slap them silly has passed, we might decide to make no response at all. Or we might gather our thoughts and respond, "I am not in choir because I have time; I do it because I make time."

There are not many people in our churches these days who are in need of things just to occupy their time. Every minute must be rationed out in many homes, and each day can be a juggling act. The commitment to choir is difficult for many; it may mean giving up relaxation, sleep, family time, work time, or even income. Many who attempt to make choir a part of their regular Christian commitment find they cannot do so. After the novelty is over, they must either find a director who is a magician and can make every rehearsal moment stimulating entertainment, or get a crush on some other choir member, or become a masochist who enjoys getting paper-cuts. Or maybe they will finally trade in the question "What's in this for me?" for the better question "How is what I am doing important to me and to the bigger picture?"

Jesus tells us this Sunday that we cannot serve both God and wealth. He tells us to not worry about food, drink, or clothing, and that we should not bother to worry at all. Can he be serious? Should we not provide for ourselves and our families? It sounds as though we can all skip choir rehearsal next week, and nobody should dare worry us about it—we're just doing what Jesus said!

Once again Jesus has told us some rather shocking things to put things in perspective and to make a point. By calling these relatively important things "unimportant," he shows us by contrast what really is ultimately important. He does not want us to be without food and clothing and shelter, but even they are unimportant compared to the kingdom of God. And they become downright idolatrous if the quest for them becomes more important than the relationship with Christ. Hymnwriter Johann Schütz bids us:

> Cast every idol from its throne,
> For God is God, and he alone:
> To God all praise and glory!
>
> "Sing Praise to God, the Highest Good"

That is the perspective Jesus is trying to teach us—to keep first things first. It is a philosophy at odds with much of the way the culture works. But it is made manifest whenever we side with values over value, others over self, activities that serve and build character over those that merely entertain or take up time. As we strive first for the kingdom of God and God's righteousness, Christ has promised that all these other things—important things—will be given to us as well.

# The Transfiguration of Our Lord
## Last Sunday after the Epiphany

The term "transfiguration" is not in the general vocabulary of most people. Even if we know that it means "to change the outward appearance of," we will not often find opportunities to use it in daily conversation.

We may give our house new shingles, shutters, paint, and shrubs, but we call it home improvement and not transfiguration. We may have plastic surgery to remove some wrinkles or tighten up some skin, but we call it a face lift and not transfiguration. We may watch Star Trek and hear the words, "Beam me up, Scotty," but that is called transmogrification and not transfiguration.

This Sunday's gospel does use this unique term. "And Jesus was transfigured before them, and his face shone like the sun, and his clothes became dazzling white." Brian Wren helps us sing of the awe and excitement in his hymn that begins:

> *Jesus on the mountain peak*
> *stands alone in glory blazing . . .*
>
> "Jesus on the Mountain Peak"

Jesus, who always looked so fully human, was once again revealed to be more. He had one foot—no, rather he had both feet—in this world and both in another. He walks up the mountain with his human disciples, but there he speaks with the long-dead Moses and Elijah. To top it all, a voice from heaven says "This is my son, the Beloved; with him I am well pleased; listen to him!" Talk about special effects! Talk about a mountain top experience!

So, the Epiphany season comes to a close as it began, with a heavenly voice confirming that this Jesus truly is the Son of God and commanding us to listen to him. The festivals of Baptism of Our Lord and the Transfiguration are the "bookends" of the Epiphany season. Both are mountain top experiences and both pack enough energy to carry us through the "ordinary" times of life.

Christ is ever present for us in our own high and low points—as present in our times of joy and assuredness as in our times of pain and doubt, in spite of our perceptions otherwise. Life, like a landscape, is not all peaks nor all valleys. And, as in music, the highs and lows define each other and need each other to express the heights and depths and richness of life.

This will be a Sunday for joyous praise and glorious alleluias. But be assured that Lent is just around the corner, and the story of salvation travels a route straight through the streets of Jerusalem on its journey to Easter.

# Ash Wednesday

*Savior, when in dust to you*
*Low we bow in homage due:*
*When, repentant, to the skies*
*Scarce we lift our weeping eyes;*
*Oh, by all your pains and woe*
*Suffered once for us below,*
*Bending from your throne on high,*
*Hear our penitential cry!*

"Savior, When in Dust to You"

In this hymn by Robert Grant we sing of such things as dust, repentance, weeping, pains, woe, suffering, and penitential cries. It can mean only one thing—Lent is upon us!

What will we give up for Lent? Even in traditions that do not emphasize a special Lenten discipline of denial, we are likely to be giving up something. Communally, it might be boisterous music and elaborate arrangements, descants and alleluias that we give up. Individually, we might hope that the spirit of the season will inspire us in our attempts to crush some old, destructive habits or start some new, beneficial ones. We pray once again that this Lenten season will have an effect on us as individuals and as a community so that we can gather all creation together at the foot of the cross. What a great reward that would be for our Lenten season.

The term "reward" will be heard extensively in the gospel for Ash Wednesday. Jesus tells of many who parade their piety by praying, fasting, or giving offerings in public, just for the sake of showing off. They already have their reward, Jesus declares, and we can imagine it is a reward that is rather empty and short-lived.

In contrast to them, Jesus tells of those who secretly give offerings and do good deeds, who pray in private, and who fast for its spiritual benefits alone. Their reward is not in earthly trinkets but rather in heavenly treasure.

There are some folks who seem to give up choir and even worship for Lent. Perhaps it is the icy cold weather that hits during this time period in many parts of the northern hemisphere. Perhaps it is the icy coldness of the pronouncement "Remember that you are dust, and to dust you shall return." That statement should give us the shivers. But they can be shivers of warm excitement rather than cold dread. For the ashes that mark our foreheads are not just dust; they are the cleansing crosses of our Baptisms. This is not to be a season for going away; it is one for coming home.

Let us enter this season awake to its rich symbolism, immersed in its purple harmonies and scarlet poetry, and treasuring the deep rewards of walking the road with Christ.

# First Sunday in Lent

It is fitting that we should come head to head with the devil this First Sunday in Lent, for that is exactly who Jesus had waiting for him as he began his ministry. Still wet from his baptism in the Jordan, no time was wasted in getting Jesus and his adversary to clash. Their encounter sets the pattern for the rest of Jesus' earthly life, as Satan would prove to be a constant thorn in his side and, ultimately, his fiercest enemy.

Though the gospel writers differ on the number and content of specific details, even the laconic Mark tells us that the encounter with the devil took place at the very beginning of Jesus' public ministry. The holy signs that convinced the disciples of his messiahship must have confirmed the fact for Satan as well, for he appears in full force. And Satan is no slouch, either, as Matthew and Luke relate. He quotes scripture like a pro, and he has a bunch of special effects in his repertoire which he uses to enhance his sales pitch.

The good news is that Jesus won this first battle. The bad news is how much even he had to endure to do it. Temptation and the power of evil are no small force, Jesus wants us to know. Martin Luther, as hymnwriter, wrote:

> The old satanic foe
> Has sworn to work us woe!
> With craft and dreadful might
> He arms himself to fight.
> On earth he has no equal.
>
> "A Mighty Fortress Is Our God"

The devil has been imagined in many ways throughout history. Even in music there is a tradition of avoiding an augmented fourth because it is the "devil's interval," and Tartini composed a piece for violin that contains the "devil's trill." And we all find passages in music that we find "devilishly" hard, and occasionally we skip a rehearsal or service because "the devil made us do it." And so we see how easy it becomes to domesticate and trivialize a power so strong that even Jesus had to ferociously fight it.

Our focus for this Sunday, as for our entire lives, should be on realizing the immense proportions of sin and evil, our utter impotence to overcome them, and, most importantly, the grace won for us by the battle-scarred Christ, who holds the field victorious.

# Second Sunday in Lent

We do a lot of lifting when we make music in a church choir. We may have to lift chairs and risers into place to get started. We lift hymnbooks and folders to put us in the correct position. We lift our eyes for instructions, and, for the singing process to begin, we lift our diaphragms and keep high the backs of our throats. If there is a high note coming up, lifting our eyebrows can give us a boost. We may even sing the hymn by George Kitchin:

> *Lift high the cross, the love of Christ proclaim*
> *Till all the world adore his sacred name.*
> "Lift High the Cross"

And we hope and pray that our efforts, blessed by God, will lift the presence of Christ and be uplifting to all present.

Lifting implies many things. It implies the exertion of energy, it gives honor, and it calls attention to that which is being lifted.

This Sunday's gospel is the moving account of Jesus with Nicodemus. Jesus tells of being born from above, of winds that blow where they will, of things heavenly and things earthly, and of the God who so loved the world that he gave his only Son. He also speaks prophetically of the Son of Man, lifted up as the serpent in the wilderness, who will grant believers eternal life.

It is an eerie comparison—Jesus and the serpent—but it is full of many profound truths. In both instances, those present are united as they focus their attention on the awesome sight being lifted up. The serpent is honored on a regal bronze pole, the Christ under a sign that says "King of the Jews." And both are energizing catalysts of life where otherwise only death would reign.

As we, like Nicodemus, seek to be faithful disciples, we do well to emulate such a pattern. We strive, in our lives and in our particular ministry of music, to draw the world's attention to the Son of Man lifted up, to honor the Crucified One, and to express the energy of life overcoming death.

# *Third Sunday in Lent*

There are very few important things in life that qualify for a quick fix, yet how many times do people claim to have simple answers for complex problems? Simple solutions are certainly desirable and should be used whenever possible, but they often prove to be wrong because of their shortsightedness.

This Sunday we shall hear the beloved story of Jesus and the woman of Samaria; the many dimensions of this episode run as deep as the well where their encounter takes place. The first portion of this story centers on the woman's shock that Jesus even dares to speak to her since the law forbids it. Then it shifts its focus as the woman misunderstands Jesus' promise to provide living water. She responds, "Sir, give me this water, that I may not thirst, nor come here to draw."

We probably would have responded in the same way. Humans are always looking for ways to make things more automatic and time-saving. Even the church gets caught in the "quick-fix-for-tough-problems" mentality. But Jesus suggests another approach.

The metaphor of water in the well is a profound one. A well, just as any place that dispenses liquids, is a place to which one must return, for physical thirst does recur. In our earthly lives we need for both our physical and spiritual thirsts to be regularly quenched.

Choir members and others who worship regularly know of this rhythm of returning often to the source. Even when we know that the church does quench us, we may fall into the habit of going only when we feel a need. Medical professionals tell us that our bodies probably do not get enough water for optimum health, since we may drink only when we feel thirsty. So it is with spiritual thirst and returning to the source that quenches it. Luther once said that the time we need to worship and receive Holy Communion the most is when we feel we need it the least. Bernard of Clairvaux also expressed this need in a hymn:

> We taste you, ever-living bread,
> And long to feast upon you still;
> We drink of you, the fountainhead;
> Our thirsty souls from you we fill.
> "O Jesus, Joy of Loving Hearts"

A well without fresh circulating water becomes stagnant. A fountain is a glorious sight, but it is just pumps and pipes without water to run through it. We have a piece of paper with words and symbols on it and we call it "music." But music really occurs only when people pick it up and turn it into sounds full of life. When the energy stops, so stops the music until the voices are again united.

In our baptisms, Jesus has given us a living water which does last for a lifetime. But our baptisms are also a well to return to day after day as we draw upon the promises of Christ. Jesus reminds us of our thirst and stands at the well, ready to refresh and fill us.

# Fourth Sunday in Lent

The words of John Newton, a hymnwriter and self-professed wretch, will no doubt be on the minds and lips of many this Sunday:

*I once was lost, but now am found;*
*Was blind but now I see.*

"Amazing Grace, How Sweet the Sound"

For in the gospel reading we will hear of yet more people coming to grips with the amazing grace of God.

The premise of the story is simple enough, at least to those who have heard of the many other healing miracles of Jesus. A man, blind from birth, receives from Jesus some mud along with the command to go and wash it away. St. John, in a matter-of-fact way, simply records, "Then he went and washed and came back able to see." What could be more beautiful or more powerful than the simple command, the faith that obeys, and the healing, as presented in this episode from the life and ministry of the Anointed One? What else is lurking in the wings that requires several additional paragraphs to complete the story?

The story is complicated by disciples who presume that someone's sin was responsible for the blindness, by observers who cannot agree if this was the same man they knew as a blind beggar or an impostor, by Pharisees who cannot believe that a rule-breaker like Jesus could have performed a healing, by the healed man's parents who decline to express their convictions out of fear of expulsion, by a heated theological discussion between the healed man and the Pharisees, and, finally, by a calm and comforting discussion with Jesus who sets things straight. How does the healed man summarize the situation? In the midst of the fury, he states, "One thing I do know, that though I was blind, now I see." Jesus, when asked who the Son of Man is, likewise sums it up and says, "You have seen him, and the one speaking to you is he." If they would have only kept it that simple, we muse, this whole episode could have been told in three verses rather than forty-one!

We all like things summarized and simplified for us. A solo is often refreshing after long passages of choral singing. Unison chant is exquisite next to polyphonic motets. The great Karl Barth summed up his immense theological work by quoting the children's song, "Jesus Loves Me, This I Know." Is simplicity simply better than complexity? Why even bother with complexity?

Oliver Wendell Holmes is quoted as saying, "I don't give a fig for the simplicity this side of complexity, but I would die for the simplicity on the other side of complexity." Complexity, it seems, is needed to define simplicity; just as order and chaos, darkness and light, allegro and adagio, piano and forte, soprano and bass, "Amazing Grace" and Bach's St. Matthew Passion need each other in order to define themselves and express great truth. Let us strive in every situation to live out the gospel in all its simple complexity and complex simplicity, by Christ's example and for his glory.

# Fifth Sunday in Lent

Have you noticed the gospel readings getting lengthier these last Sundays in Lent? They contain so much drama, so much power, and so many facets of faith that hours could be spent unpacking just a few of their treasures. Even then, we could not exhaust all that is contained in these endless wells of gospel riches.

This Sunday's gospel of 45 verses recounts the dramatic event of the raising of Lazarus from the dead. We encounter the faith and emotions of his sisters, Mary and Martha, whom we remember from other biblical accounts. We try to experience the events through the anxious eyes of the disciples. We ponder Jesus' actions as he waits before going to Bethany, weeps upon his arrival, prays aloud for the benefit of the bystanders, and performs the raising of the dead-for-days Lazarus in full drama. He utters the spine-tingling words, "I am the resurrection and the life. Those who believe in me, even though they die, will live, and everyone who lives and believes in me will never die."

The same Spirit that was at work that day in Bethany is still present among us, and a command from that same Jesus still works the miracle of calling life from death. Hymnwriter Delores Dufner tells of this powerful word:

> The Word of God is breath and life;
> it comes to heal and wake and save.
> So let the Spirit touch and mend
> and rouse your dry bones from their grave.
> "The Word of God Is Source and Seed"

Does the Lazarus story speak so powerfully because it is good drama, or because it portrays supernatural powers, or because it has characters we already know and has a happy ending? Yes, and much more; for it is a story about us. We are the bystanders, taking it all in. We are the disciples, knowing who Jesus is, yet still surprised by his words and actions. We are Mary and Martha, mourning our loved one, having faith that Jesus could have healed, yet confused and even angry over his delay. And we are Lazarus, repulsive by the stench of disease and decay, dead beyond every power except the potent, life-giving call of the Savior to "come out!"

What power and pathos are present in this story! We may worry that our meager attempts at praising and proclaiming these truths will not be up to the task. But we need not worry—of course they won't! To claim ability on our own to be worthy and capable of such a task is utter arrogance. A well-known eucharistic prayer reminds us that we make our offerings "not as we ought, but as we are able." It is only as God's Spirit blesses our offerings and speaks through them that we participate in the noble calling to proclaim to a dying world the resurrection that God has planned for it.

# Sunday of the Passion/Palm Sunday

For most Sundays of the church year we strive for thematic unity. Worship planners spend time and use their expertise organizing services where the preaching, scriptures, prayers, music, art, and all other parts of the liturgy unite in proclaiming some facet of the good news of God.

This Sunday stands at a unique place in the rhythm of the church's life. Even its name, Sunday of the Passion/Palm Sunday, exposes the specialness of the day. It is a day of dualities when we will hear two gospel readings—that of Jesus' triumphal entry into Jerusalem, and by contrast, that lengthiest of all Gospel pericopes—the Passion of our Lord. We gather for a palm procession; we depart, immersed in the heaviness of Holy Week.

The people of Jerusalem knew only the festivity of the day as they expected Jesus to be ushering in the triumph of Israel. Jesus obviously had a different scenario on his mind, for he knew this was only the beginning of the end. "Ignorance is bliss," goes the saying. Anyone can praise a victor, but even the disciples departed once they realized what was happening in the days that followed. Sadly, the same is true for many in our congregation and even in our choirs. "Let me know when the big, happy festivals are coming up," some say. "I don't want to ruin my good mood by going on a somber day," they might as well add. Those who worship faithfully know the risks of coming on a day when we will be confronted with the crimson details of the passion story. But it is worth the risk, for we trade in a superficial, feel-good experience for a deeper, richer encounter with the Christ who has himself gone through it all.

The function of our worship this Sunday will be, as always, to praise the triune God, proclaim the gospel, pray together, offer ourselves in service, and be fed by Christ's communion with us and by our communion with each other. But we will not merely remember that first Palm Sunday; we will experience it anew. For Christ continues to be praised and lauded, continues to display his scars, continues to come to us and feed us, continues to save and redeem us.

Our music will be a part of that experience. With voices and instruments united we will relive the festivity of Christ's coming and ponder the depths of his suffering and death. Hymnwriter Samuel Crossman allows us to eloquently profess:

> Here might I stay and sing
> No story so divine!
> Never was love, dear King,
> Never was grief like thine.
>
> "My Song Is Love Unknown"

As Holy Week is ushered in once again, we pray that our minds and hearts will be open and ready to ponder and receive such a high and deep declaration of love.

# Holy Week/The Three Days

Christians do some amazing things this week. Some will make a pilgrimage to their church every single day, whether to worship, pray, rehearse, decorate, clean, or even to help with all the extra worship bulletins. Our daily routines of work, school, or family care will go on much as usual, but on top of these we still add additional tasks. We also anticipate Easter Sunday by planning for meals, company, clothing, and even decorating the eggs. But, rather than ignoring or working straight through these intervening weekdays, we plan to savor and struggle with them.

Thousands of words will be spoken and heard in the course of these days, for there is so much to tell and express. But such wondrous things are encapsulated best in poetry from the church's hymnwriters. The gospel readings for Monday, Tuesday, and Wednesday in Holy Week bring Jesus and us ever closer to the time and place of sacrifice. James Montgomery bids us:

> *Go to dark Gethsemane,*
> *All who feel the tempter's power;*
> *Your Redeemer's conflict see.*
> *Watch with him one bitter hour;*
> *Turn not from his griefs away;*
> *Learn from Jesus Christ to pray.*
>
> "Go to Dark Gethsemane"

On Maundy Thursday (or Holy Thursday) we receive Jesus' command to love each other, and he seals that command with his own gifts of bread and wine, water and towel. An ancient Latin hymn expresses our unity with the church in all times and places:

> *Where true charity and love abide, God is dwelling there.*
> *Ubi caritas et amor, Deus ibi est.*
>
> "Ubi Caritas et Amor/Where True Charity and Love Abide"

On a Friday that Christians dare to call "good," we contemplate the ultimate sacrifice, pray for ourselves and each other in the shadow of the cross, and adore the one crucified for the salvation of the world. Bernard of Clairvaux, along with Paul Gerhardt and other translators, asks with us:

> *What language shall I borrow To thank thee, dearest friend,*
> *For this thy dying sorrow, Thy pity without end?*
>
> "O Sacred Head, Now Wounded"

Finally, on the Vigil of Easter, the climax is reached. The risen Christ is proclaimed as new light in the darkness, the history of God's salvation is recounted, new members are incorporated into the death and resurrection of Jesus, baptisms are renewed, and we eat and drink in the presence of the Risen Lord. Surrounded by such richness, we can only rise up and proclaim in the splendid poetry of John Geyer:

> *We know that Christ is raised and dies no more.*
> *Embraced by death, he broke its fearful hold,*
> *And our despair he turned to blazing joy. Hallelujah!*
>
> "We Know that Christ Is Raised"

# The Resurrection of Our Lord

There's light at the end of the tunnel! Though we are still in the midst of Holy Week, we can count down the days and hours rather than the weeks of the Lent behind us. Though we have some music to still polish and much to still deliver, we can already taste that post-Easter peace we have come to savor. Church musicians, especially at the final worship service on Easter Day, can sing with great conviction (and with a little chuckle at its double meaning) the ancient Easter hymn:

> *The strife is o'er, the battle done;*
> *Now is the victor's triumph won!*
> *Now be the song of praise begun. Alleluia!*
> "The Strife Is O'er, the Battle Done"

As long as we have done our best, we need not feel ashamed of the relief we may feel once Lent is over. Our alleluias will sound more joyous because of their sabbatical. The whites and golds will sparkle more brightly because the purples and scarlets have told us their story. The sunlight streaming through the windows will carry more intensity because of the times we met in darkness. The organ and other instruments will sound more jubilant after the deep, rich sonorities of Lent. We will treasure more our rejoicing because we have grieved.

Jesus probably experienced some relief, too, as he saw the light at the opening of the tomb. Salvation's song had reached the highest notes of its intense climax; it was time for the coda and the cadence. What great joy must have been his as he shared the jubilant news of his resurrection with those he loved the most! Their fright must have given way quickly to joy and peace, made all the more intense because of the deep sorrow they had experienced. That was Jesus' special gift to those who had known him the best. It is a gift he continues to give to us as we walk with him on the passion path to Jerusalem and as we invite him to walk with us on our rocky roads.

Just as Jesus reveled in the satisfaction of a tough job well done, the relief we feel as another Holy Week and Easter are reached surely goes beyond our creaturely comforts. For all is made new. We have caught a glimpse of the Paschal candle piercing the darkness, and we recognize it as the light of Christ which he has planted within us. We have seen the first rays of daylight illuminating the far corners of the cave, and we know that tomb is ours. And we have visited the garden, expecting only to grieve, but instead we are surprised and comforted by his living presence.

There is indeed light at the end of the tunnel—it is the rest of our lives! Christ has fought and won a tremendous battle for the sake of that light which blesses our baptisms, guides our living, hallows our dying, and promises our resurrections. We cannot help but sing praises and proclaim such good news.

# Second Sunday of Easter

**M**uch of the culture around us has already packed Easter away until next year—or at least it has been marked down to half price! But the church has the audacity to keep celebrating Easter for 50 days! In spite of this Sunday's nickname of "Low Sunday," we continue to sing our alleluias and proclaim that Christ is risen to all who will hear. This season is a time to rejoice and reflect on the meaning of the resurrection and to try to fashion our lives to be the Easter people that Christ has made us.

This Sunday we will hear the wonderful story from John's Gospel that tells of the resurrected Jesus appearing to his disciples. It might make for a good test question—when Jesus suddenly appears to his fearful disciples meeting behind locked doors, what are his first words to them? Perhaps "surprise" or "cheer up" or "it's me" might be understandable responses. But Jesus surprises us almost as much as he must have surprised his disciples when he says, "Peace be with you." Many hymnwriters, including Jean Tisserand, have made note of this:

> *That night the apostles met in fear;*
> *Among them came their master dear,*
> *And said, "My peace be with you here."*
> *Alleluia!*

"O Sons and Daughters of the King"

Peace is a hard concept to define. We usually describe it as the absence of strife whether between nations, families, or individuals. As important as such arenas are for peace, these are not the same as the peace Jesus gives.

Sometimes we feel peace through some outside stimulus. Drugs or manipulative words or music can cause us to ignore the reality of life around us. This is likewise not the peace that Jesus gives.

Some have objected to the sharing of the peace in worship, arguing that well-wishing and personal greetings are not appropriate for something as important as the worship time. If that was all that was taking place, then the critics would be correct. But the peace we give and receive is not merely an expression of good wishes. It is the peace of Christ that we give, and he has given us the opportunity and responsibility to be channels of this peace to each other. Christ's peace is deep in meaning, rich in scope, and full of the power that only a dying and rising Savior can give. It is a release from real forces and a rescue from ourselves. Christ's words do not merely wish us peace—they grant it.

That is the peace we mean to share in worship—in the word, in the sacraments, in the fellowship, in the holy surroundings, and in the music whether it be jubilant or meditative. May the peace of Christ dwell in us richly this Easter season as we are called to be channels and recipients of the peace Christ has won for us.

# Third Sunday of Easter

How lucky were those two followers of Jesus who encountered him on the Emmaus road! They did not know the identity of their traveling companion, but he had such a friendly and caring manner. He gave an attentive ear as they related their experiences of the last few days and as they lamented their dashed hopes and discouragement. When he did speak he helped them understand so much about the scriptures and the prophecy about the Messiah. His words and presence were so powerful that they later exclaimed, "Were not our hearts burning within us?" They invited him to stay and, to their joy, he accepted. At mealtime he took bread, blessed and broke it, and gave it to them. Then their eyes were opened as he vanished from their sight.

How fortunate to be in the presence of the resurrected Christ—to hear his teachings and words of acceptance, to share a meal with him and with so many others who also knew him, to feel the amazement upon realizing in whose presence they found themselves. There could surely be no doubts in the minds of those who were so fortunate to have been there. They had known him, grown up with him, learned from him, and been fed by him.

How fortunate they were and how fortunate we are, for the same happens to us each and every time we gather for worship! The church has always loved this passage from Luke's Gospel, not only because of its drama and excitement, but because it affirms our encounters with Christ in worship. The two central features of the Emmaus story are the same as the two major parts of liturgical worship services—teaching and sharing, feeding of the mind and feeding of the body, scriptures and sacraments, word and eucharist.

Those two on the Emmaus Road did not initially know Jesus because, we are told, "their eyes were kept from recognizing him." Jesus wanted them to recognize him not by physical features, which they knew, but instead by his words and actions, which he felt were much more important.

So were they the only lucky ones? We, too, are in a community of Jesus' followers who tell each other of encounters with him. We keep hearing and seeing the words and works of Jesus. Jesus continues to be made known to us in the breaking of the bread. In addition we have the benefit of 2,000 more years of Christ's promise, still unbroken. If our eyes are kept from recognizing him it is not of his doing, for now we have the blessing of the Holy Spirit who makes known this Christ crucified and risen.

We are those disciples on the Emmaus Road, and we pray with disciples of every time and place in Herbert Brokering's hymn:

> Stay with us, till night has come:
> our praise to you this day be sung.
> Bless our bread, open our eyes:
> Jesus, be our great surprise.
>
> "Stay with Us"

May the Holy Spirit assist and open our eyes to see how fortunate we are to be in the presence of the resurrected Christ.

# *Fourth Sunday of Easter*

This Fourth Sunday of Easter has the nickname of "Good Shepherd Sunday" because the scripture readings always deal with some aspect of shepherds and sheep. Our first impulse might be to observe the Sunday with green-colored glasses and dwell on images of pastoral hillsides and babbling brooks, playful sheep and a smiling shepherd. How wonderful when life is just like that! But how dishonest to proclaim such a perspective as the norm or as the only acceptable Christian life. We must be sure our preaching and our music do not proclaim such a narrow view. For our own lives tell a different story. We know of hillsides with mudslides, of brooks that run dry or overflow their banks, and of sheep that often doubt or wander from the shepherd. More importantly, our shepherd knows a reality that is less than picture-perfect. For he has lived on this very same earth a life that included rejection, torture, death, and the grave.

In this Sunday's gospel Jesus tells us about thieves and bandits who enter the fold by some way other than the gate, and that they come to kill and destroy the sheep. Jesus wants us to know about enemies of the faith so that we will recognize them for what they are and resist them. When the church hides important issues by ignoring or squelching them it is resisting the example of Christ who was straightforward about telling his followers the truth, no matter how distasteful. The church, when following Christ's example, is to be at the forefront of exposing evil and teaching about the ways of the world.

Why? We can handle the truth because we have a God who is stronger than all the forces of evil. We can stand and face the tragedies and prejudices of society because we know that God holds the ultimate answers and grants the power to overcome. We want to tackle the tough tasks because God is never proclaimed and praised more fully than when truth encounters untruth, when good encounters evil. How can we discern who are the thieves and bandits of the faith, and how can we be prepared to tackle them head-on?

The Good Shepherd knows his sheep by name and they know his voice. Though they can sometimes disagree, Christians come to know through a life of worship, learning, fellowship, and prayer what is the voice of the Good Shepherd and what is the voice of the impostor. The thief comes only to kill and destroy. The Good Shepherd comes that we might have life, and have it abundantly. We hear the Shepherd's encouraging words through the hymnwriting of Marjorie Jillson:

> *Have good cheer, little flock;*
> *Have good cheer, little flock,*
> *For the Father will keep you in his love forever;*
> *Have good cheer, little flock!*
> "Have No Fear, Little Flock"

John 10:1-10

# Fifth Sunday of Easter

In this Sunday's gospel Jesus seems to be tying up loose ends and giving answers to the uttered and unuttered questions of his disciples.

To the question "In whom should we believe, God or you?" he answers, "Believe in God, believe also in me."

To the question "Where and why are you going?" he answers, "I go to my father's house to prepare a place for you."

To the question "Why must you go?" he answers, "So I can come again and take you to myself."

To the question "How can we know the way?" he answers "I am the way, and the truth, and the life."

To the request "Show us the Father," Jesus replies "They who have seen me have seen the Father."

In each instance Jesus' response is positive and filled with hope, asking only that we believe. Human beings, though, are often uncomfortable with answers that seem to raise even more questions. We prefer times when we are told exactly what to believe and do in each instance. We want a personal octavo for living, with our own part highlighted so we can know each pitch, each note value, each dynamic, each tempo change, and each syllable expected of us at any given moment. Simply believing seems too easy, too vague, and too dangerous all at the same time.

Perhaps the closing verses give us a point of focus. "Very truly, I tell you, the one who believes in me will also do the works that I do."

We have a marvelous record of what Jesus did in his earthly life and what he has continued to do through his body, the church. Jesus doesn't need to list all that he wants us to do—he has shown us. He has healed the sick, cared for the outcast, blessed the young and the aged, and given of himself in order that the Father be praised and proclaimed.

For Jesus, believing equals doing, and he asks the same of those who claim his lordship. Our assignments will not always be laid out as neatly as rehearsal plans on a chalkboard. Christ gives us strength to stay centered on the way, the truth, and the life so that we can discern his call and be empowered by his example. George Herbert's masterful hymn tells of this communion with Christ:

> *Come, my way, my truth, my life:*
> *Such a way as gives us breath;*
> *Such a truth as ends all strife;*
> *Such a life as conquers death.*
>
> "Come, My Way, My Truth, My Life"

# Sixth Sunday of Easter

If there is any word that stands out by extensive use in this Sunday's gospel it is the word "will." Many of the "will" statements predict things that Jesus knows are about to happen: "I will ask the Father and he will give you another Advocate, to be with you forever . . . He will be in you . . . The world will no longer see me." How good to hear these promises that were so soon fulfilled.

Other statements are promises of what is to happen for his followers: "You will see me . . . you will also live . . . you will know that I am in the Father." How comforting to hear that Jesus has promised eternal life and full knowledge of God.

There is still another type of "will" in this passage. In the opening and again in the closing lines, Jesus tells them, "If you love me, you will keep my commandments." This gets a little worrisome. We have come to trust his unconditional promises, but this seems to put a condition on us. And we know we do not have such a great record at keeping promises.

The beloved motet by Thomas Tallis wonderfully sets this text but uses an older translation. It sings, "If you love me, keep my commandments." What could be more straightforward than such a command? In newer translations, however, we may hear, "If you love me, you will keep my commandments." Here it seems to be more like a statement of fact—that love of Christ naturally leads to keeping the commandments.

Which then is it correct to say, that these words are a command or a declaration? Probably both, for we need to remember Christ's definition of love. For him, love is not a mere feeling; it is action. Feelings cannot be commanded, but actions can. And practicing love leads to feelings of love. It is futile to ask whether love or service comes first; they come together, as Christ has continually said and shown. Moreover, they come not by our own willing but as a gift from the one who is love incarnate. Bianco da Siena penned a sumptuous prayer with this in mind:

> Come down, O Love divine;
> Seek thou this soul of mine
> And visit it with thine own ardor glowing;
> O Comforter, draw near;
> Within my heart appear
> And kindle it, thy holy flame bestowing.
>
> "Come Down, O Love Divine"

Christ's command to love is connected with a declaration. More importantly, they are united into one by a promise. And this promise is from the very one who has proven to be the ultimate giver and keeper of promises.

# The Ascension of Our Lord

The symbolically strong number of forty is held up once again as we celebrate the Ascension of Our Lord forty days after his day of resurrection. These have been forty days of rejoicing, learning, and eating with the Risen One and, through him, with his disciples throughout history. The summaries of the faith he gives are so helpful; the peace he grants is so comforting; the promises he makes are so uplifting. It is with high but mixed emotions that we see him carried up into heaven. Though he has promised to still be with us in new and even better ways, we know things will never be quite the same. And although we cannot understand why he must go in order to be present, we are willing to believe his promise. William Chatterton Dix addresses this mystery in a great hymn;

*Alleluia! Not as orphans are we left in sorrow now;*
*Alleluia! He is near us; faith believes, nor questions how.*
"Alleluia! Sing to Jesus"

There are many who have trouble with some aspects of the Ascension story. Talk of monarchs and enthronements does not hold as much positive meaning as in earlier times. Perhaps our greatest difficulty lies in the concept of heaven as up in the sky, someplace above the clouds, somewhere over the rainbow. Having traveled millions of miles into space, we have a less literal belief in the location of heaven, if indeed it is a location at all. But if we feel we can no longer look toward heaven, do we instead cast our eyes downward or even close them altogether?

Looking upward is still our best bet. Looking upward is how navigators steer their course. Looking upward is how we stay together when singing in a choir. Looking upward gives us new perspectives, new vistas, new comrades, new opportunities, and new energies. Looking upward moves our focus beyond ourselves. The disciples looked upward on that day of Jesus' ascension. Yes, they saw his departure with bittersweet emotions. But as they looked upward they received his blessing, his promise to send power from on high, and his great energy that sent them rejoicing back to Jerusalem. St. Luke records that they worshipped him and were continually in the temple blessing God.

Does it not seem strange that they returned and went to the temple? Did not Jesus call them his witnesses and did he not charge them to proclaim all they had seen and heard? Were their priorities misplaced already?

Hardly! Their worship of the Ascended One began right there at Bethany, in response to his glorious and gracious presence. It continued on their journey back to Jerusalem, and they were drawn magnetically to the house of worship. From there, they were energized by his Spirit to live lives of proclamation and service, even to the point martyrdom. Such is the power of Christ's promises, of vibrant worship, and of lifting our eyes to the Ascended One. Look up! The time for singing has come!

# Seventh Sunday of Easter

On this seventh and final Sunday of the Easter season we will hear Jesus pray what is often called his "high priestly prayer." Though taking place just before his crucifixion, this reading says so much to us when proclaimed these days around Ascension, and as we look forward to Pentecost.

A key theme in this Sunday's portion of the prayer is unity. Jesus speaks of his unity with the Father and with all people. And he prays that God will make known this unity so that we, too, will know of the unity which is ours with the Father and with each other. He prays that we would live as if we are in unity because, as he points out, we truly are.

We probably do not feel very much at unity. We know of so many world religions, so many denominations within Christianity, so many differences between congregations, and so many rifts between parishioners. Still, Jesus not only prays for unity, he claims it is already here.

As musicians we are often called to be in unity. We may need to stand or sit or move as one body. We need to be precise in our attacks and releases. We need to purify our vowels and tone so that we will blend together into one sound. We may even wear identical vestments so that our individuality gives way to visual unity. And what could be more exciting than a good unison sound? Truly, a choir is a lesson in itself on unity.

But wait—our experience tells us more. Are two voices ever exactly alike? Do not voices have different timbres and ranges? Are there not times when some must sing louder and some softer? Where would music be without the non-unison sounds of harmony and counterpoint? These examples do not negate the lesson on unity; they make it even stronger. Unity does not require identical sounds, but a common goal. Unity does not deny diversity, but rather celebrates it.

Fights and schisms among Christians do harm the message we try to proclaim, but rejoicing in the diversity of God's people proclaims the gospel. When we sing in parts we demonstrate the beauty of diversity and model harmonious living. When we sing polyphony we share in the excitement of different melodies, beautiful on their own, complementing each other when combined, and creating a glorious tapestry of sound that is much more colorful than any individual part. This, too, manifests the gospel.

We do have much for which to work and pray when it comes to this matter of unity. But it is not because it does not exist. We pray for the eyes of faith to see the unity that transcends diversity—and to feel it, work for it, and to rejoice in it. Our prayer is that of the hymnwriter Jeffrey Rowthorn:

> Give us all new fervor, draw us closer in community.
> With the Spirit's gifts empower us for the work of ministry.
> "Lord, You Give the Great Commission"

John 17:1-11

# The Day of Pentecost

On the festival of Pentecost we look to the reading from Acts to set the stage. We get caught up in the action of that historic day, feeling the rush of the wind, seeing the tongues of fire, hearing the many languages, experiencing the bewilderment of both the participants and onlookers, and believing the message of Peter's powerful preaching. We might have a hard time concentrating on or even remembering the other readings after such an action scene. What even is the gospel for the day? It tells of the resurrected Jesus appearing to his frightened disciples. There he says, "Peace be with you," and "Receive the Holy Spirit." He shows them his hands and side, and he sends them on their way with the charge to forgive and retain sins.

Oh, yes, he did one more thing—he breathed on them. How strange to hear and picture that! But what might be considered a rude act in our day was then a meaningful and powerful gesture. Breath and wind have long been signs and symbols of God and the Holy Spirit. In many languages the words are similar or even identical. Can wind, air, and breath mean such great things to us? We may use electric fans and air conditioners to do it, but we still crave the refreshment of moving air. We may not need the wind to pump our water or propel our boats, but we still know the awesome power of a tornado or a hurricane. We may know it takes more than breath to stay alive, but we still know what it means when we are told that someone has stopped breathing.

Jesus has chosen an ancient yet universal symbol to convey the giving of the Holy Spirit. Air is so plentiful and so necessary for life; yet it is invisible and so often taken for granted. Every time we breathe we make use of this wonderful gift from God. How much we are aware of this gift is often exhibited in how we use it. One of the most grateful ways to use breath is in music. Wind instruments, whether a single flute or an organ of thousands of pipes, use columns of air to produce sounds. And all instrumental families use the resonating air to carry their sounds. In the prime instrument of worship—the human voice—tones unite with words, and they carry each other from the depths of one soul to others and to God. It is no wonder that the church has promoted music with integrity and looked with suspicion at anything that is artificial or superficial. Live music made by live people proclaims the living, breathing presence of the Holy Spirit. The Spirit dwells with us and within us—as close as our very breath and as constant as the rhythm of our breathing. Hymnwriter Michael Hewlett calls us to use our breath in proclamation:

> Tell of how the ascended Jesus armed a people for his own;
> how a hundred men and women turned the known world upside down,
> to its dark and furthest corners by the wind of heaven blown.
>
> "Praise the Spirit in Creation"

Let us be grateful receivers and users of God's life-giving breath.

# The Holy Trinity
## First Sunday after Pentecost

This Sunday stands at a pivotal point in many respects. God's self-revelation has reached an apex with the sending of the Holy Spirit at Pentecost, and we celebrate unity and diversity in God's trinitarian presence. And there is a new chapter beginning in Jesus' story. We have just walked with him through his earthly life, experienced anew his passion, celebrated with renewed joy his resurrection, reveled in the peace of his final weeks on earth, felt the twangs of his ascension, and been swept up by the coming of the Spirit. But now his separateness from the Father and the Spirit has been blurred. The One from Galilee now transcends all time and space and is in unity with the Creator and Sanctifier. Things can never be quite the same.

One more turning point is reached this Trinity Sunday as we hear the final verses of Matthew's Gospel. Jesus assumes full authority and delivers the great commission to go and make disciples, to baptize them in the name of this Holy Trinity, and to teach them what it means to be a created, redeemed, and sanctified people of God. As Matthew's proclamation of the good news is coming to an end, ours is just beginning.

Such lofty ideals for such weak and faulty individuals! We may feel that Jesus has left us with a "commission impossible." How can we do all those things that he has commanded of us? Won't he settle for just a few of them?

In truth, we have a greater chance of doing everything Jesus commanded of us than of doing only a few. For his commands throughout scripture are usually coupled with the means to bring them about. The great commission concludes with a plan equal to the task. "Remember" is the command; "I am with you always" is the power; ". . . to the end of the age" is the promise.

Our first and most important duty is to remember. And we remember by savoring the presence of the Holy Trinity in worship and in fellowship, in song and solitude, and in prayer and praise with the community of believers in all times and places. We join with them in the great Te Deum hymn:

> *Holy Father, holy Son,*
> *Holy Spirit, three we name you,*
> *Though in essence only one;*
> *Undivided God we claim you*
> *And, adoring, bend the knee*
> *While we own the mystery.*
> "Holy God, We Praise Your Name"

Matthew 28:16-20

# *Proper 3*

## *Sunday between May 24 and 28 inclusive*
### *(if after Trinity Sunday)*

Have you ever had someone say to you, "Oh, you sing in a church choir? That must be fun. I wish I had extra time to do things like that." After the urge to slap them silly has passed, we might decide to make no response at all. Or we might gather our thoughts and respond, "I am not in choir because I have time; I do it because I make time."

There are not many people in our churches these days who are in need of things just to occupy their time. Every minute must be rationed out in many homes, and each day can be a juggling act. The commitment to choir is difficult for many; it may mean giving up relaxation, sleep, family time, work time, or even income. Many who attempt to make choir a part of their regular Christian commitment find they cannot do so. After the novelty is over, they must either find a director who is a magician and can make every rehearsal moment stimulating entertainment, or get a crush on some other choir member, or become a masochist who enjoys getting paper-cuts. Or maybe they will finally trade in the question "what's in this for me?" for the better question "how is what I am doing important to me and to the bigger picture?"

Jesus tells us this Sunday that we cannot serve both God and wealth. He tells us to not worry about food, drink, or clothing, and that we should not bother to worry at all. Can he be serious? Should we not provide for ourselves and our families? It sounds as though we can all skip choir rehearsal next week, and nobody should dare worry us about it—we're just doing what Jesus said!

Once again Jesus has told us some rather shocking things to put things in perspective and to make a point. By calling these relatively important things "unimportant," he shows us by contrast what really is ultimately important. He does not want us to be without food and clothing and shelter, but even they are unimportant compared to the kingdom of God. And they become downright idolatrous if the quest for them becomes more important than the relationship with Christ. Hymnwriter Johann Schütz bids us:

> *Cast every idol from its throne,*
> *For God is God, and he alone:*
> *To God all praise and glory!*
> "Sing Praise to God, the Highest Good"

That is the perspective Jesus is trying to teach us—to keep first things first. It is a philosophy at odds with much of the way the culture works. But it is made manifest whenever we side with values over value, others over self, activities that serve and build character over those that merely entertain or take up time. As we strive first for the kingdom of God and God's righteousness, Christ has promised that all these other things—important things—will be given to us as well.

# Proper 4

## Sunday between May 29 and June 4
### (if after Trinity Sunday)

Starting with a firm foundation is necessary whether building structures, skills, or lives. The footers must be straight and sturdy for a building to be useful and safe. The "three R's" of education must be firmly grasped for higher levels of learning to take place. The elements of rhythm, pitch, and technique must be mastered for musical proficiency to be achieved. Knowing and following the basic rules of civility are necessary to get along in society. In short, the concept of firm foundations is itself foundational to every discipline.

Jesus teaches an important lesson on foundations in this Sunday's gospel. It is the memorable story of two men, each building a house. One wisely chooses to build on top of rock, the other on sand. Once the storms come, the consequences of their choices are as obvious as the point Jesus is making. Building our lives upon the foundation of Christ is the sure and wise choice—all other options are foolish and dangerous.

We often celebrate this story in song. Perhaps we have sung the children's song that tells with voices and actions of the rains falling down, the floods coming up, and the fate of the two houses. Or perhaps we have confessed in the hymn of Edward Mote:

> His oath, his covenant, his blood
> Sustain me in the raging flood;
> When all supports are washed away,
> He then is all my hope and stay.
> On Christ, the solid rock, I stand;
> All other ground is sinking sand.
>
> "My Hope Is Built on Nothing Less"

How great to know that Christ will be there if needed. How much nicer, we may think, if we ourselves escape disasters altogether. Then we need not bother Christ at all, and we may feel better not having to put our faith to the test. This pattern of thought, however, is definitely not based on a firm foundation.

This short story has two more important points to teach us. The wise man's house did not stand because of his superior building talents, better materials, or even harder work. Its survival was due to something beyond himself and his control—the strength of solid rock. Being wise, then, depends not on our own wisdom but in acknowledging our own inability to survive on our own and in trusting the one who saves us.

Furthermore, the wise man's choice of foundation was not just as an insurance policy in the event of a rare disaster; the storms visited him just as surely and with as much fury as they visited the foolish man. Jesus has not promised an absence of storms for the wise or for the foolish. But he has promised his presence through the best and worst of times—a presence that keeps us afloat and rescues us for living lives of praise.

# *Proper 5*

## *Sunday between June 5 and 11 inclusive*
### *(if after Trinity Sunday)*

If everyone would pay attention and stop talking we could get so much more music learned and polished!" we lament at choir practice. "I could have had this project completed much earlier if it weren't for all the phone calls about trivial matters," we complain at work. "My free evening was barely restful, filled with one bothersome distraction after another," we moan at home.

We may feel we are doomed to mediocrity unless we can achieve an unencumbered life. Even our faith and prayer life is plagued by many distractions; it is no wonder the cloistered life appeals to many. Yes, distractions are bothersome, and we should do what we can to keep focused on those things that are most important to life and faith. But we need only look at Christ and his disciples to know that our situation is not unique to this generation.

As we listen to the gospel reading this Sunday, we will hear of many interruptions. As Jesus tries to eat dinner with his disciples, he is soon joined by many tax collectors and sinners. And the Pharisees add to the commotion by asking why he eats with such people. Then a synagogue leader comes to ask Jesus to bring his daughter back to life. Before he can complete the first miracle, a woman in need of healing comes from behind and touches his cloak. He heals her and hurries on to the leader's house. But before he can go inside, he has to contend with the commotion of the flute players and the crowd at the door. They laugh when Jesus tells them the girl is not dead but sleeping, and they have to be put outside before he can perform his life-giving miracle. Matthew's passage concludes with the statement, "And the report of this spread throughout that district." We can only wonder if the report was more concerned with the miracles or with the amazing feat of accomplishing anything at all amid such chaos!

Fortunately, Jesus was not overwhelmed as we might be. He saw each interruption as a cry for help, a chance to minister, an opportunity for grace, a proclamation of God's mercy. His care and compassion went beyond mere inconvenience and discomfort—they took him to the cross and grave. Frederick W. Faber's classic hymn contemplates the vastness of such love:

> *There's a wideness in God's mercy,*
> *Like the wideness of the sea;*
> *There's a kindness in his justice*
> *Which is more than liberty.*
>
> "There's a Wideness in God's Mercy"

There is yet one more interruption described in this passage. Way back in the opening lines, Jesus sees Matthew hard at work in his tax booth. Over the details and duties of his daily work, Matthew hears, "Follow me." It was to be the most important call of his lifetime. And he got up and followed. May we, too, be always ready to hear and heed such important, life-changing interruptions from the Savior Jesus.

# Proper 6

## Sunday between June 12 and 18 inclusive
### (if after Trinity Sunday)

"Remember to start the procession on stanza one," shouts the director as the choir gets ready to leave the choir room for the worship service. "And don't forget to sing parts on the inner stanzas of the outer hymns and the outer stanzas of the inner hymns, except the last one when the sopranos sing the tenor line an octave higher and the tenors sing the soprano line an octave lower," the instructions continue. "And watch me for the changes in dynamics on the piece we didn't get to practice, and remember to sing the first repeat but not the second on the offertory. And the choir communes before the congregation this week, so get up before the ushers tell you to. And remember that we sing at the early service next Sunday, and we rehearse Wednesday instead of Thursday this week. Oh, one more thing—don't forget to enjoy yourself and smile!"

The choir members smile, all right, but going through their minds are not all the things to remember but rather a firm commitment to keep their eyes on the person in front of them. Surely they heard and remembered all those instructions! How worried we would be if we knew that the very person we intend to watch was making the same plan to depend on us!

This Sunday's gospel reading is filled with instructions, too. Jesus, seeing how much shepherding there is to be done, summons his twelve disciples and gives them authority and instructions for being his emissaries to the lost sheep of Israel. The instructions are not easy, nor are the scenes he depicts pleasant. They include rejection, flogging, persecution, and even death. Maybe we should carry a copy of this passage from Matthew to whip out whenever someone approaches us wearing a "Love Jesus and Be Happy" button. How can we remember all the instructions, especially with our minds on all the calamities that might befall us?

Jesus wants to be honest with his disciples, so he does not gild the lily. But even stronger than his warnings are his promises: "Do not worry about how you are to speak or what you are to say, for it is not you who speak, but the Spirit of your Father speaking through you," he says. Besides divine guidance, Jesus' disciples have each other to lend support, to share the load, and to remind each other of the Lord's instructions and promises. With such help, they can do what is asked of them.

It is the same for modern-day disciples, as well. By keeping in fellowship with Christ and with other disciples, our instructions are made more memorable and our loads more bearable. We can confess in a hymn by Margaret R. Seebach:

> Stumbling and blind, we strive to do your will,
> Trusting the word you surely will fulfill,
> That all are yours, however far they roam,
> That love shall triumph, and your kingdom come.
>
> "Your Kingdom Come"

Amen. Let it be so with us.

# *Proper 7*

## *Sunday between June 19 and 25 inclusive*
### *(if after Trinity Sunday)*

How good we feel when Jesus speaks poetically of God's great love and concern for each one of us. We feel safe when we hear that the care God has for sparrows is exceeded by his great care for us. And we feel important when we hear that God knows every hair on our head—something most of us will never even know about ourselves. We are told these things, Jesus says, so that we will have no fear. This message of love and care is an important one, and we shall take great delight in proclaiming it this Sunday in word, sacrament, and song.

But, lest we pack up the message too soon, we had better ask why Jesus spoke so forcefully on this theme of protection. The lines that frame this lovely landscape depict a harsh world that lies in waiting for his disciples. They will be maligned, Jesus tells them. His coming brings not peace but confrontation, even within their families. They must be ready to love Jesus more than anything, including their own lives.

Why would anyone sign up for such a program? Did he hope to gain followers by telling of such things? He surely would have flunked many modern evangelism courses. Couldn't we improve the church's drawing power by emphasizing the sparrow-protecting and hair-counting stuff and playing down the other parts?

Jesus chose to tell the harsh truth rather than attractive lies. And he did it for the sake of honesty and integrity, for the gospel, and, ultimately, for us. The prophecy is paired with the promise so that we will not be surprised when trouble comes, and we will be ready to do battle, knowing that God is for us.

As music ministers, our call is to be faithful proclaimers of the gospel message—the whole message. Only a faith that is this radical and life-changing can preach a God who loves and protects with such passion. Attempts to make the gospel easier, more attractive, or more palatable to contemporary culture are ultimately deceitful and heretical. And such a watered-down faith is not worth our time and attention, much less our effort and devotion.

Jesus instead presents a faith of great substance. It is one that was worthy of his own life and death, and he lovingly offers it to us, in all its richness. Losing our lives for the sake of Christ, we find them in his revolutionary love and radical care. The hymn collector J. Rippon preserved for us this stanza of God's promise:

> *Fear not, I am with you, oh, be not dismayed,*
> *For I am your God and will still give you aid;*
> *I'll strengthen you, help you, and cause you to stand,*
> *Upheld by my righteous, omnipotent hand.*
> "How Firm a Foundation"

# *Proper 8*
## *Sunday between June 26 and July 2 inclusive*

D o you remember those long readings during the Lenten season? This Sunday's gospel makes up for it, as it is only three verses long. But despite its brevity Jesus makes some firm pledges that have long-term impact on his disciples' work. Those who welcome his disciples are welcoming Christ himself, and hence the one who sent him. Likewise, welcoming a prophet or a righteous person is a deed that does more than just share kindness. Furthermore, even giving a cup of cold water to a little one in the name of a disciple is an act of divine worship. In short, Jesus is identifying himself with his message, with all who carry it, and with all who receive it.

Such a pledge of solidarity is possible only from one who has both the divine power to bring about what he pledges and the selfless love to share the honor rightfully due him alone. We stand amazed at such a power and such a love. We also stand amazed at what this revelation means to our discipleship. Our honor is due wherever God's presence is celebrated and his word proclaimed. And our mission field is everywhere and anywhere there is a need.

But Christ's pledge means much to our individual selves, too. For we are blessed and called in baptism to be givers, receivers, and vessels of Christ. As we witness to the salvation he has won, we carry his redemption to all we encounter, finding it true for us as well.

We can pledge our discipleship to Jesus only because he has first pledged his presence and power to us. Sigismund von Birken, in a classic German hymn, lets us sing our pledge of allegiance. Following stanzas that begin "Let us ever walk with Jesus," "Let us suffer here with Jesus," and "Let us gladly die with Jesus," we conclude with:

> *Let us also live with Jesus.*
> *He has risen from the dead*
> *That to life we may awaken.*
> *Jesus, since you are our head,*
> *We are your own living members;*
> *Where you live, there we shall be*
> *in your presence constantly,*
> *Living there with you forever.*
> *Jesus, if I faithful be,*
> *Life eternal grant to me.*
>
> "Let Us Ever Walk with Jesus"

# *Proper 9*
## *Sunday between July 3 and 9 inclusive*

Many involved with the church's worship and music lament their generation's fickleness. Some feel that sound theological tenets and worthy traditions are being threatened and even overtaken by whims and fads of transient culture. Others feel that a changing world and an active Holy Spirit call for newness, unencumbered by the habits of the past or the lethargy of those unwilling to learn new skills. Very little can be taken for granted these days. But one thing is certain—amid all the battles are those who quietly and diligently work, search, and pray for God's call to be made known to them. Their concerns are not so much with taking sides and winning battles, but rather with sharing in the struggle and being open enough to hear the voice of wisdom and truth.

Jesus knew of fickleness in his generation. He pointed out how they criticized John the Baptist for not joining their eating or drinking and Jesus for doing just the opposite. He can't win with this bunch! But he does not dwell on the situation. Instead, Matthew records that Jesus prayed to the Father in gratitude that the great truths have been hidden from the wise and intelligent and revealed instead to infants. As important as are knowledge and skill, Jesus shows that they take a secondary role to humility and dependency on God.

After weeks and weeks of hearing about the tough work, tough road, and tough love of God's kingdom, this Sunday's gospel might be seen by many people as contradictory. Horatius Bonar has set much of its closing paragraph in hymn form:

> I heard the voice of Jesus say, "Come unto me and rest;
> Lay down, O weary one, lay down Your head upon my breast."
> "I Heard the Voice of Jesus Say"

Jesus goes on to tell of a yoke he has for each of us. Even though a yoke is a tool for doing hard work, he tells us that his yoke is easy and his burden light. As beautiful as this imagery is, we can only marvel how it contrasts with his other metaphors for discipleship. Is Jesus in reality the fickle one? Is he telling his followers what they want to hear rather than what they need to hear? Is this the watering down and dumbing down we so fear for disciples of our generation?

If we give our critical impulses a rest and let Christ speak to us, we can hear him being just the opposite of fickle. He is proclaiming his unwavering presence with us at work and at rest, in our times of energy and of weariness, when exercising our fortes and wallowing in our insecurities. Even the work of the kingdom is subservient to the loving relationship Christ wants with his disciples. Work, knowledge, and skill receive their deepest rooting and highest calling as they grow out of such a relationship. Bonar's hymn also voices a disciple's response:

> I came to Jesus as I was, So weary, worn, and sad;
> I found in him a resting place, And he has made me glad.

To the one who gives us rest, gladness, and custom-made yokes, let us join our voices in humble praise. And let us open our minds to receive the wisdom we need to live in a fickle world.

Matthew 11:16-19, 25-30

# Proper 10
## Sunday between July 10 and 16 inclusive

Does everyone in your congregation keep silent and reverent during the prelude? Are your people always attentive when the choir sings? Do your preachers and presiders catch every nuance of the choir's message in word and melody? Do your choir members pay close attention to every word and action of the liturgy? Do we ever have to call out, "Listen!"

Now that just about everybody has been accused and reprimanded, let us return to reality. It is human nature to be selective about our listening habits. And it is the nature of good music and full, rich, spiritual worship to contain more than we can ever appreciate and comprehend. Even in the presence of Christ himself we need to be reminded to listen. And so it has been with disciples of every age.

In this Sunday's gospel Jesus announces his forthcoming parable by calling out, "Listen!" And he concludes the parable with the charge, "Let anyone with ears listen!" In between these two exclamations is the story of seeds which fall on a variety of surfaces. The ones that fell on the hard pathway, on rocky ground, or among thorns fail to thrive. But those that fell in the good soil flourish and produce much grain. The message is clear—how much better it is for us to be good soil rather than hard, shallow, or thorny ground. Though we do not hold the power in ourselves to control the kingdom of God, we are blessed as God plants and brings about growth in and through us. In a hymn by John Newton, so appropriately sung at the close of a worship service, we pray:

> On what has now been sown Your blessing, Lord, bestow;
> The power is yours alone To make it sprout and grow.
>
> "On What Has Now Been Sown"

But let us open our ears and listen to one more part of this parable. What about that wasteful sower? Shouldn't he have been more careful with his seeds than to scatter them on a path, in the rocks, or among the thorns in the first place? Likewise, as we answer the call to minister in our own unique ways, shouldn't we be careful to not waste the precious gift of the kingdom?

Jesus' parable is not about smart farming, it is about God's work and the assisting role we are privileged to share. We are not responsible for supplying the seed or causing it to grow—that is God's role. Under God's management, the seed is so plentiful, the nurturing so effective, and the potential for growth so great that we can be excessive and even extravagant in our sowing.

We may never know where the seeds fall and what becomes of them. But, even in those who are not paying attention to our musical offerings, maybe a seed is being planted. And just maybe, in those sermons, readings, and prayers whose full impact we may miss, seeds have been planted in us. Let us be about our calling to be doers and hearers, not only in worship, but in every aspect of our lives.

# *Proper 11*
## *Sunday between July 17 and 23 inclusive*

Jesus often used the metaphor of seeds to teach important lessons about God's kingdom. Seeds are tiny, yet they can grow into huge plants. Seeds are plentiful, yet not all will sprout and grow. And a seed's productivity is affected by the ground on which it falls. Such big pictures of the kingdom he has given us from such tiny creations!

This week's gospel contains yet another "seedy" story. This time an enemy has sown weeds among the wheat, and the hungry sprouts threaten the success of the crop. The workers are ready to pull out all the weeds, but the wisdom of the householder points to a different solution. Eliminating the weeds will endanger the wheat, he fears. Let them grow and ripen together; the harvest will be the time for separating the wheat and the weeds.

There is indeed much wisdom in this teaching, but we may wish Jesus' message had been more definitive. Oh, the call for tolerance and patience is clear, but we are not given much help in separating the wheat from the weeds. What is the key to wise discernment?

Church musicians with some years of experience often look back to times when the music sung or played was quite different from what it is now. "Can you believe we used to do this stuff and felt it was good?" we might muse. Or we might ponder in amazement how certain musical styles we feel called to use now would have offended our better judgment even a decade ago. How do we separate the worthy from the unworthy or even from the less worthy? Truly, our greatest need in separating the weeds from the wheat is wise discernment. It is a commodity hard to define; it is even harder to obtain and administer.

Just as the farm hands had to be guided by their master's wisdom, the discernment we seek most is the will of Christ. We are also reminded in this story that the most important answers in life are seldom easy to do or even easy to understand. Zeal and quickness are not always virtues. And those who claim to speak for God must be cautious and ever open to change lest they stifle or deny the continuing creativity of the Holy Spirit. Hymnwriter Michael Schirmer expressed this need centuries ago when he wrote:

> *Left to ourselves, we surely stray;*
> *Oh, lead us on the narrow way,*
> *With wisest counsel guide us;*
> *And give us steadfastness, that we*
> *May follow you forever free,*
> *No matter who derides us.*
>
> "O Holy Spirit, Enter In"

We work, pray, and struggle for the skills, artistry, insights, patience, and humility to be faithful caretakers of the seeds growing in and about God's kingdom.

# Proper 12
## Sunday between July 24 and 30 inclusive

Have you ever been introduced to a group and then been told, "Tell us all about yourself!"? It can be a frightening request. Do you tell about your family, hometown, education, employment, hobbies, faith, or your choir membership? Do you tell how you spent your summer vacation? How about expressing the anxiety you feel by being put on the spot and having to summarize what's most important to and about you, all in a few sentences? We are simply too complex to sum up in a few cheery comments.

This Sunday's gospel may sound as if Jesus has just been asked to explain God's kingdom in ten sentences or less, for Matthew has recorded for us a series of mini-parables. In twelve short verses Jesus says the kingdom is like a mustard seed, some yeast, a treasure in the field, a pearl of great value, and a fishing net. And those who encounter the kingdom are compared to sowers, birds, bread bakers, treasure hunters, pearl merchants, and fish. What a combination of descriptions! It is no wonder that we can have an identity complex as we try to discover and define our place in God's kingdom.

Jesus is, of course, speaking metaphorically. Why, instead of telling us what the kingdom is like, couldn't he tell us what it really is? Ideal as that sounds, we simply couldn't handle it. It is beyond our capabilities to understand such wonders. Only a few things within our experience can give us even a glimpse of the greatness, so Jesus piled up the helpful images, creating a composite picture far greater than what any one description could do by itself.

Christians need not be ashamed of the many ways we think and speak of the triune God and the workings of the kingdom. Many of our metaphors come right from scripture; others come from faithful disciples of distant times and cultures. And many new ones are graciously offered to us for our consideration and inspiration. We continue to discover that good metaphoric language does not disguise or distort the truth—it reveals it.

There is even one more mini-parable in this full package from Matthew. Jesus tells the crowds, "Therefore every scribe who has been trained for the kingdom of heaven is like the master of a household who brings out of his treasure what is new and what is old." We, too, are truly rich when we treasure the best poetic images from the past as well as make room for new ones that express the wide diversity of God's world and God's people. Hymnody continues to be both a classroom and a playground for new images to mingle with the old. Twentieth-century hymnwiter Cesáreo Gabaraín had some surprising things to describe our calling as Christians:

> *You are the dawn that will bring a new day;*
> *you're the wheat that will bear golden grain;*
> *you are a sting and a soft, gentle touch,*
> *to witness wherever you go.*

"You Are the Seed/Sois la Semilla"

Will the addition of more metaphors bring even more confusion to our task of understanding and working in God's kingdom? Not if we realize that it is not an identity complex that we have—what we have as Christians are richly complex identities!

Matthew 13:31-33, 44-52

# Proper 13
## Sunday between July 31 and August 6 inclusive

I vant to be alone!" was the dramatic cry of legendary actress Greta Garbo. Most of us will never experience or understand the intense pressures faced by celebrities, but at least their fame and financial means often give them the opportunity to get the solitude they want.

We may utter the same cry at times in our lives. "I want to be alone," pleads the practicing organist upon seeing the custodian entering with the vacuum cleaner. "We want to be alone," complains the choir after hearing how the full congregation soaks up the resonant, lively sound they produced when the room was empty. "We want to be left alone," warn worship leaders as they feel pressures from many directions to alter the liturgy and its music. Wanting to be left alone can be a cop-out at times. But being alone can also be a time of retreat, reflection, and renewal.

Jesus is presented to us in a very human fashion as this Sunday's gospel reading opens. He has just heard of the tragic beheading of John the Baptist. Matthew records that Jesus withdrew in a boat to a deserted place by himself. He had much to contemplate. John was his relative, his forerunner, his baptizer, his preacher! How different John's life would have been had he not gotten involved with Jesus! What did this mean for all the others who proclaimed him as the Savior? Was he signing their death warrants, too?

But Jesus' retreat time, deserved as it was, was cut short; the crowds heard where he was headed and followed. Seeing them, he had compassion and cured their sick. And there is even more work to do, for the crowd stays through the evening. The disciples are concerned for the people's mealtime, for the high cost of providing enough food, and for the chaos that could ensue. Shouldn't they give a supper break so the people can go into the villages to buy food? Jesus chooses another storyline, one that creates a sensation of its own and proclaims the kingdom of God in a most profound way. More than five thousand are fed from five loaves and two fish, and the copious leftovers are a sermon in themselves! There is nothing reposeful about this day!

Sorrow and joy stand side by side on this day in Jesus' life. It is a day of weariness and great activity, of retreat and full charge ahead, of solitude and massive crowds, of bad news and exuberant Gospel. Is it that Jesus cannot make up his mind? No, his day is one of contrasts because he is responding to the diverse needs around him. As his messengers in this world, we want nothing other than this for ourselves. We hear Albert F. Bayly's hymn:

> Father, providing food for your children,
> By your wise guiding teach us to share
> One with another, so that, rejoicing
> With us, all others may know your care.
>
> "Praise and Thanksgiving"

Yes, we want to be alone at times. But, more importantly, we want to join with Jesus in his daily routine of meeting needs.

# Proper 14

## Sunday between August 7 and 13 inclusive

Have you ever experienced performance anxiety? Even soloists who always appear calm and collected admit to being nervous at times. They fear their voice might crack, or they might forget where to breathe, or they might jumble the words, or someone might laugh, or the ceiling might collapse, or . . . you fill in the blank. Why would we put ourselves through such anguish? Psychologists tell us that the worst nightmare for many persons is the fear of performing music in public. They also tell us what is the ultimate goal of these same people—it is to perform music in public! Go figure! It is a strange, paradoxical force that drives us to embark on that first performance. It fulfills deeply, but what separates success from failure is only a thin layer of confidence. It can feel much like walking on water.

Lest you think we're hinting for volunteers to make their solo debuts, we should point out that it is St. Peter who is going "solo" this Sunday. The scene is familiar—Jesus' disciples are in a boat when a storm hits. Seeing someone walking toward them on the water, their fear is magnified. "It is a ghost!" they cry. "Take heart, it is I; do not be afraid," is the comforting response from their master. Peter, needing more assurance that this really is Jesus, makes the suggestion, "Lord, if it is you, command me to come to you on the water." Jesus' response is brief. "Come," he says.

What was going though Peters' mind as he took those first tentative steps? His thoughts probably bounced between confidence and doubt, much like our own mental conversations. "Me and my big mouth! Why didn't I leave this to the pros? Well, maybe I can do it. No, I'll just have to dry off and leave town. But if I can do this it will make me famous. Maybe I should picture the others in their underwear. I wish a fire drill would happen right now. I can count on Jesus' help, but I'm not so sure of myself. Yes, I can do it! Then again . . ."

You probably know how the story turned out. Reviewers of his performance could truthfully say that Peter was all wet. But let's not forget those first few steps he did take before his focus shifted from Jesus to his own fear. Jesus called his faith "little," but by doing so he did acknowledge its presence. And by testing it he gave Peter a valuable lesson. Yes, even a little faith can work wonders, and it can be the ripple that grows into a wave. But, ultimately, we must take no pride in the magnitude of our faith, for it is not of our own creation. It is a gift from the Faithful One who calms the storms, holds out a gracious hand, and bids us come.

Though we usually think of sailors when we hear it, the hymn by William Whiting is meaningful to all who face the storms:

> *O Savior, whose almighty word*
> *The winds and waves submissive heard,*
> *Who walked upon the foaming deep,*
> *And calm amid the storm didst sleep.*
> "Eternal Father, Strong to Save"

In times of confidence or doubt, surrounded by a chorus or singing solo, Jesus says, "Take heart, it is I; do not be afraid."

# *Proper 15*

## *Sunday between August 14 and 20 inclusive*

Have you ever been involved in a remodeling project during which an old wall was removed? The newly enlarged room has a new and different feel all its own. Though some parts may continue to resemble the old rooms, their combination is a new creation, and the possibilities it opens up are exciting.

Walls serve many important practical purposes. They provide protection from elements and enemies, they reflect sound and light, and they give us a place to hang our pictures. They provide a rich metaphoric purpose, as well. Whenever peoples are divided by race or religion, culture or custom, we inevitably turn to "wall-talk" to describe the situation. And how vivid the image is in our minds whenever we hear of walls coming down.

Jesus tore down many walls during his earthly ministry. This Sunday's gospel tells of a particularly tough wall, and breaking it down gives a new, panoramic view of his ministry. Jesus and his disciples are confronted by a woman who requests healing for her daughter. That should sound familiar, for such requests are plentiful in the Gospels. But this woman is a Canaanite, and one of the thickest, tallest walls in all history existed between her people and the Jews. The disciples knew of this wall, and they presumed it was impenetrable. "Send her away, for she keeps shouting after us," they plead. Jesus' response is also shocking. "I was sent only to the lost sheep of the house of Israel," he says, defending his refusal. But she persists, provoking an even more scandalous response from Jesus, "It is not fair to take the children's food and throw it to the dogs." Was he serious in his protests? Were there other incidents, perhaps unrecorded, where he refused healing when he was asked? Did he actually change his mind? Was he playing along just to make a point?

Let's leave those questions for the preachers. What is important for us to note is how her clever response caused Jesus to pronounce her faith great and her daughter healed. This episode signifies walls of huge proportions being scaled, shot full of holes, and brought crashing to the ground. The walls of racism, classism, sexism, and sectarianism have their very foundations undermined by this outrageous act of Christ.

But many of the same walls are still standing, we argue, and some seem stronger and taller than ever before. We may sing and hope for a world described in John Oxenham's hymn:

> In Christ now meet both east and west,
> In him meet south and north;
> All Christly souls are one in him
> Throughout the whole wide earth.
>
> "In Christ There Is No East or West"

But are we naive or even mistaken to believe it?

The world that does not recognize Christ is also yet unaware that its walls are hollow. The chipping away goes slowly, it seems. But every deed of mercy done in Christ's name loosens a stone or two. Every note of music that proclaims God's way over the world's way leaves a dent in the plaster. The barriers are doomed; we can live as if they don't exist, walking freely the paths cleared by the wall-demolishing Christ. The new room looks marvelous, and the possibilities it opens up are exhilarating!

# Proper 16

## Sunday between August 21 and 27 inclusive

We all know the type of conversation that begins with the phrase, "I thought you should know what others are saying . . ." After such a disclaimer the speakers feel free to say whatever they wish, confident that by quoting others they are immune from any responsibility for what is being said. Perhaps the best way to respond to such "helpful" reporting is to say, "But what do you think?" Their tune will usually change!

In this Sunday's gospel we will hear a similar dialogue between Jesus and his disciples. "Who do people say that the Son of Man is?" he asks. The disciples are repeating what they have heard as they report, "Some say John the Baptist, but others Elijah, and still others Jeremiah or one of the prophets." Then Jesus digs deeper and asks, "But who do you say that I am?"

Matthew does not indicate how much time passed before Peter responded with his famous confession, "You are the Messiah, the Son of the living God!" "Blessed are you," Jesus responds. He goes on to pronounce Peter's confession as a divine revelation and that on this rock will be built his Church; hell itself will not be able to prevail against it. This insight must have been of phenomenal importance to elicit such a response from Jesus. Nikolai Grundtvig captured this excitement in the sturdy hymn:

> Built on a rock the church shall stand,
> Even when steeples are falling;
> Crumbled have spires in every land,
> Bells still are chiming and calling.

"Built on a Rock"

There is nothing warm and fuzzy about a rock. And there is nothing sentimental about the keys of the kingdom and the power to bind and loose which Jesus grants to his disciples. How can we ever with a clear conscience proclaim Christ in minimizing or marginalizing language? Peter has given us an example to follow. Get past what others say; proclaim boldly in word and deed that Jesus is the Messiah, the Son of the living God. We want to stay close to that which is rock-solid, and we pledge our loyalties to a faith so strongly rooted in the living God.

"Rock solid" is a term we often use to describe someone's personality, dependability, or emotional stability. It is also used in music when describing someone with a strong sense of rhythm. They can keep the beat no matter what others are doing around them. Far from being boring, a steady beat provides the basis from which endless variations can be created. A rock-solid beat is the common language, the steady support, the living pulse.

May our music, our worship, and our lives find their foundation and inspiration in the solid presence of the living God.

Matthew 16:13-20

# *Proper 17*

## *Sunday between August 28 and September 3 inclusive*

This Sunday we shall be hearing again about Peter in the gospel reading. Last week he was the proclaimer of Jesus as "the Christ, the Son of the living God!" This week Jesus addresses Peter with the stern rebuke, "Get behind me, Satan!" Why the change? Is Peter, after all, the rock or a hindrance?

Truthfully, he is both for he is very human. Peter receives his strong admonition after a dispute with Jesus. Jesus says he must go to Jerusalem, suffer, be killed, and be raised up. Peter is quick to protest, hoping as we all would, that such drastic measures will not be necessary. Jesus' harshness shows how important he knows his mission to be. He will not let Peter soft pedal it or suggest an easy way out. We should likewise remember Jesus' admonition whenever we are tempted to proclaim a non-crucified Savior, whenever we encounter a watered-down Christianity, or whenever the ways of the world are embraced as the ways of God.

We acknowledge the world's situation and plead for release in the words of hymn-writer Somerset C. Lowry:

> *Come, O Christ, and reign among us,*
> *King of love and Prince of Peace;*
> *Hush the storm of strife and passion,*
> *Bid its cruel discords cease.*
>
> "Son of God, Eternal Savior"

God's ways, as Jesus has shown us again, are often paradox. To follow Jesus one must take up one's cross. Those who try to save their own lives will lose them, and those who lose their lives for Christ's sake will find them. Those who gain the world forfeit their lives, and, ultimately, to live is to die. Such are the dynamic truths of Christianity. "They must be true" goes the old saying, "for no human could have invented such a preposterous faith."

This, then, is the paradoxical truth to which we witness whenever we gather for worship. Such fantastic and unbelievable truths must be constantly rehearsed and continually proclaimed for us to learn them. Even then, we must ultimately rely on God's gift of faith to believe such claims and on God's grace to fulfill them. Such a God is not for us to fully understand—only to trust, serve, imitate, worship, and praise.

# *Proper 18*
## *Sunday between September 4 and 10 inclusive*

One of Jesus' primary concerns was that of unity and camaraderie among his followers. He told parables and prayed at length for the unity of individuals with each other and with God. His great emphasis shows how crucial he felt unity to be and, perhaps even more importantly, how difficult he knew unity is to achieve. The state of the church proves his concerns were correct. There are differences between Eastern and Western Christianity; between Catholics, Protestants, and in-betweens; between denominations that may even carry the same name, within synods and districts, between parishes, between groups within congregations, and even within small groups such as choirs and classes. We need to earnestly pray with the hymnwriter Olive Wise Spannaus:

> *Lord of all nations, grant me grace*
> *To love all peoples every race;*
> *And in each person may I see*
> *My kindred, loved, redeemed by thee.*
>
> "Lord of All Nations, Grant Me Grace"

We would not blame Jesus one bit if the tone of his voice had been cynical or even sarcastic when he spoke the words we shall hear in this Sunday's gospel—"If two of you agree on earth about anything you ask; it will be done for you by my Father in heaven." Jesus the realist was decrying the divisiveness and uncooperativeness of his followers. Yet, within this lament lies a promise—"For where two or three are gathered in my name, I am there among them."

We surely have a special relationship with God on a one-to-one basis. It is a promise sealed in baptism and crucially important for every Christian life. But over and over we are told of the special presence of Christ with the community—the assembly of people, be it as large as thousands or as small as two or three. That special presence is the reason we assemble for corporate worship time after time. It is precisely in the corporateness of gathering, confessing, hearing, responding, baptizing, communing, speaking, and singing together that this lesson is proclaimed and learned anew. We are people, and we are a people.

Have you noticed that some of the same terms can describe relationships and music? Unison and harmony we recognize as positive attributes both inside and outside of the choir loft. Dissonance and other off-key descriptions describe something else.

Fortunately, Christ's promise to be present whenever two or three are gathered in his name is not conditional upon all people being in agreement. At those times of conflict we may be less likely to sense the presence of Jesus, but, regardless, his promise remains.

Our efforts at music-making proclaim the word and are parables in themselves on what greatness can happen when individuality is offered up for the benefit of the whole body, and when diversity is woven into harmony. For even here, in the midst of us who have gathered in his name, is the Lord.

Matthew 18:15-20

# *Proper 19*

## *Sunday between September 11 and 17 inclusive*

Numbers, numbers everywhere! They mark our houses and postal zones, run our telephones and calculators, identify our charge accounts and tax withholdings, and mark the passing of time on clocks and calendars. Accurate counting is essential in making music, as well. Numbers help us to find pages and measures, and counting helps us to read rhythms and stay together. As a choir, we depend heavily on our numbers.

Numbers and counting are indeed essential tools we use every day and in nearly every area of life. But Jesus tells us in this Sunday's gospel of one very important area where numbers and counting are not to be used. Once again, it is Peter who has asked a question. "Lord, if another member of the church sins against me, how often should I forgive? As many as seven times?" Jesus' first response is short. "Not seven times, but, I tell you, seventy-seven times," Jesus seems initially to be just as caught up with numbers as was Peter. But a parable quickly follows which tells about a servant who was forgiven many debts and then hypocritically went out and dealt forcefully with one who owed him a mere pittance.

It all seems so obvious when Jesus teaches us, but applying it to our own situations is often another matter. We can relate to the hymn stanza by Rosamond E. Herklots that asks:

> How can your pardon reach and bless
> The unforgiving heart
> That broods on wrongs and will not let
> Old bitterness depart?
>
> "Forgive Our Sins as We Forgive"

We are not to withhold forgiveness, Jesus tells us, no matter how deeply we feel we are owed, because we have been forgiven a debt of cosmic proportions. Just as we are to love because God first loved us, we are to forgive because God has first forgiven us.

How often need we forgive? As often as necessary! And may God grant us the wisdom to know when we should remember to count and when we should remember to forget!

# *Proper 20*

## *Sunday between September 18 and 24 inclusive*

Justice is a noble goal. Much of our government and society works so that all are treated as equally as possible, that lawbreakers are punished, and that exemplary service is rewarded. We try to model our personal relationships on the same ideals of just treatment and equality.

Many day-to-day activities of the congregation follow the practice of rewarding good workers. Long-time members are called "pillars of the church," and leadership positions are likely to be given to those who have proven themselves capable. Those who have been in choir the longest usually form the core group and may be first in line for honors. Such systems usually work well, except, of course, when good ideas are ignored because they come from new people, or when newcomers are not made to feel welcome by the old guard. Such are the ups and downs of the world's varied understandings of justice.

In this Sunday's gospel Jesus tells a parable on a rather controversial topic—that of equitable pay for comparable work. Just try to find a day when this topic does not come up in some form or another! In this parable, those who labored all day are paid the same as those who worked only the last hour. The workers are understandably upset at such a policy, forcing the employer to explain his actions. Justice has been done, he explains, because he gave to each worker the amount that was agreed upon. It is within his right to do what he pleases with his wealth. What the workers are really upset about is his generosity!

Obviously, such a parable is not about how to run a business; it is yet another glimpse into the kingdom of God. Is Jesus saying that God has no sense of justice? Surely not, for God is our very model of justice, and God surely wants justice to prevail in all earthly matters. But here Jesus is saying that God's justice is on so large a scale that we may have a hard time seeing it from our limited perspective. God's love and saving grace is for all people, not just for those who have been loyal the longest or show the most obvious signs, noble as those attributes may be. In one of the Reformation's earliest hymns, Paul Speratus set into verse this pillar of the faith:

> *Salvation unto us has come*
> *By God's free grace and favor;*
> *Good works cannot avert our doom,*
> *They help and save us never.*
> *Faith looks to Jesus Christ alone,*
> *Who did for all the world atone;*
> *He is our mediator.*
>
> "Salvation unto Us Has Come"

Under God's rule we are not paid according to what we deserve, and we thank God for that! We are all given the same gracious gift from the same generous God, and that is more than any deserve. We, equally undeserving yet equally forgiven, live our lives in gratitude and sing our songs of praise to God, the lavish giver.

Matthew 20:1-16

# *Proper 21*

## *Sunday between September 25 and October 1 inclusive*

In this Sunday's gospel we will hear Jesus' parable of a man with two sons. Both sons are told to go work in the vineyard. One says no but later does go and work. The other says yes but does not go and work. Once again Jesus has told a parable about a situation to which many can relate. Parents and children, students and teachers, bosses and workers, and even choir members and directors can recognize times when this behavior occurs.

It probably didn't take the disciples any longer than it takes us to figure out which son was looked upon favorably. Obviously, it is the one who, in the end, does the work that the father requested. Christ is calling his followers to action, to be doers and not just hearers or agree-ers.

But, lest we conclude this parable's message too soon, let us consider one more angle. Jesus' parable is about two people-one who said yes but did no and one who said no but did yes. Could not the story have included two more siblings? How about one who says no and indeed does not work and another who says yes and follows through? Surely these two additional cases would be very easy to judge with condemnation for one and high praise for the other.

Do such consistently good or consistently bad persons exist? They are not a part of this story, at least. That is probably because most of us are found in that gray, in-between area inhabited by those who often say yes and do no and often say no and do yes. By telling of two imperfect and inconsistent individuals Jesus is acknowledging the reality of the human condition. Still marred by the evils of our selves and the world, God's work in us is strong enough to turn no's into yes's. This parable speaks to us about repentance—the turning around of attitude as well as actions.

In the midst of all the glory proclaimed in her hymn which begins "At the Name of Jesus," Caroline M. Noel placed this charge:

> *In your hearts enthrone him; there let him subdue*
> *All that is not holy, all that is not true.*
> *Crown him as your captain in temptation's hour;*
> *Let his will enfold you in its light and power.*
>
> "At the Name of Jesus"

This is the earnest hope and highest goal of those who know they are not perfect, but who, with God's help and forgiveness, can experience the relationship God wants with us and can do the work God has planned for us.

# Proper 22
## Sunday between October 2 and 8 inclusive

Twenty-twenty hindsight" is the term often used to describe our ability to look back on a past event and know now what would have been the best path to take. "We should have bought that parcel of land where the shopping mall now stands. We should not have accepted those first job offers. We should have nurtured that friendship rather than let it die. We should not have quit music lessons when we were young."

The list could be endless, but, since clairvoyance is not within the grasp of most of us, we are destined to win a few and lose a few, to make some wrong choices and even some right ones, all based on our best judgments at the time.

In this Sunday's gospel we will hear a parable about people who use poor judgment. They are tenants, working on a farm owned by someone else. Yet, when the householder sends messengers to collect his rightful dues, they are treated shamefully. The ultimate blow comes when the owner's son is sent as a special emissary, and even he is cast out and killed. Will the tenants now get to keep what they fought for? Certainly not! Because of their rebellion even what they have will be taken away. Had they known the consequences they surely would have done things differently.

Jesus concludes this parable by quoting the Old Testament: "The very stone which the builders rejected has become the head of the corner." Just as a cornerstone supports the building, identifies it, and contains its treasures, Christ is both the sure foundation and cornerstone of the church. We who live on this side of the resurrection have the benefit of this 20-20 hindsight. We need not doubt his words, actions, commands, and promises which are proclaimed through the church in word, sacrament, and song. Still, in light of our tendency to make poor choices at times, we cannot help but wonder and pray with the hymnic words of W. Russel Bowie:

> New advent of the love of Christ,
> Will we again refuse you,
> Till in the night of hate and war
> We perish as we lose you?
> "Lord Christ, When First You Came to Earth"

We have one more, even greater, gift from now on—the gift of 20-20 foresight. Jesus has shown us that he is this one who was once rejected but now is the cornerstone of our lives in the present and in the future. We live our lives, do our deeds, sing our songs, proclaim the promises, and trust the future to this one who is the sure foundation.

Matthew 21:33-46

# *Proper 23*
## *Sunday between October 9 and 15 inclusive*

Charles Dickens was referring to the French Revolution when he penned, "It was the best of times; it was the worst of times." But he could have just as appropriately been writing about another event that can involve battles, bayonets, and even beheadings—church weddings! They can be times of high emotions, high expectations, and high anxieties—all pointing to the importance we place on them. For a marriage ceremony is a most important rite of passage, a sign of ongoing life, and an embodiment of divine and human love. If only the details of processions and programs, signals and solos, cousins and carnations weren't so complicated!

Jesus tells of a highly complicated wedding in this Sunday's gospel. Though many customs differed in his day, guest lists and food preparations were as crucial then as they are now. But this father-of-the-groom is having trouble. The slaves he sends out to gather the invited guests are receiving troublesome responses. Some treat the invitation lightly, others are too stuck to their work, and some are so hostile that they actually kill the messengers. What would the host do after being treated so badly?

Since the banquet was already prepared, there was no time to write to Dear Abby. After sending troops to take revenge on those who killed his messengers, he gives his slaves new orders. This time they are to go into the streets, inviting anybody and everybody to come. Even after the hall is filled, there is yet one more episode—someone is there without a wedding robe, and he must be punished and banished. Jesus' closing words are brief, "For many are called, but few are chosen." Is that all he can say to us after such a complicated story about such a complicated wedding banquet?

If we have spent time with this parable before, we probably already know that this is not about an average, every-day wedding. This is the messianic banquet, the supreme fulfillment of God's own kingdom, the ultimate Holy Communion, the marriage feast of the Lamb.

This is one wedding we do not want to miss; it truly will be one to remember. Just how can we properly acknowledge the invitation and be best prepared to honor the host? Forget the formal wear and the matching shoes and flowers. Just what is the proper wedding robe?

The robe is that of Jesus' righteousness given to us in baptism. Any further adornments spring from our joy at being invited. In a classic communion hymn, Johann Franck bids us:

> *Soul, adorn yourself with gladness,*
> *Leave the gloomy haunts of sadness,*
> *Come into the daylight's splendor,*
> *There with joy your praises render.*
> *Bless the one whose grace unbounded*
> *This amazing banquet founded;*
> *He, though heavenly, high, and holy,*
> *Deigns to dwell with you most lowly.*
>
> "Soul, Adorn Yourself with Gladness"

For all who accept the invitation, this wedding will surely be the "best of times!"

# Proper 24

## *Sunday between October 16 and 22 inclusive*

Some people keep separate sets of clothes just for church. Perhaps they do not dress up much on other days of the week, or perhaps they just want to keep something special for such a special place. Some people do the same with their manners, speech, and behavior. Some even have a special "church-singing" tone, saving their other voices for the opera house, the cabaret, the Sweet Adelines, or the shower. Sometimes what we reserve for the church is truly our "Sunday best." Other times, we may feel second- and third-rate stuff is good enough for the church. There truly are singers, instrumentalists, poets, and composers out there who compromise their art and skill, believing that pious intentions and a willing market are all the requirements they need. We, too, can be tempted to treat the church as one small organization among the millions that make up this world. And we can be tempted to compartmentalize our Christianity as just one activity among the dozens in which we participate. We hang up our Christian identity right next to our Sunday clothes; there they wait until the next time we need them.

It is not easy to define and identify what is truly sacred in this world and what is purely secular. The Pharisees were dealing with such labels when they tried to trick Jesus into speaking out against the government. In this Sunday's gospel, we hear them ask if it is lawful for religious people to pay taxes. Jesus chooses to not answer the entrapping question; instead he points to the image appearing on the coin. "Give therefore to the emperor the things that are the emperor's, and to God the things that are God's," is his memorable reply. At first hearing, he seems to be making a clear distinction between sacred and secular. But just what, we might ask, are God's things?

Most of us probably belong to denominations which encourage us to pay our fair share of taxes, for even the work of the church benefits from the safety, education, transportation, and conveniences taxes help provide. Some of our taxes even go to feeding the hungry, helping the sick, and keeping world peace. That's quite different from the way things were in Jesus' day. It might be that the lines between sacred and secular work are even more intertwined now than back then. How can we give the "emperor" what is due? More importantly, how can we discern what belongs to God so we can make our offering?

Hymnwriter F. Pratt Green turned this dilemma into a prayer. Referring to what happens at worship, he writes:

> *Here the servants of the Servant seek in worship to explore*
> *what it means in daily living to believe and to adore.*
> "God Is Here"

In Christ's incarnation, God has placed a blessing on the things of this world. God makes holy the skills, arts, voices, labors, and all good works done to God's honor. We give to God not our dregs, nor our second-best, nor even our Sunday best. We offer every part of our lives—our very best—to honor and to serve.

# *Proper 25*

## *Sunday between October 23 and 29 inclusive*

A choir member asks the director, "Are we to watch you or look at the printed music?" A child asks a parent, "Do you love me or are you going to discipline me?" A parishoner asks the pastor, "Do Christians benefit from the word or the sacraments?"

Obviously, the answer in each of these cases is "both." That quick response would likely be followed by a longer explanation to point out that the two parts of each of those questions are not in competition with each other. They are not options but different aspects of the same truth. Both sides are necessary; they depend and build on each other. Simplistic and legalistic minds always want one correct answer. But simple answers have one thing in common—they are usually incomplete.

So it is in this Sunday's gospel when the Pharisees ask, "Which commandment of the law is the greatest?" Jesus answers, "You shall love the Lord your God with all your heart, and with all your soul, and with all your mind." His answer is firmly rooted in the scriptures and Jewish tradition, and he can boldly proclaim the correct answer to their test question.

But he cannot let it drop there; he needs to tell them the rest of the story, adding, "And a second is like it: You shall love your neighbor as yourself." Jesus refuses to separate these two pillars of the faith. Neither is quite right without the other, he wants them to know.

Some might think, "There is no way I can do a good job at obeying both of those tough commandments, so I will choose one and try to do it really well." It sounds silly, doesn't it? But we need not look very far to see those who try to ignore the distractions of the world so they can concentrate on being holy, or those who are so preoccupied with what they can do for others that they forget the source and sustainer of life. We can also find choir members who try to rely solely on the director or solely on the printed page, or parents who discipline without love or love without discipline, or church members who are undernourished from refusing the promised means of grace. Such people are all around us, and they are often in us.

Is it, then, simply a matter of valuing both sides of the issue and trying to balance them? That's still not quite right. Jesus tells us that upon these two commandments hang all the law and the prophets. They have been boiled down to one ultimate commandment with two, interdependent sides. Love of God results in love of neighbor; we can love our neighbor only because God loves us. Such a balanced faith frees us from attempting the balancing act, frees us from keeping track of points, frees us from ourselves, and frees us for service.

How can such a faith be ours? It is given as a gift from the one who proclaimed and lived a life of integrated love and service. Hymnwriter Brian Wren tells us where we might look to learn Christ's example:

> *We strain to glimpse your mercy seat*
> *and find you kneeling at our feet.*
> "Great God, Your Love Has Called Us"

# *Proper 26*
## *Sunday between October 30 and November 5 inclusive*

Isn't it hard to be humble when you're as good as we are? Okay, maybe we have one or two things we could be humble about, but we'll work on that whenever humility is coming up in the lectionary. Thank goodness we get warnings about such topics; we'll wear less jewelry that day, pack away the great masters and dust off the folk songs, and exchange our smiles for looks of intense earnestness.

Consider this your warning. For in this Sunday's gospel Jesus condemns the scribes and Pharisees for not doing what they teach others to do, for giving out burdens they do not themselves bear, for doing their deeds in public just for show, and for taking the seats of honor and demanding high respect wherever they go. In short, their humility rating is an F.

Jesus was a different sort of rabbi, and it showed. His behavior and demeanor provoked the Pharisees and puzzled the people. His eccentricities made it easy for the Pharisees to dismiss his claims. "If you really were a rabbi, you would act like one!" they might have charged. The people took to him on account of this same unique quality. "Here is one who exhibits all the signs of being in close communion with God, yet he treats us as equals," they might have exclaimed. In spite of their varied reactions to Jesus, both sides could agree on one thing—he was radically consistent in his words, deeds, and treatment of others.

"The greatest among you will be your servant. All who exalt themselves will be humbled, and all who humble themselves will be exalted," Jesus concludes. Is there any way to get that humility for ourselves? Probably not, for as soon as we make it our goal we will spend so much time and effort examining ourselves and checking our progress that it will defeat the purpose. We certainly want to avoid a false humility—that's even harder to take than arrogance. And we do not want to deny all the good that we can do, for that dishonors the God who gave us our talents and the ability to develop our skills. It really is hard to be humble, isn't it? Even when we try.

That is probably our best hope—to stop trying so hard to be humble and strive rather for consistency—our actions consistent with our thoughts, our words consistent with our deeds, our lives consistent with the example of Christ. With this kind of humility we need never worry that it will start to take pride in itself—we'll never be able to perfect it. Bianco da Siena prayed for this humility in the early 15th century:

> *Let holy charity mine outward vesture be,*
> *And lowliness become my inner clothing -*
> *True lowliness of heart, which takes the humbler part,*
> *And o'er its own shortcomings weeps with loathing.*
>
> "Come Down, O Love Divine"

As choir members, we embody the paradox of which Jesus speaks. It may seem to others and even to ourselves that we are worthy of great accolades on account of our talents and commitments. We even sit in places of honor and command attention. Yet, we are the servants of the worshiping community and of the Lord we love. We are set apart, called into a ministry of service. With such a high calling, it is indeed hard to be humble.

Matthew 23:1-12

# *Proper 27*
## *Sunday between November 6 and 12 inclusive*

We have probably all heard or made light-hearted comments about how being in a church choir is a preparation for heaven where all God's saved will be united into one big heavenly chorus. We may muse that our experience here gives us a head start on the hereafter and maybe we'll be first in line for solos or at least as section leaders! Philipp Nicolai's great chorale "Wake, Awake, for Night Is Flying" abounds in musical imagery when describing heaven:

> *Now let all the heavens adore you,*
> *And saints and angels sing before you,*
> *The harps and cymbals all unite.*
> *Of one pearl each shining portal,*
> *Where, dwelling with the choir immortal,*
> *We gather round your dazzling light.*
> *No eye has seen, no ear*
> *Has yet been trained to hear.*
> *What joy is ours!*
> *Crescendos rise; your halls resound;*
> *Hosannas blend in cosmic sound.*

"Wake, Awake, for Night Is Flying"

In these last days of the church year thoughts again turn to the ending of the present world and to the second coming of Christ. Thoughts of such a time thrill and yet disturb us, for we wonder what will be our part in such extraordinary times.

This Sunday's gospel is Jesus' parable of the wise and foolish bridesmaids. The wise five have taken extra oil with them so they are prepared for even a late arrival of the bridegroom. The foolish five have not been so thoughtful and prudent, and they find themselves absent and unprepared for the arrival. "Keep awake therefore, for you know neither the day nor the hour," concludes the reading.

Such a parable surely casts condemnation on the foolish who were not prepared as it honors with praise those who were wise. But just how, we must ask, are we to be prepared? Advent comes just in time with such answers. For now, let us simply remember that the first important step is to keep awake.

The wise ones were not considered wise because they knew with confidence the time of arrival. On the contrary, their wisdom lies in being watchful and ready for the arrival at any hour. It was the foolish ones who arrogantly thought they knew the estimated time of arrival!

We are called to a humble, patient, watchful life of waiting and working. Can we do it on our own? Probably not. To each other we say, "Work and wait with me." To God we pray, "Give me oil in my lamp, keep me burning." God has promised to be with us and to fill us, even in our waiting. The heavenly choir has been rehearsing for eons; everyone knows their part perfectly, and it surely must sound great! All it takes is for the conductor to say, "Let the music begin!"

# Proper 28
## Sunday between November 13 and 19 inclusive

What a marvelous piece of work is each and every person God has created! And what a marvelous piece of work is humanity as a whole, for at any given time in history, there are those gifted with skills in science, art, government, education, agriculture, and whatever else is needed for society. When a culture works well, it is easy to point out how each person has something important to contribute to the whole. But on an individual level we may struggle with personal issues. "What is my unique role in the big picture of humanity? Am I doing what I should be doing? Some seem to have so many abilities; do I even have any skills? Are my skills up to those around me? " Such questions show we do care about the big picture and our role in it, but they can still be troubling.

This Sunday's gospel is Jesus' parable of the talents. A wealthy man entrusts his workers with varying amounts of cash as he leaves on a trip. Upon his return he gets reports from all the workers. Two have doubled their investment; one has buried his share and simply dug it back up to return. It is upon him that the master's anger falls. It is not the amount that was important; it was the lack of initiative, the wasting of an opportunity, the failing to do something good.

Though "talents" here refers to money, Christians of every era have understood the connection to skills and abilities. And there are many important lessons that we can learn from this parable. First of all, talents are given not so much as gifts but as loans. Repayment is assumed; interest is expected. Secondly, not all are given the same amount. We need not waste time worrying about or lamenting our portion; our time is best spent using and increasing what we have been given. Sharing is preferable to comparing. Lastly, those who make good use of their talents receive even more abilities and more opportunities to use them. Those who do not use what they have find that they have lost their abilities altogether. Jesus has described for us the proverbial admonition, "use it or lose it."

As a church choir, we are a body that has received large doses of talent. And we have also been provided with a wonderful arena for our talents to be shared, invested, and returned with dividends. In Christian worship, our talents in music join with those who have been gifted in many other ways. We depend on each other, encourage each other, honor each other, and pray for each other in our various ministries. Above all, we unite to proclaim and praise the source and inspiration for all our gifts. In a hymn by Howell E. Lewis, we make this prayer;

> Lord of light, your name out-shining
> All the stars and suns of space,
> Use our talents in your kingdom
> As the servants of your grace.
>
> "Lord of Light"

Do we want more talent? Then let us wisely and generously use what we have. We may discover that we already have more than we ever imagined.

Matthew 25:14-30

# Christ the King

## Last Sunday after Pentecost
### Proper 29

The church year comes to a festive close on this Sunday of Christ the King. It is the church's "New Year's Eve" when we try to sum up the past year and look forward to the next with new eyes and renewed hope.

The church year walks us through the life of Christ by bringing to remembrance all that the Lord has done. It is simultaneously the life of the church and of each of its members, as well. For a Savior who was born, lived, and died on this earth knows our lives intimately. And a Savior who came back to life and grants the same to his followers is a story worth repeating.

And repeat it we do. Though different seasons and festivals highlight specific parts at different times, each time we worship we recount the story. Its familiarity is comforting; its repetition forms and builds up the community. And yet, it is ever new, for the Holy Spirit comes to each person as it will.

On a day called "Christ the King" we proclaim the glory of God as we are able. Boisterous music and full liturgical celebrations are ways we proclaim and experience the specialness of the festival. It would be easy to turn the whole day into a jubilant party—too easy, in fact. Fortunately, the gospel reading comes along to remind us of the rest of the story. It tells us of the nature of this King. This is not a king made in our image, for no earthly king claims such solidarity with his subjects as does Christ. "When you feed the hungry, you feed me," he says. "When you don't feed the hungry, you don't feed me," completes the equation.

As much as we'd rather just tell of Christ's glory, we realize that telling only part of the story is not telling the story at all. God's message is of grace and judgment; Christ's life was one of the cross and the crown; human life is made up of joy and sorrow.

The sovereign has given orders to work, watch, wait, and the grace and power to carry them out. Most importantly, he promises to remain with us through it all. Thomas Kelly's classic hymn celebrates this king's solidarity with his subjects:

> They suffer with their Lord below;
> They reign with him above;
> Their profit and their joy to know
> The mystery of his love.
>
> "The Head that Once Was Crowned"

God comes to us in both our suffering and in our celebrating to lead us through yet another year of grace—a year for telling and singing and living the gift of salvation.

# CYCLE B

# First Sunday in Advent

"Keep awake! Look up! Be ready! Watch!" Such warnings we hear often in making music. Being prepared and alert is necessary for such basic procedures as attacks and releases, tempos and dynamics, even standing and sitting. A choir that is alert and ready can respond to the director's cues, regardless of whether such cues were rehearsed, the result of sudden inspiration, or even in the rare chance of getting lost!

"Beware, keep alert, for you do not know when the time will come" and "Keep awake." These are warnings found in our gospel reading this Sunday as we begin another church year with the Advent season. Along with these warnings are images of a sun and moon that give no light, stars falling as heaven is shaken, the Son of Man coming with angels to gather the elect, the fig tree which tells that summer is near, and the story of a man who goes on a journey, leaving each servant with work to do. The time of his return is unknown, but all are expected to be in readiness at any time.

Do we prepare for Christ's return by attempting to figure out when it will take place? That would surely help us be better prepared. No, we are told to be ready at all times for we do not and we cannot know the time of God's choosing.

The season of Advent is a time to call to mind all the "comings" of God. Jesus came and will come again. He wants us to be a part of that new world, and he helps us and leads us on that journey to the kingdom. When we are confident that Christ will come again we can live as if it has already taken place. We are prepared when we live under the reign of God—even now before its fulfillment.

Is Advent a time of somber yearning or one of joyful anticipation? It is surely both, and our worship and music reflect the duality. We might sing Charles Wesley's

> *Lo! He comes with clouds descending . . .*
> *Alleluia! Christ the Lord returns to reign.*
>
> "Lo! He Comes with Clouds Descending"

alongside the spiritual

> *My Lord, what a morning,*
> *When the stars begin to fall.*
>
> "My Lord, What a Morning"

We lament the state of the world and those parts of ourselves which do not acknowledge the presence of God. Yet, we must also rejoice, for the coming God is already the God among us.

May this new Advent season be a time for us to be proclaimers and receivers of the thrilling word, "Prepare the way of the Lord."

Mark 13:24-37

# Second Sunday in Advent

What a character John the Baptist must have been! We get the itches when we think of his clothes made of camel hair. We can probably understand the wild honey, but eating locusts and living in the wilderness?! John could well be the patron saint of eccentrics.

His message sounded equally strange—calling everyone to repentance and baptism and telling of the one who was to come. But soon the people saw that the one who came was indeed the Messiah; then they looked back to John with gratitude for giving the warning. They called him a prophet and a forerunner of Jesus.

Through the ages numerous churches have been named for this character who takes such an important position each Advent, and we will hear and sing much about him this Second Sunday in Advent. We may even proclaim his message in the words of hymn-writer Alberto Taulé:

> *Mountains and valleys will have to be prepared;*
> *new highways opened, new protocols declared.*
> *Almost here! God is nearing, in beauty and grace!*
> *All clear every gateway, in haste, come out in haste!*
> "All Earth Is Hopeful"

We honor John for having been chosen by God to prepare the way, and we marvel that his 2,000-year-old message is as potent now as it was then. But we must not dwell on John so much that we fail to catch his message for ourselves. For he did not gloat in his special role; he claimed to be unworthy to even untie the sandal thong of the one who was coming.

Have you ever considered the similarities between John and choir members? We may not wear camel hair garments, but choirs often wear special vestments that are unlike those of other worshipers. We probably do not munch on locusts, but singers have been known to alter their eating habits for the sake of their voices. We may not live in the wilderness, but some of our choir lofts can be in some pretty remote places!

Ultimately, we hope that our closest resemblance to John is in proclamation. Just like John's message, our music can call to repentance, assure of forgiveness, comfort those who sit in darkness, and share the promise of the one who has come and will come again. Are we worthy to take on such a role? Along with John we can confess that we are not. But God did not wait for others more worthy to come along. We should consider the saying, "God does not choose the qualified; God qualifies the chosen."

God called John and God calls us into ministry. We are made worthy because of that baptismal call and graced with the worthiness that Christ has won for us.

# Third Sunday in Advent

The Third Sunday in Advent could well be subtitled "John the Baptizer—Part Two." In last week's gospel reading we heard a description of what John looked like, how he dressed, and where he lived. More importantly, we heard of what he said and did. He told of the imminent coming of the Messiah, admonished people to repent and to make straight the way, and he baptized them with water.

This Sunday the focus will be more on the people's reaction to the baptizer. News of John and his message spread far and wide, and soon the priests and Levites were dispatched from Jerusalem to the Jordan in order that they might investigate. Their ultimate question—"Who are you?"

John honestly answers their cross-examination. "No," he replies, "I am neither the Messiah, nor Elijah, nor the prophet." So they press further, "Who are you? Let us have an answer!" John answers with a quote from Isaiah, "I am the voice of one crying out in the wilderness, 'Make straight the way of the Lord.'" John again refuses to claim any divine nature for himself, wishing only to be known as "a voice."

Choir members know what it is like to be known as a voice. We may simply be known as an alto, a soprano, a tenor, or a bass. Members of the congregation or even other members of the same choir may not know our names or what our individual voices sound like. Yet, our presence is important; we are parts of the whole and we each have something unique to contribute. Though abilities may differ, nobody ever has any more than one voice to offer. But, in most cases, everyone has no less than one voice either.

Our voice can be the instrument used by God to proclaim, to uplift, and to comfort those who hear it. An early Latin Advent hymn celebrates the "voice" and calls us to bear and heed its message:

> Hark, a thrilling voice is sounding,
> Christ is nigh, we hear the cry;
> Cast away the works of darkness,
> All you children of the day!
>
> "Hark! A Thrilling Voice Is Sounding!"

God calls us to use our varied voices and to join the chorus of proclaimers that is ancient and ever new. Awesome indeed is the power of a voice that answers the call to prepare the way of the Lord.

John 1:6-8, 19-28

# Fourth Sunday in Advent

During the Advent season we have been hearing much about messengers. We have been reminded once again of Old Testament prophets who had to keep telling the people, "God will come to save you." We have spent much time considering John the Baptizer, that messenger who was only six months older than the Christ he proclaimed. And we have been reminded of our own roles as messengers—in our individual lives and in our united voice of music ministry.

This is about it! Christmas truly is just around the corner—the corner which we call the Fourth Sunday in Advent. Are we ready? Have we done all we can? Has our congregation heard and caught the message? Have we? Perhaps we become perplexed and anxious when we ponder such questions. If so, we are in good company. For these words describe the state of still one more messenger—the Virgin Mary.

This Sunday's gospel is the stirring story of the Annunciation. The angel Gabriel (another messenger, by the way) appears and utters the world premiere of "Ave, Maria." Gabriel calls Mary the favored one and proclaims God's presence with her. Mary's first reaction is perplexity over such a blessed visitor with such shocking news. Gabriel continues to spin out the details of what will be taking place, and Mary responds, "How can this be?" Gabriel uses as an example the once-barren, now-pregnant Elizabeth and assures Mary, "For nothing will be impossible with God."

What good advice for us, as well. We can feel perplexed, anxious, and even guilty over our own lack of preparedness and effectiveness both inside and outside the choir loft. But, ultimately, we must turn it over to God and trust that our questions will be answered, our anxieties calmed. Our response can echo Mary's, "Here am I, the servant of the Lord; let it be with me according to your word." All that remains is for us to join our voices in the ancient prayer:

> Oh, come, blest Dayspring, come and cheer
> Our spirits by your advent here;
> Disperse the gloomy clouds of night,
> And death's dark shadows put to flight.
> Rejoice, rejoice, Emmanuel
> Shall come to you, O Israel!
>
> "Oh, Come, Oh, Come, Emmanuel"

# The Nativity of Our Lord

*Silent night, holy night!*
*All is calm, all is bright*

"Silent Night, Holy Night!"

It is rather ironic that this hymn has become one of the most popular Christmas songs of all time. We hear it in churches, on television specials, and piped into the mall. It is everywhere! Yes, it does have a worthy text and a pleasant tune, and they do complement each other. The ironic part lies in its description of the night. We have a hard enough time picturing a Christmas night that is holy and bright, much less one that is calm. And silent? That hymn must be for those who lived in ages past, not for our modern, noisy days. Or maybe it still speaks to the "worship consumers," those folks in our congregation who just show up for a Christmas worship experience. Pastors, musicians, and other worship leaders are not meant to understand a silent, holy night, where all is calm and bright.

We have worked hard in our preparations for leading Christmas worship. We do it out of commitment and contracts, out of heart and habit. We give it as a gift to our God, to our congregation, and to ourselves. Celebrating and proclaiming the incarnation of our God is worth all we can give and so much more. We would probably feel guilty if we did experience a calm, restful, stress-free Christmas.

If that is the type of Christmas we think we want, we should think again. What was so calm about being in a strange town at the time a baby is to be born? What is so stress-free about trying to find a room in a sold-out town? What is so silent about animals? And, if the child Jesus was resting so quietly, why does so much of our Christmas music keep telling him to hush up and go to sleep?

The calm, the silence, the peace of Christmas is so noticeable because it is the exception; it stands in stark contrast to its surroundings, as much now as it did then. Peace is present, not in absence of its competition, but amidst it.

Joseph Mohr did not author "Silent Night, Holy Night" because he had nothing else to do or because he was so inspired by the sense of calm and peace around him. He created it frantically, on the very day it was needed, upon finding that the church's organ was broken and the scheduled music could not be used. The organist, Franz Gruber, was probably not thrilled when his pastor showed up with the news of the organ's condition and asked for a new tune on the spot. Christmas Eve was not the time to discuss job descriptions, unreasonable expectations, or staff relations. All was probably not calm nor bright as they rushed to write, prepare, and perform their new work that very evening. But, we hope that they were able to experience at least a small amount of the heavenly peace their creation has brought to the world. May our music be such a generous gift to all we will touch.

Luke 2:1-20; John 1:1-14

# First Sunday after Christmas

Does it bother you when someone asks a question with an obvious answer? "Hello," we say when answering the telephone. "Are you home?" comes the response. How we answer back depends a lot on our toleration of the person calling, our mood, and our ability to put little aggravations into perspective.

When singing, we do not seem to mind it as much. Even though we can look ahead or even remember the answer, we rather enjoy asking the obvious in William Chatterton Dix's hymn:

> *What child is this, who, laid to rest,*
> *On Mary's lap is sleeping?*
> *Whom angels greet with anthems sweet*
> *While shepherds watch are keeping?*
> "What Child Is This"

We know the answer given by Christians throughout the ages; it is, hopefully, our personal creed, as well:

> *This, this is Christ the king,*
> *Whom shepherds guard and angels sing;*
> *Haste, haste to bring him laud,*
> *The babe, the son of Mary!*

Those in attendance at the birth in Bethlehem seemed to know the answer to the question, "What child is this?" But, just outside the stable, it was a different story. In this Sunday's gospel we hear of the holy family as they visit the temple. They are there to fulfill two sacred rites—the ritual purification of Mary, as required after childbirth, and the presentation of their first-born son to God. Thousands of such rites took place in the temple, and the holy family, to most eyes, just blended in with the others. What child is this? Just any child.

But some special eyes were alert in God's temple that day. The righteous and devout Simeon, in this child whom he has never seen, recognizes the Lord's Messiah. His poetic "Nunc Dimittis," preserved in Luke's Gospel and treasured in the church's liturgy, he utters as thanksgiving for God's revelation to him. He can die now, he says, for he has seen God's plan for salvation.

Before Mary and Joseph have time to react to such pronouncements, they are met by the aged prophet, Anna. She, too, has the eyes of faith to see the fulfillment of her fasting and praying. Luke records that she "began to praise God and to speak about the child to all who were looking for the redemption of Jerusalem."

What models of piety, prayer, patience, and proclamation we have in Anna and Simeon! May our eyes be as open to see the Christ, our arms as open to receive him, and our voices as eager to proclaim, "This, this is Christ the King!"

# Second Sunday after Christmas

Some folks say they are in the home building or home improvement business, but what they really mean is that they work on houses. Calling them homes makes it more pleasant and warm because of what the title conveys. We might recall Guest's poem "It takes a heap of living to make a house a home."

An author writes hundreds of pages of a story with great action and suspense, but the editor says the main character does not seem real. "Put some flesh and blood on him," the editor advises.

A politician tries to run a campaign using only signs and media ads. Her advisor tells her she better get out, meet folks, and "press some flesh" if she hopes to gain a following.

In choir we say we have to keep track of our music, but what we are referring to are pieces of paper printed with words and symbols. With them we plan to make music.

Rather than bother with a real instrument or work with a real accompanist, a church opts for pre-recorded soundtracks. The notes are perfect, the technology impressive, but the final product lacks a sense of presence. It's hard to take seriously a musical offering created at another time, at another place, and by anonymous musicians.

What is missing from an empty house, a dry novel, a distant politician, a piece of paper with symbols, or canned music? The human touch, the genuine article.

Such is the world described by St. John in the opening paragraphs of his Gospel. The world came into being through the Word, but the world knew him not. What was the Father to do? In the words of a Bohemian carol:

> *Into flesh is made the Word. Hallelujah!*
> *He, our refuge and our Lord. Hallelujah!*
> *On this day God gave us*
> *Christ, his Son, to save us.*
>
> "Let Our Gladness Have No End"

In the incarnation of Christ, God made the ultimate leap. The Word made Flesh makes all of human life the realm of God's presence. The divine has entered humanity's house and has made it a home.

# The Epiphany of Our Lord

A central symbol of the festival and season of Epiphany is the star. The vision of the Bethlehem star thrills those of every age. On this festival of Epiphany we will again hear of that brilliant glow which captured the attention of the Magi from the East. They came a long distance, from a foreign culture, not knowing exactly where they were going, but having enough trust in the holy sign to keep following it. That star did not disappoint them—it faithfully led them to the very doorway of the Christ they sought to worship and honor with precious gifts.

Stars are truly amazing things. From earliest history they have inspired astronomers and astrologers, navigators and nomads, poets and painters. To our eyes, stars are never static; they sparkle, change colors, and move with the passing of time and seasons. They seem alive. Science has taught us even more amazing things about stars. Those whose light we see now may not even be in existence anymore. Just like the saints, their legacy lives on. The imagery of stars enters into the church's hymnody, as well. The great Danish hymnwriter Nikolai Gruntvig wrote:

> As a star, God's holy Word
> Leads us to our King and Lord;
>> "Bright and Glorious Is the Sky"

German hymnwriter/composer Philipp Nicolai addresses Jesus:

> O Morning Star, how fair and bright!
> You shine with God's own truth and light,
> Aglow with grace and mercy!
>> "O Morning Star, How Fair and Bright!"

Contemporary American hymnwriter Kathleen Thomerson professes:

> God set the stars to give light to the world.
> The star of my life is Jesus.
>> "I Want to Walk as a Child of the Light"

Stars indeed are metaphors for Christ, for the gospel, for creation, and for our calling as Christians to let our lights shine in a dark world. The season when it is easy and even fashionable to shine has just passed. Many folks pack away their shine along with the tinsel and electric lights until next Christmas. But now, exactly when the rest of the world has hidden it all away, is the most important time for Christians to keep shining. Just how can we keep up our sparkle? We cannot do it on our own, for our light is not of our own making. Rather, we stay close to Christ, the true "star" of Christmas, for he is that life-giving presence which the world so desperately needs. And we stay close to each other in this church community, called to shine in work, worship, praise, song, and prayer to Christ, our light.

# The Baptism of Our Lord
## First Sunday after the Epiphany

Many of us can recall the decade-long news stories about the struggles of the working people in Poland. Their leaders' names became household words, and the name of their union gave new meaning to the word "solidarity." That word still brings to mind images of struggling, standing firm, banding together, working for just causes, and identifying with each other. The people came to trust in the union and join its cause not so much because of its name, as good as it was, but because of its actions. The people heard with their ears and saw with their eyes that this union was of them and for them.

This Sunday we will hear of an even greater pledge of solidarity. Once again we will proclaim and celebrate the beginning of Jesus' public ministry as he is baptized by John in the Jordan River. The Spirit descends like a dove, and a voice from heaven proclaims, "This is my Son, the Beloved, with whom I am well pleased." Jesus' baptism is the great sign that God is in solidarity with him.

Though he is God's beloved Son, Jesus still comes to be baptized. Who would have thought that Jesus would need to be baptized? Surely not John, who felt himself unworthy to even untie the thong of his sandal. Surely we would not have guessed it—we who are baptized for the forgiveness of sins and into the death and resurrection of this very Jesus. F. Pratt Green explores this paradox in a hymn:

> When Jesus came to Jordan to be baptized by John,
> He did not come for pardon but as the Sinless One.
> He came to share repentance with all who mourn their sins,
> To speak the vital sentence with which good news begins.
>
> "When Jesus Came to Jordan"

Jesus' baptism is an example of what we are called to do. His and our baptisms are the source and sustenance of our ministries on this earth. His and our baptisms are the proclamation of God's solidarity with us in this life, in our deaths, and in the life to come. In our baptisms, God is well pleased; it is the assurance that God's promises are true. And that is a pledge of solidarity worth singing about!

Mark 1:4-11

# Second Sunday after the Epiphany

The continuing epiphanies of Jesus dominate our gospel readings these Sundays. From the star and the wise men to his baptism and the assuring voice from heaven, we are witnesses again this Sunday as Jesus calls his first disciples. His works and words were to gain for him large numbers of followers. But, rather than just waiting for the curious to come, Jesus begins his ministry by calling specific persons. Perhaps he knew the benefits of having an inner circle. Perhaps he wanted pupils and witnesses from the very beginning. Regardless of his exact motives, it is a scenario rather hard to imagine; for he calls those who have not yet seen his works and who may not even know his name! It is even more amazing then, that when Jesus calls "Follow me," they do it. It must be no ordinary call. It is surely a call full of power and promise.

An important role of the church in all generations has been to continue making this call to follow Jesus. Our music plays no small part in this mission. As we respond to his call as musicians, we have been given the power and the promise that blesses our efforts and joins them to the great commission to make disciples for the Savior. Many find a hymn refrain by Daniel Schutte to ring true for them:

> Here I am, Lord. Is it I, Lord?
> I have heard you calling in the night.
> I will go, Lord, if you lead me.
> I will hold your people in my heart.
>
> "I, the Lord of Sea and Sky"

All this from the short phrase "Follow me!" But, there is still one more short phrase in this gospel reading. As Jesus' first disciples are telling others of their new-found life, they issue the invitation, "Come and see!"

So many things cannot be put into words or captured in pictures. Only the real thing will do. So it is with faith. Perhaps the best favor we can do for our neighbors and friends is to provide the invitation, opportunity, and encouragement to "come and see." Our worship and its music can be a vital part of how they hear God's call to them.

It has been said that the response we should most desire from visitors to our church is not what a "great place," or "great people," or "great preaching," or "great music" we have. We hope their response from what they see and hear will be "what a great God they have!"

"Follow me" and "come and see"—short phrases that are still calling disciples and still accomplishing miracles because they bid us look to Christ, the shining star.

# Third Sunday after the Epiphany

There is something "fishy" about many of the gospel readings for these Sundays in the Epiphany season. Several times we hear that Jesus is passing by the Sea of Galilee. There he sees people on the shore, mending their nets, or in boats, casting them out. Fishing is the occupation of many whom Jesus called to be his first and closest disciples. He calls to them, "Follow me," and they actually do it! This sounds remarkably like the proverbial "fish story," where details become more exaggerated and unbelievable at each telling. But, with Jesus, they simply hear the call and they follow him. "You should have seen the one that got away!" does not seem to be a part of this fish story.

Fishing gets even more visibility in this Sunday's gospel. Jesus says to Simon and Andrew, "Follow me and I will make you fish for people." With that short declaration, Jesus has given a definition of discipleship. It is a role with a goal, a call with a promise.

Evangelism is not easy. We may get confused by the different techniques used between and within denominations. We have all probably encountered evangelism styles that turn us off, and which, in all reality, may have done more damage than good. The relationship between worship, music, and evangelism is a controversial one, and we worry about adopting styles that cheapen the message or manipulate the receivers. We may give up witnessing altogether, preferring to leave that to the "professionals."

Before we reel in the line for good, let us examine Jesus' metaphor one more time. Fishing, whether by net or hook, is an act of catching. And "catching" is a term with many layers of meaning. If something attracts and intrigues us we may say it is "catching." Furthermore, catching is not a one-sided activity; it requires a giver and a receiver and the right opportunity for their encounter to take place.

It has often been said that the Christian faith is not so much "taught" as "caught." The Holy Spirit uses us and those around us in this catching ministry. Our call, then, is to be simultaneously casters and receivers. We do this inside the church—through our prayers and offerings of time, talent, and treasure—and in our daily lives.

Especially in the Epiphany season, we often pray for Christ to shine on us, as in Johann Heermann's hymn:

> O Christ, our light, O Radiance true,
> Shine forth on those estranged from you,
> And bring them to your home again,
> Where their delight shall never end.
> > "O Christ, Our Light, O Radiance True"

But we also pray that Christ will shine through us, reflecting and magnifying his glory, like the rays of sun off the Sea of Galilee.

# Fourth Sunday after the Epiphany

We humans have a love-hate relationship with authority. Generally, we love it when we have it over others and hate it when others have it over us. If there is any middle ground, it is probably those situations where the authority over us does not ask too much, or where we gladly give up a bit of authority over our selves for the sake of a greater goal. Such is the situation in a musical group, where it is necessary to synchronize tempos and dynamics for the sake of unity over chaos.

There is a difference, however, between authority and power. We often find ourselves in situations where we may technically hold authority but lack the power to accomplish what we want. Tensions between parents and children, bosses and employees, governments and citizens, even church leaders and congregations can turn into battles over such issues. What really are authority and power, and who really holds them?

Twice in this Sunday's gospel we will hear the people gasp in wonderment because Jesus seems to have authority. He teaches in the synagogue as they haven't been taught before, and Mark records, "they were astounded at his teaching, for he taught them as having authority." Immediately enters a man possessed by an unclean spirit. Jesus commands the spirit to leave, and it does. Then the people exclaim, "What is this? A new teaching-with authority!"

Jesus is actively making himself known in these early days of his ministry. Christopher Wordsworth declares in a hymn:

> *Manifest in making whole palsied limbs and fainting soul;*
> *Manifest in valiant fight, quelling all the devils might;*
> *Manifest in gracious will, ever bringing good from ill:*
> *Anthems be to thee addressed, God in flesh made manifest.*
> "Songs of Thankfulness and Praise"

That, then, is the crucial difference between Jesus and others with some sort of authority—he wills only that which is good, and he alone has the power to make it happen. We are often aghast and dismayed by the power of evil in the world, and we would be fools to deny such powers. But evil is a lesser authority and a lesser power than the crucified and risen one whose authority and power are continually being made manifest. We rejoice that we are called to embody and proclaim the presence of such a teacher, healer, and Savior.

# Fifth Sunday after the Epiphany

Jesus models a marvelous paradigm for us in the opening verses of this Sunday's gospel. Mark tells us that "as soon as Jesus and the disciples left the synagogue, they entered the house of Simon and Andrew." There they find Simon's mother-in-law sick, and Jesus heals her. The pattern for the rest of his day has now been set, for at sundown many more were brought to him for healing and casting out of demons. The whole city was gathered at his door, Mark relates.

We rejoice in the Anointed One doing the work of the kingdom, but, we may ask, how is this a model for us? We can do some good works in Jesus' name and at his command, but how can we keep up with him? It was, after all, his full-time job. Even Jesus grew weary, and the same reading tells of him getting up early to go find a deserted place. Still the people found him and he resumed curing their ills. How can we do that?

Perhaps we should look not only at Jesus' works but also to the spaces in between. The visit to Andrew's and Simon's house followed his attendance at the synagogue service. And Jesus, getting up early to find some place and time for himself, uses it in prayer. Much of the gospel story reinforces this pattern of worship alternating with work.

Worship and work are two sides of the same coin. Worship which does not encourage and equip the saints for work and ministry is incomplete, and work which does not have as its basis a spirit of praise and worship is not sufficiently grounded. Each is weaker without the other. But together they form a solid partnership and pattern for walking with our Lord, finding sustenance for life, and doing the work of the kingdom. It is a pattern followed by Jesus and commended to us out of love. Georgia Harkness paints a vivid picture of work and worship in a hymn:

> Hope of the world, afoot on dusty highways,
> Showing to wandering souls the path of light:
> Walk thou beside us lest the tempting byways
> Lure us away from thee to endless night.
>
> "Hope of the World"

May we, in a steady rhythm of work and worship, strive to follow Jesus, the hope of the world.

Mark 1: 29-39

# Sixth Sunday after the Epiphany
## *Proper 1*

W̲e need only consider the church year, the liturgy, and the lectionary to see how numerous and varied are the ways to speak of God and God's relationship with us. Each time a worship service takes place, the gospel is enacted and proclaimed anew. While we search for new ways to proclaim the gospel, it is still, in essence, the same gospel which we seek to convey, the same truths we seek to grasp.

Few places contain definitions of faith and grace as clearly and compactly as this Sunday's gospel. It tells of a man with leprosy who comes to Jesus and says, "If you choose, you can make me clean." What a great example of faith! Faith does not presume to know what God *will* do; but it does trust in what God *can* do.

In his reply, Jesus responds with pure grace. "I do choose. Be made clean!" It is not out of some requirement that he does it, nor some deal, nor a reward, but a choice.

There are many theories why Jesus told the healed man to keep quiet about the healing. Whatever the reason for Jesus' warning, it didn't work. And there has never been a time when we can more forgive someone for disobeying Jesus. The response to grace is uncontrollable joy and gratitude, and it irrepressibly pursues an outlet. The spiritual "There Is a Balm in Gilead" counsels us:

> *If you cannot preach like Peter,*
> *if you cannot pray like Paul,*
> *you can tell the love of Jesus*
> *and say, "He died for all."*
> "There Is a Balm in Gilead"

In the creative spirit of the spirituals, we might add a stanza that says "you can sing the love of Jesus," for that is our humble but heartfelt response to the grace-filled gift of faith.

# Seventh Sunday after the Epiphany
## Proper 2

We have come to expect that our gospel readings will end in exclamations these days. We hear either of Jesus' fame spreading far and wide, or of the officials murmuring against him, or of the crowds clamoring for his attention. This Sunday's reading closes with, "they were all amazed and glorified God saying, 'We have never seen anything like this!'"

What led up to such an acclamation this time? It is the story of one who came, literally, through the roof. A paralyzed man desperately wants to see Jesus for healing, but the crowds around the house are so thick he cannot even get close. The paralyzed man finally makes it into the inner circle after being lowered through a hole in the roof. There he meets the master healer, who forgives his sins and heals him.

There are innumerable ways of studying and discussing this account, but let us imagine that there was someone present who asked the healed man for his comments. Surely he would be overjoyed, and we hope he would go on to thank all those who helped. Jesus would be at the top of the list, to be sure. But next he would most likely express his gratitude to his four friends. They, after all, attempted to break through the crowd; they devised the idea and dug through the roof; they hauled their friend up there and lowered him to the ground. Jesus praised them for their faith, but he could have just as well commended them for their ingenuity, hard work, and love. This account is as much a lesson on friendship and cooperation as it is on faith.

Love and support carry us through many harried and desperate scenes. They lift us up, they calm us down, they bring us to a place of healing. By its very nature and definition, the church is a place of community—a community that acknowledges Jesus as Lord and that is called together in worship, work, and fellowship. The church choir is no less an example of Christian community. Our ministry is a model of response to a high calling, support and dependency on each other, and bonding together into a union that is stronger than any one individual.

We need not limit our concept of community to the choir or congregational level. Our support system includes the servants of God in every time and place. As the paralyzed man's friends lifted their sights upward, we can join with them and with hymnwriter Henry Lyte to call out:

> Angels help us to adore him,
> Who behold him face to face.
> Sun and moon bow down before him;
> All who dwell in time and space.
> Alleluia! Alleluia!
> Praise with us the God of grace.
>
> "Praise, My Soul, the King of Heaven"

When we consider all those who support us in our journey we too can exclaim, "We have never seen anything like this!"

Mark 2:1-12

# Eighth Sunday after the Epiphany
## Proper 3

Have you ever been complimented by an insult? "That was surely a depressing organ piece you played today!" states a parishoner, assuming that prettiness is the goal of church music. "Thank you!" we reply. "Since today is Good Friday, I was hoping it would express just that. Thanks for noticing!"

Jesus receives a similar "put-down" in this Sunday's gospel. Seeing him at the table with those they considered unworthy, the scribes of the Pharisees ask, "Why does he eat with tax collectors and sinners?" They cannot understand why he would do something so scandalous to the tradition; but Jesus is obviously doing something new. Hymnwriter John Newton expresses this in a hymn:

> When he lived on earth they scorned him;
> "Friend of sinners" was his name.
> Though the angels have adored him,
> Still he answers to that claim.

"One There Is, above All Others"

The reading goes on to relate another encounter with the Pharisees. Seeing that Jesus' disciples did not take part in the customary fast, they demand to know why. "The wedding guests cannot fast while the bridegroom is with them, can they?" Jesus asks. He is creating a new set of rules, and thanks for noticing!

In the final portion of this reading we hear Jesus speaking metaphorically of new patches pulling away from old cloth and new wine bursting old wineskins. He is definitely telling of new things! While he doesn't wish to rile people up just for the sake of conflict, he does use each instance to proclaim and explain his new world order.

The mini-parable of the old and new wineskins has sometimes been used in arguments over what types of music and liturgy are best for modern worship. Surely it is a complex issue, and we should feel a greater affinity for those who struggle with the issue than for those who have an easy answer or those who claim there is no issue at all. Just as new wine bursts old skins gone rigid over time, the call to the church to speak new languages and sing new songs is an invitation to add to the wine cellar. But the new wineskin expands only if the new wine is a good, lively batch. As does the ever-renewing church, it expands to contain the new mixture, making room for that which is good, and casting off that which is less worthy, regardless of its vintage.

"That music sounds like it came from a thousand years ago!" someone comments. "You're absolutely right!" we respond. "Doesn't it effectively proclaim a gospel that transcends our culture?" "That music sounds like it came from some foreign country halfway across the world!" someone says to us. "You're absolutely right!" we respond. "Doesn't it proclaim the gospel with a wonderful new voice? Thanks for noticing!"

# The Transfiguration of Our Lord
## Last Sunday after the Epiphany

The term "transfiguration" is not in the general vocabulary of most people. Even if we know that it means "to change the outward appearance of," we will not often find opportunities to use it in daily conversation.

We may give our house new shingles, shutters, paint, and shrubs, but we call it home improvement and not transfiguration. We may have plastic surgery to remove some wrinkles or tighten up some skin, but we call it a face lift and not transfiguration. We may watch Star Trek and hear the words, "Beam me up, Scotty," but that is called transmogrification and not transfiguration.

This Sunday's gospel does use this unique term. "And Jesus was transfigured before them, and his face shone like the sun, and his clothes became dazzling white." Brian Wren helps us sing of the awe and excitement in his hymn that begins:

> *Jesus on the mountain peak*
> *stands alone in glory blazing . . .*
>
> "Jesus on the Mountain Peak"

Jesus, who always looked so fully human, was once again revealed to be more. He had one foot—no, rather he had both feet—in this world and both in another. He walks up the mountain with his human disciples, but there he speaks with the long-dead Moses and Elijah. To top it all, a voice from heaven says "This is my son, the Beloved; with him I am well pleased; listen to him!" Talk about special effects! Talk about a mountain top experience!

So, the Epiphany season comes to a close as it began, with a heavenly voice confirming that this Jesus truly is the Son of God and commanding us to listen to him. The festivals of Baptism of Our Lord and the Transfiguration are the "bookends" of the Epiphany season. Both are mountain top experiences and both pack enough energy to carry us through the "ordinary" times of life.

Christ is ever present for us in our own high and low points—as present in our times of joy and assuredness as in our times of pain and doubt, in spite of our perceptions otherwise. Life, like a landscape, is not all peaks nor all valleys. And, as in music, the highs and lows define each other and need each other to express the heights and depths and richness of life.

This will be a Sunday for joyous praise and glorious alleluias. But be assured that Lent is just around the corner, and the story of salvation travels a route straight through the streets Jerusalem on its journey to Easter.

# Ash Wednesday

*Savior, when in dust to you*
*Low we bow in homage due:*
*When, repentant, to the skies*
*Scarce we lift our weeping eyes;*
*Oh, by all your pains and woe*
*Suffered once for us below,*
*Bending from your throne on high,*
*Hear our penitential cry!*

"Savior, When in Dust to You"

In this hymn by Robert Grant we sing of such things as dust, repentance, weeping, pains, woe, suffering, and penitential cries. It can mean only one thing—Lent is upon us!

What will we give up for Lent? Even in traditions that do not emphasize a special Lenten discipline of denial, we are likely to be giving up something. Communally, it might be boisterous music and elaborate arrangements, descants and alleluias that we give up. Individually, we might hope that the spirit of the season will inspire us in our attempts to crush some old, destructive habits or start some new, beneficial ones. We pray once again that this Lenten season will have an effect on us as individuals and as a community so that we can gather all creation together at the foot of the cross. What a great reward that would be for our Lenten season.

The term "reward" will be heard extensively in the gospel for Ash Wednesday. Jesus tells of many who parade their piety by praying, fasting, or giving offerings in public, just for the sake of showing off. They already have their reward, Jesus declares, and we can imagine it is a reward that is rather empty and short-lived.

In contrast to them, Jesus tells of those who secretly give offerings and do good deeds, who pray in private, and who fast for its spiritual benefits alone. Their reward is not in earthly trinkets but rather in heavenly treasure.

There are some folks who seem to give up choir and even worship for Lent. Perhaps it is the icy cold weather that hits during this time period in many parts of the northern hemisphere. Perhaps it is the icy coldness of the pronouncement "Remember that you are dust, and to dust you shall return." That statement should give us the shivers. But they can be shivers of warm excitement rather than cold dread. For the ashes that mark our foreheads are not just dust, they are the cleansing crosses of our Baptisms. This is not to be a season for going away; it is one for coming home.

Let us enter this season awake to its rich symbolism, immersed in its purple harmonies and scarlet poetry, and treasuring the deep rewards of walking the road with Christ.

# First Sunday in Lent

It is fitting that we should come head to head with the devil this First Sunday in Lent, for that is exactly who Jesus had waiting for him as he began his ministry. Still wet from his baptism in the Jordan, no time was wasted in getting Jesus and his adversary to clash. Their encounter sets the pattern for the rest of Jesus' earthly life, as Satan would prove to be a constant thorn in his side and, ultimately, his fiercest enemy.

Though the gospel writers differ on the number and content of specific details, even the laconic Mark tells us that the encounter with the devil took place at the very beginning of Jesus' public ministry. The holy signs that convinced the disciples of his messiahship must have confirmed the fact for Satan as well, for he appears in full force. And Satan is no slouch, either, as Matthew and Luke relate. He quotes scripture like a pro, and he has a bunch of special effects in his repertoire which he uses to enhance his sales pitch.

The good news is that Jesus won this first battle. The bad news is how much even he had to endure to do it. Temptation and the power of evil are no small force, Jesus wants us to know. Martin Luther, as hymnwriter, wrote:

> *The old satanic foe*
> *Has sworn to work us woe!*
> *With craft and dreadful might*
> *He arms himself to fight.*
> *On earth he has no equal.*
>
> "A Mighty Fortress Is Our God"

The devil has been imagined in many ways throughout history. Even in music there is a tradition of avoiding an augmented fourth because it is the "devil's interval," and Tartini composed a piece for violin that contains the "devil's trill." And we all find passages in music that we find "devilishly" hard, and occasionally we skip a rehearsal or service because "the devil made us do it." And so we see how easy it becomes to domesticate and trivialize a power so strong that even Jesus had to ferociously fight it.

Our focus for this Sunday, as for our entire lives, should be on realizing the immense proportions of sin and evil, our utter impotence to overcome them, and, most importantly, the grace won for us by the battle-scarred Christ, who holds the field victorious.

# Second Sunday in Lent

The teachings of Jesus are often rich in paradox. One need only consider the Beatitudes and many of the parables to hear the message from Jesus that things are often not as they seem. The real truth is often just the opposite of evidence and human reason.

This Sunday's gospel has a few more examples to add to our paradox list. Jesus tells us that to become his followers, we should deny ourselves and take up our crosses and follow him. Those who would save their lives should lose them, and those who lose their lives for his sake, and for the sake of the gospel, will save them. He even adds that it is possible to gain the whole world and still forfeit one's life.

Have we learned that lesson now that we have heard it? Hardly! In fact, we have probably heard it often and we still have trouble comprehending it, much less believing and living it. The central teachings of Jesus must continually be proclaimed, surely because of their importance, but especially because they are so opposite of our natural way of doing things. We need to be confronted with such truths straightforwardly, consistently, and frequently.

"Repetitious" is what some call our liturgies and lectionaries, hymns and holy communions, confessions and creeds, alms and anthems. "Yes," we admit, "but we need them. The story is too important to ignore and too much of a paradox to ever fully comprehend. We need to hear it again and again. We need to proclaim the gospel truths as much for ourselves as for those whom we want to hear them." Hymnwriter Martin Schalling helps us to plead:

> Lord grant that I in every place
> May glorify thy lavish grace
> And serve and help my neighbor.
>
> "Lord, Thee I Love with All My Heart"

How can we base our hopes on something so unbelievable as the gospel paradoxes? Surely God hasn't asked us to abandon the common sense with which we have been graced? How can we be sure that we are losing our lives to something that really is the only way to save them?

We look to Christ for these answers. Jesus has told us to do nothing that he hasn't done himself. He's been there—or rather, he's been here. He has told us and shown us about taking up crosses and losing life so it can be gained eternally. That should convince even our common sense that the paradoxes of God are trustworthy. It is a story worth singing about and worth repeating and repeating and repeating and repeating . . .

# Third Sunday in Lent

Those who prefer to picture Jesus as always meek and mild will probably be uncomfortable this Sunday. For in the gospel we will hear of an angry, temple-charging Jesus who takes matters into his own hands by making a whip, driving out animals, turning over the tables of the money changers, and commanding the people to stop making his Father's house a marketplace. Many preachers will use this as a jumping off point to take on things which need to be driven from the modern-day church. And, no doubt, many in the choir lofts and on organ benches will be fantasizing about what they wish Jesus would drive out of the church and its worship. Plenty food for thought—this radical act by Jesus.

But tucked away near the end of this reading we find another, quieter encounter that is just as rich in scope. Jesus predicts that he will destroy the temple and, in three days, will raise it up. The disciples are curious about this statement, since they are standing in a building which had been under construction for 46 years. The gospel writer comments, "But he was speaking of the temple of his body. After he was raised from the dead, his disciples remembered that he had said this." What seemed like a confusing statement at the time became, upon reflection, a tenet of the faith. In fact, everything Jesus said and did started to make infinitely more sense when viewed from the post-resurrection side of his life.

We see many such parallels in life. Children learn to repeat sounds, words, and even phrases long before they begin to understand what they mean. But once they understand the concept, they already have the means to express it. Much of music training involves learning the symbols and techniques that won't be fully realized until later, but they will be there when artistry calls for them. In worship, the words and actions of the liturgy are picked up without necessarily knowing what they are all about. But, suddenly during the 499th repetition of a creed, something new is made known to us. Likewise, we memorize Bible verses, catechisms, and prayers long before we know their importance, but they are there for us when faith needs them.

These cases are similar in that each contains so much more than we can ever fully comprehend. And they hold something else in common—each involves a unique language that is the channel for something great. We learn our words, musical skills, liturgies, Bibles, catechisms, and prayers so that the basic proficiencies are already in place when the fullness of life has need of them.

Knowledge is just the beginning, of course. The words of hymnwriter Harry Emerson Fosdick encourage us to pray that God would grant us wisdom and courage for specific challenges—

> . . . *For the facing of this hour,*
> . . . *For the living of these days,*
> . . . *Lest we miss your kingdom's goal,*
> and . . . *Serving you whom we adore.*
> "God of Grace and God of Glory"

# Fourth Sunday in Lent

Mention the word "snakes" and many people cringe. Snakes are things that populate phobias, horror films, and nightmares. Even those who don't have a phobia about snakes would rather not run across one unexpectedly. Snakes and serpents have had a bad reputation from the very first book of the Old Testament, and they are still used often as symbols for Satan and the forces of evil.

How surprising, then, that this Sunday's readings will contain quite different references to serpents. Jesus speaks, "Just as Moses lifted up the serpent in the wilderness, so must the Son of Man be lifted up, that whoever believes in him may have eternal life." He refers, of course, to the bronze serpent on a pole which God had commanded Moses to raise up. All who looked upon it would be saved from the bites of the real serpents.

Here Jesus is comparing himself to, of all things, a serpent! What do they possibly have in common? Quite a lot, says Jesus. For both have been provided and anointed by God to bring saving grace to those who believe. By using the Moses story he was affirming his unity with the past and proclaiming that his mission was not a different and separate story but rather a new and vital chapter in the continuing saga of God saving God's own people.

But was it necessary to use as an example something so repulsive as a snake? Perhaps that's exactly why he used it. God's saving grace reaches to all people, not just to the cute and cuddly. In the very next verse of John's Gospel we will hear the beloved John 3:16, "For God so loved the world that he gave his only Son, so that everyone who believes in him may not perish but may have eternal life."

Yes, we believe that God loved, though we have a harder time believing that what God loved was this world. But God did redeem this very world, full of its natural disasters, its pollution, its warring tribes, its unlovable serpents, and, even harder to believe, its people. What God has loved, we are to love. We love the world enough to take care of it. We love others enough to treat them as God wishes and enough that we want them to know of God's love for them. We love the world's people and we join with them in the song of the ages:

> To God and to the Lamb, who is the great I Am,
> While millions join the theme I will sing.
>> "What Wondrous Love Is This"

As musicians in the church we have a high calling—to be partners in proclaiming the good news and in helping each other receive and believe it. That's no small call, but we are not alone. God's unhidden agenda is to save the world, snakes and all. With God on our side, who can fall?

# Fifth Sunday in Lent

A few years ago there was a popular show with the humorous title, "Stop the World, I Want to Get Off." We have probably said that ourselves whenever things reach the pressure point. Fortunately, we usually use the phrase to express or relieve frustration, for the results are devastating for us and all around us if we take the expression literally.

Can we imagine Jesus ever making such a statement? If there ever was one who could become weary from carrying the weight of the world, it surely was him. Not only that, he had the added burden of knowing what was to be his violent fate. Most other problems fade by comparison to such strength and fortitude in the face of severe suffering.

This Sunday's gospel contains many small episodes and sayings from Jesus, all for the sake of his followers who were facing much they did not understand. He compares himself to a grain of wheat which must die in order to bear fruit. He tells them that those who lose their lives will keep them. He promises that, when he is lifted up from the earth, he will draw all people to himself. Poignantly, he admits that his soul is troubled, but he will still not ask the Father to save him from what is to come. "No," he says decisively, "it is for this reason that I have come to this hour."

We owe a great debt of gratitude to Jesus for such strength and single-mindedness of mission. It is important for us to know that it was not easy, even for one both human and divine. For not only did his endurance help bring about the salvation of the world, it continues to help us in those times when we need to be strong.

"Costly grace" is the phrase coined by Dietrich Bonhöffer to help us grasp the sacrificial nature of Christ's salvation. And Bonhöffer's hymn binds Christ's suffering to our own:

> And when this cup you give is filled to brimming
> with bitter suffering, hard to understand,
> we take it thankfully and without trembling
> out of so good and so beloved a hand.
>
> "By Gracious Powers"

Christ's definition of strength is not the same as the world's—it is often just the opposite. But Christ's strength is more powerful than the world's because he has overcome the world. Fortunately, his cry was not "Stop the world, I want to get off." Rather, his costly life, death, and resurrection truly stopped the world as we know it; and he now bids us to follow him and serve others in his new, grace-filled world.

# Sunday of the Passion/Palm Sunday

For most Sundays of the church year we strive for thematic unity. Worship planners spend time and use their expertise organizing services where the preaching, scriptures, prayers, music, art, and all other parts of the liturgy unite in proclaiming some facet of the good news of God.

This Sunday stands at a unique place in the rhythm of the church's life. Even its name, Sunday of the Passion/Palm Sunday, exposes the specialness of the day. It is a day of dualities when we will hear two gospel readings—that of Jesus' triumphal entry into Jerusalem, and by contrast, that lengthiest of all Gospel pericopes—the Passion of our Lord. We gather for a palm procession; we depart, immersed in the heaviness of Holy Week.

The people of Jerusalem knew only the festivity of the day as they expected Jesus to be ushering in the triumph of Israel. Jesus obviously had a different scenario on his mind, for he knew this was only the beginning of the end. "Ignorance is bliss," goes the saying. Anyone can praise a victor, but even the disciples departed once they realized what was happening in the days that followed. Sadly, the same is true for many in our congregation and even in our choirs. "Let me know when the big, happy festivals are coming up," some say. "I don't want to ruin my good mood by going on a somber day," they might as well add. Those who worship faithfully know the risks of coming on a day when we will be confronted with the crimson details of the passion story. But it is worth the risk, for we trade in a superficial, feel-good experience for a deeper, richer encounter with the Christ who has himself gone through it all.

The function of our worship this Sunday will be, as always, to praise the triune God, proclaim the gospel, pray together, offer ourselves in service, and be fed by Christ's communion with us and by our communion with each other. But we will not merely remember that first Palm Sunday; we will experience it anew. For Christ continues to be praised and lauded, continues to display his scars, continues to come to us and feed us, continues to save and redeem us.

Our music will be a part of that experience. With voices and instruments united we will relive the festivity of Christ's coming and ponder the depths of his suffering and death. Hymnwriter Samuel Crossman allows us to eloquently profess:

> *Here might I stay and sing*
> *No story so divine!*
> *Never was love, dear King,*
> *Never was grief like thine.*
> "My Song Is Love Unknown"

As Holy Week is ushered in once again, we pray that our minds and hearts will be open and ready to ponder and receive such a high and deep declaration of love.

# Holy Week/The Three Days

Christians do some amazing things this week. Some will make a pilgrimage to their church every single day, whether to worship, pray, rehearse, decorate, clean, or even to help with all the extra worship bulletins. Our daily routines of work, school, or family care will go on much as usual, but on top of these we still add additional tasks. We also anticipate Easter Sunday by planning for meals, company, clothing, and even decorating the eggs. But, rather than ignoring or working straight through these intervening weekdays, we plan to savor and struggle with them.

Thousands of words will be spoken and heard in the course of these days, for there is so much to tell and express. But such wondrous things are encapsulated best in poetry from the church's hymnwriters. The gospel readings for Monday, Tuesday, and Wednesday in Holy Week bring Jesus and us ever closer to the time and place of sacrifice. James Montgomery bids us:

> *Go to dark Gethsemane,*
> *All who feel the tempter's power;*
> *Your Redeemer's conflict see.*
> *Watch with him one bitter hour;*
> *Turn not from his griefs away;*
> *Learn from Jesus Christ to pray.*
> "Go to Dark Gethsemane"

On Maundy Thursday (or Holy Thursday) we receive Jesus' command to love each other, and he seals that command with his own gifts of bread and wine, water and towel. An ancient Latin hymn expresses our unity with the church in all times and places:

> *Where true charity and love abide, God is dwelling there.*
> *Ubi caritas et amor, Deus ibi est.*
> "Ubi Caritas et Amor/Where True Charity and Love Abide"

On a Friday that Christians dare to call "good," we contemplate the ultimate sacrifice, pray for ourselves and each other in the shadow of the cross, and adore the one crucified for the salvation of the world. Bernard of Clairvaux, along with Paul Gerhardt and other translators, asks with us:

> *What language shall I borrow To thank thee, dearest friend,*
> *For this thy dying sorrow, Thy pity without end?*
> "O Sacred Head, Now Wounded"

Finally, on the Vigil of Easter, the climax is reached. The risen Christ is proclaimed as new light in the darkness, the history of God's salvation is recounted, new members are incorporated into the death and resurrection of Jesus, baptisms are renewed, and we eat and drink in the presence of the risen Lord. Surrounded by such richness, we can only rise up and proclaim in the splendid poetry of John Geyer:

> *We know that Christ is raised and dies no more.*
> *Embraced by death, he broke its fearful hold,*
> *And our despair he turned to blazing joy. Hallelujah!*
> "We Know that Christ Is Raised"

# The Resurrection of Our Lord

There's light at the end of the tunnel! Though we are still in the midst of Holy Week, we can count down the days and hours rather than the weeks of the Lent behind us. Though we have some music to still polish and much to still deliver, we can already taste that post-Easter peace we have come to savor. Church musicians, especially at the final worship service on Easter Day, can sing with great conviction (and with a little chuckle at its double meaning) the ancient Easter hymn:

> The strife is o'er, the battle done;
> Now is the victor's triumph won!
> Now be the song of praise begun. Alleluia!
> "The Strife Is O'er, the Battle Done"

As long as we have done our best, we need not feel ashamed of the relief we may feel once Lent is over. Our alleluias will sound more joyous because of their sabbatical. The whites and golds will sparkle more brightly because the purples and scarlets have told us their story. The sunlight streaming through the windows will carry more intensity because of the times we met in darkness. The organ and other instruments will sound more jubilant after the deep, rich sonorities of Lent. We will treasure more our rejoicing because we have grieved.

Jesus probably experienced some relief, too, as he saw the light at the opening of the tomb. Salvation's song had reached the highest notes of its intense climax; it was time for the coda and the cadence. What great joy must have been his as he shared the jubilant news of his resurrection with those he loved the most! Their fright must have given way quickly to joy and peace, made all the more intense because of the deep of sorrow they had experienced. That was Jesus' special gift to those who had known him the best. It is a gift he continues to give to us as we walk with him on the passion path to Jerusalem and as we invite him to walk with us on our rocky roads.

Just as Jesus reveled in the satisfaction of a tough job well done, the relief we feel as another Holy Week and Easter are reached surely goes beyond our creaturely comforts. For all is made new. We have caught a glimpse of the Paschal candle piercing the darkness, and we recognize it as the light of Christ which he has planted within us. We have seen the first rays of daylight illuminating the far corners of the cave, and we know that tomb is ours. And we have visited the garden, expecting only to grieve, but instead we are surprised and comforted by his living presence.

There is indeed light at the end of the tunnel—it is the rest of our lives! Christ has fought and won a tremendous battle for the sake of that light which blesses our baptisms, guides our living, hallows our dying, and promises our resurrections. We cannot help but sing praises and proclaim such good news.

# Second Sunday of Easter

Much of the culture around us has already packed Easter away until next year—or at least it has been marked down to half price! But the church has the audacity to keep celebrating Easter for 50 days! In spite of this Sunday's nickname of "Low Sunday," we continue to sing our alleluias and proclaim that Christ is risen to all who will hear. This season is a time to rejoice and reflect on the meaning of the resurrection and to try to fashion our lives to be the Easter people that Christ has made us.

This Sunday we will hear the wonderful story from John's Gospel that tells of the resurrected Jesus appearing to his disciples. It might make for a good test question—when Jesus suddenly appears to his fearful disciples meeting behind locked doors, what are his first words to them? Perhaps "surprise" or "cheer up" or "it's me" might be understandable responses. But Jesus surprises us almost as much as he must have surprised his disciples when he says, "Peace be with you." Many hymnwriters, including Jean Tisserand, have made note of this:

> That night the apostles met in fear;
> Among them came their master dear,
> And said, "My peace be with you here."
> Alleluia!

"O Sons and Daughters of the King"

Peace is a hard concept to define. We usually describe it as the absence of strife whether between nations, families, or individuals. As important as such arenas are for peace, these are not the same as the peace Jesus gives.

Sometimes we feel peace through some outside stimulus. Drugs or manipulative words or music can cause us to ignore the reality of life around us. This is likewise not the peace that Jesus gives.

Some have objected to the sharing of the peace in worship, arguing that well-wishing and personal greetings are not appropriate for something as important as the worship time. If that was all that was taking place, then the critics would be correct. But the peace we give and receive is not merely an expression of good wishes. It is the peace of Christ that we give, and he has given us the opportunity and responsibility to be channels of this peace to each other. Christ's peace is deep in meaning, rich in scope, and full of the power that only a dying and rising Savior can give. It is a release from real forces and a rescue from ourselves. Christ's words do not merely wish us peace—they grant it.

That is the peace we mean to share in worship—in the word, in the sacraments, in the fellowship, in the holy surroundings, and in the music whether it be jubilant or meditative. May the peace of Christ dwell in us richly this Easter season as we are called to be channels and recipients of the peace Christ has won for us.

# *Third Sunday of Easter*

The entertainment world seems caught up in repeats. Television shows are often rerun, but usually they are less popular the second time around. A successful movie may beget a sequel or two, but they rarely are as successful as the first. It seems to be the same way with food—leftovers seldom carry the importance or appeal of the original meal.

But there are instances where repeats are welcomed and even celebrated. Surely the most soul-stirring are the recounts of Jesus appearing after his resurrection. This Sunday, as last, we will hear of Jesus appearing to his disciples and saying, "Peace be with you." Whether such appearances were numerous or just that we have several reports of the same appearance will have to be a matter for the biblical scholars to determine. For us, we rejoice in each and every account of this Jesus, once dead, now alive and present to his disciples. His words and actions seem to carry even more power than before, and they are full of promise.

Jesus needs to convince his disciples that he can be trusted. He encourages them to look upon his pierced hands and feet to show that he is the very same Jesus they saw crucified. He encourages them to touch him so they will know he is not a ghost or mirage but the real thing. He even eats in their presence as a further sign of his reality. He reminds them what he told them when he was with them before, and he opens their minds to the scriptures.

But here Jesus adds a new dimension. In the same sentence in which he reminds them that his suffering, death, and resurrection were all foretold in the scriptures, he tells them that repentance and forgiveness of sins is to be proclaimed in his name to all nations. Must the pleasure of his company end so abruptly? Can't we sit and savor his presence a little longer?

Seeing is believing, Jesus says, but believing is doing. They are all parts of the same truth, two sides of the same coin. As many hymnwriters have done, Georg Vetter ties together worship and witness:

> *Let praises ring; give thanks and bring*
> *To Christ our Lord adoration.*
> *His honor speed by word and deed*
> *To every land and nation.*
> "With High Delight Let Us Unite"

The church models this divinely instituted paradigm. In worship we are provided opportunities for God to speak to us through scriptures, preaching, sacraments, architecture, art, music, and the presence of people around us. And we respond in confessions, professions, prayers, receiving sacraments, making music, giving offerings, and pledging to go into the world and share what we have received. It is a pattern of call and response, and it bears repeating for a lifetime!

# Fourth Sunday of Easter

This Sunday we celebrate the Fourth Sunday of Easter, also known as "Good Shepherd Sunday" because of the themes that run through the readings and the much-loved 23rd Psalm. For some it is a day to take verbal and musical romps through idyllic hillsides where the grass is always green, the weather perfect, the shepherd restful, and the sheep playful. Their music gently flows along in 6/8 meter, with few dissonances upsetting the lush, comforting, peaceful sounds that seem to please everybody in the pew. Sounds like quite a Sunday, doesn't it?

Just in time come the words of Jesus to pull us out of this fairy-tale land. Not all is calm and pretty in this scene, says this shepherd who has seen it all. This one talks of wolves who snatch and scatter the sheep and of hired hands who run away in fright, caring more for themselves than for their charges. "I am the good shepherd," says Jesus, "because I lay down my life for the sheep."

Jesus' rescue of us is not gentle gamboling in pleasant pastures. It is a battle complete with fights, sneak attacks, and pretenders. The pasture is more like a battlefield for good and evil, life and death. Most importantly, this shepherd above all others, has the power and the will to do what has to be done.

Is this, then, a call to bash our images of a gentle shepherd and do away with peaceful music and moments of comfort and assurance? Certainly not! Such images are indeed a part of life, and they are a part of that life this Savior-shepherd has won for us. But those who know the most terror can know also the most peace. The suffering and dying Prince of Life has taught us that with his very self. It is his gift and wish for each of his sheep to know that peace in our own lives and to be instruments of that peace to others. A realistic peace is what he crave for us.

Peace comes after the storms and, perhaps, because of the storms, but never by ignoring or denying the storms. The Good Shepherd knows that and wants to be present in all our storms.

There are many hymn versions of the 23rd Psalm. One by Henry W. Baker voices this pledge:

> And so, through all the length of days,
> Thy goodness faileth never.
> Good Shepherd, may I sing thy praise
> Within thy house forever.
>
> "The King of Love My Shepherd Is"

Within and without, we might add, for Christ has won his peace for the whole world.

# Fifth Sunday of Easter

Vines are amazing organisms. In the wild, you might have to search for hours to find where one comes out of the ground. Even a houseplant vine can stretch for yards around a room. It may take some detective work to trace it back to the small container from whence it came. Big or small, all vines have one thing in common—if you should find their source, and if you should sever them from their roots, in a very short time you would see yards of foliage shrivel and die. Each cell must be connected to the other ones for them to share the juice of life, and being connected back to the root is absolutely necessary for living.

The people around Jesus knew about vines, especially the ones that were cultivated for grapes. So it is a meaningful example when he told them as he will tell us in this Sunday's gospel, "I am the vine, you are the branches." He develops the metaphor by telling of his Father, the vinegrower, who lovingly planted the vines, wisely prunes them, cuts out the unproductive parts when necessary, and encourages them to fulfill their purpose of bearing fruit. The hymnwriter Jaroslav Vajda put it this way:

> His love selected this terrain
> His vine with love he planted here
> To bear the choicest fruit for him.
> "Amid the World's Bleak Wilderness"

This is the type of story that can give us focus and purpose in our lives. But we should not stop the story too soon. For even when we know we are to bear fruit, and even when it is commanded of us, we may have a hard time sticking to our commitments. Whenever a relationship is abandoned, a project cut short, or an occupation switched, we often hear as the reason, "It no longer fit my needs." "What's in it for me?" has a notorious habit of winning out over the most fervent intentions to simply be bearers of fruit.

Feeding, then, is another part of Jesus' story of the vine and the branches. Just as each branch must be continually connected to the rest of the vine and to its source, so must we. Jesus is expressing a sad reality of the human condition, but it is also a promise. He promises to be that constant source of the juice of life. We need not, moreover, we cannot run on empty. Feeding and being fed, serving and being served, giving and receiving are as intertwined and inseparable as vines in the life Jesus wants for us. "My father is glorified by this," says Jesus, "that you bear much fruit and become my disciples."

Thank God for providing for us the church with its word and sacraments, prayer, music, fellowship, and all the countless known and unknown ways the divine vinegrower cares for us and empowers us to be fruitful for the kingdom.

# Sixth Sunday of Easter

You can lead a horse to water, but you can't make it drink," goes the old saying. "I'll say I'm sorry, but I won't mean it," screams a child when forced to apologize. "I'll do it, but my heart won't be in it," sighs an adult, admitting that, once again, responsibility wins out over personal preference.

Such examples tell us real truths about human nature, ones which we see all too often in those around us and in ourselves. Jesus was more than acquainted with what it is like to be human—he lived it; and he surely had a realistic understanding of human nature—he confronted it every day. It seems strange, then, to hear his words in this Sunday's gospel, "This is my commandment, that you love one another as I have loved you." How can we have warm feelings for those we do not know? Even harder, how can we love many of those whom we do know? How can we obey some command to love when we can't even force ourselves to love those we would like to love?

Leading horses to water, making necessary apologies, and doing things out of a sense of responsibility are simple in comparison because they involve actions—something concrete. We know when we have fulfilled such commands. We've sung all the notes on the page so we know that the song is over and it is time to sit down. But can a command to keep the love song going perpetually, even coming from Jesus, be a realistic expectation?

We must review our definition of love before we can solve this. If we think of love as warm feelings and attraction we surely cannot fulfill the command. But if we adopt Christ's definition of love we can see a glimmer of hope. For Christ, love is an action verb. Actions of love can take place where warm feelings and attraction are weak or even absent. A hymn by Somerset Lowry puts it in this perspective:

> As you, Lord, have lived for others,
> So may we for others live.
> Freely have your gifts been granted,
> Freely may your servants give.
>
> "Son of God, Eternal Savior"

Someone once said, "Thank God we were not commanded to like everybody! There are too many different and difficult personalities for that to be possible. But, with God's help and Christ's example, I think I can take part in loving others." May the presence of the resurrected Christ keep us singing love's song and doing love's deeds.

# The Ascension of Our Lord

The symbolically strong number of forty is held up once again as we celebrate the Ascension of Our Lord forty days after his day of resurrection. These have been forty days of rejoicing, learning, and eating with the Risen One and, through him, with his disciples throughout history. The summaries of the faith he gives are so helpful; the peace he grants is so comforting; the promises he makes are so uplifting. It is with high but mixed emotions that we see him carried up into heaven. Though he has promised to still be with us in new and even better ways, we know things will never be quite the same. And although we cannot understand why he must go in order to be present, we are willing to believe his promise. William Chatterton Dix addresses this mystery in a great hymn;

> *Alleluia! Not as orphans are we left in sorrow now;*
> *Alleluia! He is near us; faith believes, nor questions how.*
> "Alleluia! Sing to Jesus"

There are many who have trouble with some aspects of the Ascension story. Talk of monarchs and enthronements does not hold as much positive meaning as in earlier times. Perhaps our greatest difficulty lies in the concept of heaven as up in the sky, someplace above the clouds, somewhere over the rainbow. Having traveled millions of miles into space, we have a less literal belief in the location of heaven, if indeed it is a location at all. But if we feel we can no longer look toward heaven, do we instead cast our eyes downward or even close them altogether?

Looking upward is still our best bet. Looking upward is how navigators steer their course. Looking upward is how we stay together when singing in a choir. Looking upward gives us new perspectives, new vistas, new comrades, new opportunities, and new energies. Looking upward moves our focus beyond ourselves. The disciples looked upward on that day of Jesus' ascension. Yes, they saw his departure with bittersweet emotions. But as they looked upward they received his blessing, his promise to send power from on high, and his great energy that sent them rejoicing back to Jerusalem. St. Luke records that they worshiped him and were continually in the temple blessing God.

Does it not seem strange that they returned and went to the temple? Did not Jesus call them his witnesses and did he not charge them to proclaim all they had seen and heard? Were their priorities misplaced already?

Hardly! Their worship of the Ascended One began right there at Bethany, in response to his glorious and gracious presence. It continued on their journey back to Jerusalem, and they were drawn magnetically to the house of worship. From there, they were energized by his Spirit to live lives of proclamation and service—even to the point of martyrdom. Such is the power of Christ's promises, of vibrant worship, and of lifting our eyes to the Ascended One. Look up! The time for singing has come!

Luke 24:44-53

# Seventh Sunday of Easter

Have you ever met a guardian angel? There are numerous stories, shows, and paintings that depict such beings. Believers and non-believers alike can usually point to times when something worked for them when it really shouldn't have. We may call them coincidences or miracles, but we really aren't too sure. There are enough examples on each side of the issue to keep us wondering if and how such special protection exists.

In this Sunday's gospel we hear Jesus pray for his people in what is often called his "high priestly prayer." Jesus prays that the Father will protect them as he protected them when he was with them. He prays for protection from the evil one and from the world which hates them. How good it is to know that God is for us!

But there is more to this prayer. Just as he prays for protection, he prays for the unity of his people. "Holy Father, protect them in your name that you have given me, so that they may be one, as we are one." There is yet more. Jesus prays that his people will be "sanctified in the truth."

Are these three things—protection, unity, and sanctification—just separate items on a list of things he prayed for? Or are they somehow related? Jesus knew times would be tough for his followers. His prayer for their unity is not only for their witness to the world but for their own protection and encouragement. His followers were set apart and made holy by the truths of God. This was their unity, and this was their protection. As we should have guessed, these things do belong together. We will have to wait until more is revealed to know if there really are guardian angels. For now, it is enough to know that God does protect us, that God wants us in community with each other, and that we are set apart and made holy by the truths which we have been given. This is expressed masterfully in an early Latin hymn:

> *Christ is made the sure foundation,*
> *Christ, our head and cornerstone,*
> *Chosen of the Lord and precious,*
> *Binding all the church in one;*
> *Holy Zion's help forever*
> *And our confidence alone.*
> "Christ Is Made the Sure Foundation"

As the Easter season comes to a close, we are commissioned by Jesus' prayer, "As you have sent me into the world, so I have sent them into the world." Not alone or unarmed, but with God the protector, unifier, and sanctifier. We do not know what the world has in store for us, but we know the ending, and we know that we are not alone.

John 17:6-19

# The Day of Pentecost

The colorful story of that first Pentecost will be told once again this Sunday. Perhaps some will be hearing it for the first time. Perhaps some who have heard it many times will hear it anew, for it is the nature of this Spirit to blow where it will. Following this dramatic reading from Acts, the gospel reading for Pentecost may sound a bit out of place since it harks back to an earlier time when Jesus was still telling of this Holy Spirit who would be sent. Never mind the anachronism—we still rejoice to hear about the source, power, and work of the promised Advocate. This Spirit has quite a job description, according to Jesus. In one of the more startling statements, Jesus declares, "I still have many things to say to you, but you cannot bear them now. When the Spirit of truth comes, he will guide you into all the truth."

Considering all the radical and powerful things already spoken by Jesus, we can only wonder what things he considered still unbearable for the disciples. Other questions, too, are raised by this statement. What have we been taught since then? Did we learn what was intended? When did new revelations take place? Are there still more to come? How are continuing revelations made? How do we know if new teachings are from the Spirit of truth instead of just the spirit of the age or even the spirit of evil?

Christians have often been suspicious of anything new that claims to be from God. Groups that claim to have unique revelations and new additions to doctrine are considered cults by Orthodoxy. On the other hand, those who arrogantly claim to know exactly what the Holy Spirit is or is not doing are in danger of stifling and denying divine intentions.

Music for worship is only one of many areas where there is often difficulty discerning the intentions of the Spirit. Is the recent emergence of world music in so many unexpected places the result of new energy by the Holy Spirit, or is it a fad? And what about the popular commercial-style music that keeps knocking on the church door? Is it the Holy Spirit calling us to something new and necessary for these days? Or is it a sign of human weakness, always looking for cheap thrills and cultural conformity?

Jesus has not promised answers that are easy, clear, or on our timetable. In fact, he has not really promised answers to our questions at all. But he has promised something better. He promised to send and keep with us his Holy Spirit for guidance. And he promised the unity of this Spirit with himself and with the Father, all for our benefit. Hymnwriter Shirley Erena Murray addresses the Spirit's care and action for us:

> *Loving Spirit, loving Spirit, you have chosen me to be—*
> *you have drawn me to your wonder,*
> *you have set your sign on me.*
> "Loving Spirit"

# The Holy Trinity
## First Sunday after Pentecost

The festival of the Holy Trinity caps off the Christmas and Easter cycles of the church year. During the first half of the year we have, at different times, celebrated the creating and acting Father, or the loving and redeeming Son, or the unifying and renewing Spirit. But, whichever of God's faces we are viewing at any given time, we are not viewing it oblivious of the others. Whenever we look upon one face of God, the others are there as well. Advent, Christmas, Epiphany, Lent, Holy Week, Easter, and Pentecost are, in essence, all festivals of the Holy Trinity. Some theologians have claimed that there should be no specific festival called the Holy Trinity since every gathering in word and sacrament is a celebration and encounter with the triune God. Regardless, the church has continued to choose this one day to celebrate this truth. We often celebrate it by singing Reginald Heber's classic hymn:

> *Holy, holy, holy, merciful and mighty!*
> *God in three Persons, blessed Trinity!*
> "Holy, Holy, Holy"

The word "trinity" appears nowhere in the Bible. But Christians see its truth inherent throughout the scriptures. One such passage serves as the gospel reading this Sunday. It opens with the story of Nicodemus who comes to Jesus to ask some deep questions in the dark of night. Jesus tells him of being born from above and of being born of water and the Spirit. And he shows how the Spirit is like the wind, blowing wherever it chooses. The passage closes with the beloved "God so loved the world . . ."

Father, Son, and Holy Spirit are once again expressed as an energized and energizing unity. But what are we to do with our trinitarian experiences of God? Trying to prove the Trinity is as futile as trying to deny it. Trying to feel love for a doctrine is as impossible as trying to explain it.

As musicians in the church, perhaps we have the best response right on the tips of our tongues. Praise and proclamation are what suits the mystery best. Through our hands and voices we are united with Christians of all times and places who have been called into relationship with the Holy Trinity. Whether singing songs of the ages or those hot-off-the-press, we are links in that chain of praise and proclamation. We owe our gratitude to those before us, our responsibility to those who will follow, and our enthusiasm to our selves and to each other in the here and now. For the mystery of God in Three Persons is at the very center of our songs of praise and lives of faith.

# *Proper 3*

## *Sunday between May 24 and 28 inclusive*
### *(if after Trinity Sunday)*

Have you ever been complimented by an insult? "That was surely a depressing organ piece you played today!" states a parishioner, assuming that prettiness is the goal of church music. "Thank you!" we reply. "Since today is Good Friday, I was hoping it would express just that. Thanks for noticing!"

Jesus receives a similar "put-down" in this Sunday's gospel. Seeing him at the table with those they considered unworthy, the scribes of the Pharisees asked, "Why does he eat with tax collectors and sinners?" They cannot understand why he would do something so scandalous to the tradition; but Jesus is obviously doing something new. Hymnwriter John Newton expresses this in a hymn:

> *When he lived on earth they scorned him;*
> *"Friend of sinners" was his name.*
> *Though the angels have adored him,*
> *Still he answers to that claim.*
>
> "One There Is, above All Others"

The reading goes on to relate another encounter with the Pharisees. Seeing that Jesus' disciples did not take part in the customary fast, they demand to know why. "The wedding guests cannot fast while the bridegroom is with them, can they?" Jesus asks. He is creating a new set of rules, and thanks for noticing!

In the final portion of this reading we hear Jesus speaking metaphorically of new patches pulling away from old cloth and new wine bursting old wineskins. He is definitely telling of new things! While he doesn't wish to rile people up just for the sake of conflict, he does use each instance to proclaim and explain his new world order.

The mini-parable of the old and new wineskins has sometimes been used in arguments over what types of music and liturgy are best for modern worship. Surely it is a complex issue, and we should feel a greater affinity for those who struggle with the issue than for those who have an easy answer or those who claim there is no issue at all. Just as new wine bursts old skins gone rigid over time, the call to the church to speak new languages and sing new songs is an invitation to add to the wine cellar. But the new wineskin expands only if the new wine is a good, lively batch. As does the ever-renewing church, it expands to contain the new mixture, making room for that which is good, and casting off that which is less worthy, regardless of its vintage.

"That music sounds like it came from a thousand years ago!" someone comments. "You're absolutely right!" we respond. "Doesn't it effectively proclaim a gospel that transcends our culture?" "That music sounds like it came from some foreign country halfway across the world!" someone says to us. "You're absolutely right!" we respond. "Doesn't it proclaim the gospel with a wonderful new voice? Thanks for noticing!"

# Proper 4

## Sunday between May 29 and June 4
### (if after Trinity Sunday)

Throughout history there have been many lively discussions over what is proper to do on the Lord's day. Still today there are many different policies and practices, sometimes even within the same denomination. Sadly, what begins as a quest to honor God and glean the most from God's Sabbath often turns into a list of burdensome restrictions. We may rejoice that many restrictive practices have passed by the wayside, and we may even enjoy the nostalgia and humor their retelling brings to us. But we can also lament the spirit of our age that, in many places, barely differentiates between the Lord's day and any other day.

People in Jesus' time struggled with this balance, too. In this Sunday's gospel we hear of the Pharisees who are trying to discredit Jesus and his disciples. They soon have enough evidence to attack. They observe the disciples plucking heads of grain on the Sabbath, and they see the Savior himself doing the work of healing. Surely Jesus and his disciples are not from God, for they break the rules with such ease.

This encounter is the catalyst for Jesus' famous pronouncement, "The Sabbath was made for humankind, and not humankind for the Sabbath." It is a profound and liberating statement, one to which we can return whenever our priorities need evaluating or adjusting. Such an important axiom can keep unnecessary and even counterproductive rules from creeping in and taking the place of God's intent for this great gift. But, once we have declared independence from outside rulers, we had better be sure we have not put a worse despot in place. What kind of Sabbath observance would we establish for ourselves? Do we know what we really need versus what we think we need?

Perhaps we better return to Jesus' words once again. He did not tell us that the Sabbath was to be made by humankind; it is rather for humankind. The Sabbath is God's gift of refreshment and renewal, and a foretaste of a world where all God's intentions are fulfilled. It is a day for us to assemble in Christ's name, to confess sins and receive God's pardon, to praise, to revel in Christ's presence in word and sacrament, to pray with and for the world, and to reaffirm our commitment to God's work in and through us. The whole day is honored by the special presence of the Sabbath God, and the rest of the week is blessed by this special day. As the pattern of days and weeks gives way to months and years, the rhythm of God's Sabbath is a sign to all creation that this God who rules the universe comes at specific times and specific places to the specific people who gather in the divine name. A hymn by Christopher Wordsworth is unique in that it is addressed not to a usual subject but to a day of the week! He has written:

> O day of rest and gladness, O day of joy and light,
> O balm for care and sadness, most beautiful, most bright:
> On you the high and lowly, through ages joined in tune,
> Sing, "Holy, holy, holy," to the great God triune.
> "O Day of Rest and Gladness"

May we treat this day as the great gift that it is—one more sure sign that God is for us.

Mark 2:23-3:6

# Proper 5

## Sunday between June 5 and 11 inclusive
### (if after Trinity Sunday)

This Sunday's gospel portrays some chaotic moments in Jesus' ministry. He has gone home, but the crowds have assembled. His family feels the need to restrain him, since tensions are running high. Some claim Jesus is out of his mind; others accuse him of being possessed by the devil himself. Jesus delivers a rather lengthy defense and explanation of his works of healing. How can anyone accuse him of being under the rule of Satan, he wants to know. Have they not seen Jesus at work? For Satan is exactly who is being cast out. Can they not see that Jesus is really Satan's worst nightmare? Do they not know how they blaspheme the Holy Spirit by suggesting Jesus is on the side of Satan?

Jesus' family makes another appearance at the end of the passage. They call inside and ask for Jesus. Surely he will respond to his mother, brothers, and sisters! In what seems like a callous reply, he questions their identity. And instead of coming out, he looks to those next to him and says, "Here are my mother and my brothers! Whoever does the will of God is my brother and sister and mother."

We hope they got over the shock of such a rebuttal, for Jesus was using the situation to teach an important lesson. In both miracles and family relations, it is the doing of God's work that is most important. His miracles speak of his unity with the Father and Spirit against the power of Satan. And his surprising comment on family relationships is not so much a distancing from his own blood relatives as it is an embracing of all who share in his mission. Jeffrey Rowthorn expresses this special relationship in a hymn:

> *Indwelling God, your gospel claims*
> *one family with a billion names;*
> *let every life be touched by grace*
> *until we praise you face to face.*
>
> "Creating God, Your Fingers Trace"

We see this dynamic at work in worship and music as well. We often cling to specific older works and composers just because of their pedigree; or we toss out something worthy simply because it does not sound catchy to modern ears; or we champion a new sound simply because it is new; or we fail to take seriously music from another world culture because it does not fit our mold.

The word "like" has become a curse to many who care deeply about worship and its music. We would not have to go back very far in history—or much beyond current Western culture, for that matter—to find a time when "liking" something was its least important attribute. In fact, finding something "likable" was usually reason enough for keeping it out of worship. Some even responded by adopting those styles of poetry and music that were homely and even intentionally ugly, fearful of the seduction by pretty things. Clearly, "liking" or "disliking" cannot be a guiding principle for faithful worship. Let us instead follow Christ's example and in all things consistently search for that which best expresses and embodies truth and faithfulness to the will of God.

# *Proper 6*

## *Sunday between June 12 and 18 inclusive*
### *(if after Trinity Sunday)*

How wonderful it is when we find that our work has accomplished some good! Our music ministry was the catalyst for someone finding or returning to the church. Our teaching made an impact on some young person who decided against a destructive behavior. Our small words of greeting received great response from someone experiencing loneliness. The few hours we spent working with a fix-up crew brought sincere thanks from someone who had forgotten what warmth and security felt like. Planting the seeds of God's kingdom is hardly work at all when we get so much positive feedback.

Jesus uses the metaphor of growing seed many times when teaching about the kingdom of God. One such time is in this Sunday's gospel, and here he has chosen to stress the smallness of the seed and how it can sprout and grow even without being aware of its origin.

Jesus points out the irony of the mustard seed, a tiny seed that grows into a great, useful shrub. The seed could have been planted by nearly anyone, unknowingly, but what a great deed it turned out to be! If we knew who had planted it, we could thank and honor them. Since we do not know the planter, we honor them by making full use of it and by being inspired to do some planting ourselves, all for the benefit of others.

Surely, the growing of God's kingdom is of God's own doing. But God has gifted us with the awesome privilege of assisting with the gardening. We may participate in the planting here, the nurturing there, perhaps even the harvesting somewhere else. We will never know all the seeds we have helped to grow; that secret is hidden in God. Likewise, we will never know all the seeds that were planted in and for us, but we are the proof of their presence.

Though many choir rehearsals and worship services may seem the same to us, each tends to the kingdom in its own way, planting seeds of which we are not always aware. So we go about our ministry of music ever improving our skill, ever rehearsing our message, ever praying that God will use us in planting the seeds of the kingdom. With each note and syllable, we embody the prayer of hymnwriter John Cawood:

> So when the precious seed is sown,
> Your quickening grace bestow,
> That all whose souls the truth receive
> Its saving power may know.
>
> "Almighty God, Your Word Is Cast"

Mark 4:26-34

# *Proper 7*

## *Sunday between June 19 and 25 inclusive*
### *(if after Trinity Sunday)*

Other than on Christmas Eve, we don't often think of Jesus sleeping. Perhaps he slept enough his first thirty years so that he did not need much during the years of his public ministry. High-action people often get by on less sleep than the rest of us. And, with all the people following and clamoring for him, we can imagine his sleep was delayed and cut short numerous times.

This Sunday's gospel does tell of one time when Jesus was asleep, catching a few winks as he and the disciples are crossing the sea in a boat. The growing storm is not enough to wake him, and the worried disciples must go and find him. They are upset with him for sleeping at such a time. "Teacher, do you not care that we are perishing?" is their wake-up call. They were finding that their master, great as he was, was not always predictable. As with many of his miracles, he did not always do what they wanted or when they wanted it. He followed his own script on his own terms.

But, if they could not predict *when* he might act, they did have faith that he *would* act and that he would respond on the side of life. "Peace! Be still!" he calls to the wind and sea, and a dead calm replaces the noisy turbulence. Mark records that they were filled with great awe and said to one another, "Who then is this, that even the wind and the sea obey him?"

Once again, Jesus' response exceeds their expectations. They hoped the storm would get no worse, but Jesus stopped it completely. They sought comforting, but they received deliverance. They hoped for a favor, but they got a miracle.

"Why are you afraid? Have you still no faith?" was Jesus' probing question to the disciples, and he asks the same of his disciples two thousand years later. We call out too seldom and ask too little of him. We may suspect that Jesus is asleep when we feel we to get no response, but it is we who need to be awakened to sense his faithful presence, as constant as the rhythmic waves on the sea. May God give us faith to believe such wonderful claims. We confess with the hymnwriter Edward Hopper:

> *As a mother stills her child,*
> *Thou canst hush the oceans wild;*
> *Boisterous waves obey thy will*
> *When thou sayest to them "Be still."*
> *Wondrous sovereign of the sea,*
> *Jesus, Savior, pilot me.*
>> "Jesus Savior, Pilot Me"

# *Proper 8*

## *Sunday between June 26 and July 2 inclusive*

Those who have had a close encounter with a famous person rarely forget about it. Being in the presence of a movie star, a popular entertainer, a religious giant, or the President of the United States will be remembered, recounted, and treasured for the rest of one's life. Encounters with Jesus enter an even higher category for Christians, for such an experience never leaves one unchanged.

It has been that way since he walked this earth. So many whom he encountered in his preaching, teaching, and healing became his followers, desiring little else than to be in his presence. For he reached their very essence, touching and blessing their innermost being, changing them forever.

This Sunday we shall hear of two individuals touched by Jesus. One is a little girl; she is very sick when her father Jairus goes to beg healing from Jesus. Before he can go, the second tragic character makes an appearance. A woman, convinced that she will be healed if she can only touch Jesus' clothes, approaches him from behind. Many in this story are at their breaking point—the woman, the little girl, Jairus, their families. Their encounter with Jesus comes at the most critical, emotional pinnacle of their lives. And they receive life, healing, and wholeness. For the rest of their lives they will remember and treasure this climactic turning point.

But what about Jesus? Did he ever become blasé after doing so many similar works of healing? Did they all blur together in his mind? Jesus waved no magic wand; he spoke no standard formulas; he handed out no cheap grace. Each tragic figure was just that to the Savior. In this healing narrative there is an especially remarkable scene. As the woman seeks healing by merely touching his cloak, Mark reports that Jesus was "immediately aware that power had gone forth from him," and he asks, "who touched my clothes?" Jesus then commends the woman for her faith. A caring ministry required great effort, even for one to whom it came so naturally. Both sides of the relationship put forth energy, both were aware of it, and both were blessed by it.

We know this from our human encounters. When we love much we put our whole selves into the relationship, and we can tell when someone does the same for us. Even in making music, we know the joy and stimulation of exerting ourselves for each other. Jesus still comes to us, still encounters us, still invests energy in us, still heals us. In a text that has enriched both hymn and anthem repertoire, Percy Dearmer's words pray for us:

> *Draw us in the Spirit's tether,*
> *for when humbly in your name*
> *two or three are met together,*
> *you are in the midst of them.*
> *Alleluia!*
> "Draw Us in the Spirit's Tether"

# Proper 9
## *Sunday between July 3 and 9 inclusive*

In the second part of this Sunday's gospel we hear Jesus sending out disciples to do ministry for the kingdom of God. Besides giving instructions and advice, he also gives them authority to cast out unclean spirits, anoint and work cures, and even to enact a testimony against those who will not welcome them. Jesus' instructions are powerful, for they convey the authority to bring them about.

The first portion of the reading is also concerned with authority, but here it sings a different tune. Jesus is teaching in a synagogue, but he is unable to bring about more than a few cures. Was he just having an off day? No, the important difference in this scene is that he is in his hometown. The people know his background, his family, and even his childhood. That's the problem—they know him too well!

We may be familiar with this attitude, too. We usually consider someone an expert only if they come a far distance. Even in the local church, it is difficult for those "home-grown" folks to serve in leadership positions. "I can't take the new pastor seriously; I taught her in fourth grade Sunday School, and she didn't behave all that well." Or, "We don't need to pay much attention to the music director's opinions; he was as common as the rest of us before he went away and got a degree." Or, "I am really excited about hearing that guest choir next week for a change; our choir is just made up of volunteer members."

It is indeed a shame when roadblocks to ministry are put in place. But, as hostile as they may seem on the surface, they are often built out of insecurities. "I don't feel worthy to be ministering to others," admits one. "That person is not much different from me; hence, he must not be worthy either," concludes the rationale.

Jesus' authority came not from his upbringing but from his divine anointing. And his disciples, common and unworthy as they were, held authority because it was granted them by the Anointed One. That is the source of our calling, as well. As important as talent, education, and training are, it is ultimately God's call and baptismal blessing that grants the privilege of speaking, singing, and working in the divine name. As God has gifted us with such opportunities, we recognize and welcome the ministry that others are called to carry out. They live and work across the globe, and they stand next to us in choir. They are total strangers and they are our own family. They are us. Omer Westendorf's marvelous hymn proclaims this vision:

> *The seed of his teaching, receptive souls reaching,*
> *Shall blossom in action for God and for all.*
> *His grace did invite us, his love shall unite us*
> *To work for God's kingdom and answer his call.*
> "Sent Forth by God's Blessing"

# Proper 10

## Sunday between July 10 and 16 inclusive

Have you ever used the expression, "That person would surely love to have my head on a platter!" If so, you were calling to mind the great John the Baptist at the point of his death. We shall hear the whole story in this Sunday's gospel reading. It is an intriguing story involving our favorite villain Herod, his wife who holds a grudge against the prophet for criticizing their marriage, their daughter who helps trick her father into ordering the execution, and, of course, John the Baptist. It is also a gruesome story, recounting how those at the birthday party were confronted with the bodyless head and how John's disciples came to take and bury the headless body. And it is ultimately an upsetting story, for John is only one of many who saw early and violent deaths as the cost of their discipleship.

What a way to spend a summer Sunday! Will those who have a preview of this week's Gospel decide to stay away? We hope not, for the good news shines even more brightly in such dark surroundings. It is an opportunity to lift up those of great faith. In hymns, such as this classic by Frederick W. Faber, we praise and proclaim the witness of our spiritual ancestors:

> Faith of our fathers, living still
> In spite of dungeon, fire, and sword.
> Oh, how our hearts beat high with joy
> Whene'er we hear that glorious word.
> "Faith of Our Fathers"

It will also be a day to take stock of our own faithfulness. Are we pleased or disturbed that nobody particularly wants our head on a platter on account of our work for the kingdom? What is the cost of our discipleship?

We are not alone in our mixed emotions to this account. For Mark tells us that even Herod was moved and torn. "Herod feared John," he writes, "knowing that he was a righteous and holy man, and he protected him. When he heard him, he was greatly perplexed; and yet he liked to listen to him." Psychologists can be as intrigued with Herod as are the theologians. Who can explain the power that attracts yet repels, that appeals yet repulses, that brings judgment yet salvation?

Most people prefer consonant sounds over dissonant ones. Yet, how bland and shallow our music sounds when the two are not in creative interplay with each other. Contrasting forces define each other, play off each other, and produce energy that excites, attracts, and sets apart. The holiness of God is proclaimed ever so strongly as we contemplate the evil deeds of Herod's family. The gift of faith is treasured ever so dearly as we consider the selfless deeds of Christian martyrs. And the call to minister in Christ's name is blessed ever so powerfully as we encounter the presence that is life-changing, life-energizing, and life-transcending.

What a way to spend a summer Sunday? What a way to spend a life!

Mark 6:14-29

# *Proper 11*
## *Sunday between July 17 and 23 inclusive*

The lives of celebrities are not always easy. Maybe we will find that out when our choir becomes famous. Then we'll be paid extravagant salaries, and companies selling throat lozenges and breath mints will be after us with huge offers hoping for our endorsements. But we will also know how hard it is to have privacy when we want it, and we'll be so tired we won't be able to much enjoy our fame and fortune. Perhaps it's best that we keep our superior abilities to our own congregation after all!

Jesus became a celebrity in his own day. This Sunday's gospel begins with his apostles relating to him all they had done and taught. He must have sensed their weariness, for he tells them, "Come away to a deserted place all by yourselves and rest a while." What a welcome suggestion this must have been! But Mark goes on to say that many recognized them and saw them leave, and they ran so quickly that they actually beat Jesus and the apostles to their destination. Unlike today's celebrities, Jesus had no Hollywood mansion where he could be secluded, no travel agent to send him to a place where he could rest incognito, and no Camp David where he could go into retreat. We hear nothing more of what happened to the apostles upon their arrival in Gennesaret, for Jesus is clearly the object of the crowd's attention. They brought sick people to him who begged that they might touch even the fringe of his cloak. This crowd surely shared many attributes with modern-day celebrity worshipers.

There is one important difference with this celebrity named Jesus. Mark reports that Jesus, even out of his weariness, had compassion for them, taught them, and healed all who struggled in faith to see and touch him. Jesus does what is good, not for the sake of positive publicity, but because his very nature is perfectly and exclusively good.

Such is the Christ we proclaim every time we gather for worship. We speak, sing, pray, enact, and share the goodness of this one who forgives, heals, gathers, empowers, and loves. When we are weary from work and need renewal for going on, Christ tells us to come away and rest. For we do not and we can not do all that begs to be done. But Christ, risen and forever present in his Holy Spirit, needs no sabbatical. His goodness is beyond our comprehension; his mercy is beyond our understanding. We pray for Christ's presence and healing in a hymn by Edward H. Plumptre:

> *Oh, be our great deliverer still,*
> *The Lord of life and death;*
> *Restore and quicken, soothe and bless,*
> *With your life-giving breath.*
> *To hands that work and eyes that see*
> *Give wisdom's healing power,*
> *That whole and sick and weak and strong*
> *May praise you evermore.*
>
> "Your Hand, O Lord, in Days of Old"

To the world we may not be celebrities, but God's unconditional love and baptismal grace give us an unmistakable identity. That is a source of great riches and an endorsement beyond our wildest imagination!

Mark 6:30-34, 53-56

# Proper 12
## Sunday between July 24 and 30 inclusive

It will take a miracle for me to hit all the right notes this Sunday," bemoans an organist. "If everyone shows up on time this week it will be a miracle," comments a choir director. "If the conductor remembers to give us all the cues she promised us, it will be truly miraculous," sighs a choir member. And who says we don't come to church expecting miracles any more?!

If the truth be told, the miracles we probably talk about the most are ones largely for our own convenience and comfort, ones spoken out of cynicism or in hopes of avoiding what should rightfully happen to us. We might not even notice if a genuine, full-scale miracle took place in our very midst.

This Sunday's gospel reading hits us with some big-time miracles of undeniable potency. Five thousand people are fed in the first scene, and there is more food left over than what they originally distributed. Each and every person in attendance tasted that delicious, extravagant miracle.

It is to be a miraculous night, as well. The disciples, crossing the sea in a boat, are frightened as the wind picks up, the waves grow rougher, and the sky grows dark. Their fear is only made worse when they see a figure walking toward them on the water. With the brief words, "It is I; do not be afraid," Jesus turns their terror into joy. Even more surprise awaits them as their boat, miles out into the sea, immediately reaches land. This miracle will have a big impact on the rest of their lives.

Oh, that we could witness such drama. Then we could stop looking for miracles in detergent boxes and stop calling things miraculous when they are merely good luck. Gospel musician Thomas A. Dorsey craved and anticipated a genuine miracle. In a hymn he helped bring to its well-known form, he provided a confession of need and a profession of faith:

> Precious Lord, take my hand, lead me on, let me stand,
> I am tired, I am weak, I am worn.
> Through the storm, through the night,
> Lead me on to the light,
> Take my hand, precious Lord, lead me home.
>
> "Precious Lord, Take My Hand"

Our music-making is a miracle in itself. How spots and lines on a page can bring back to life that which was imagined long ago and far away truly defies the logic of time and space. How diverse people can combine their talents to express such profound truths and great beauty is surely a sign of divine blessing.

As we gather in Christ's name for worship, we are fed. Each and every one present can taste in word and sacrament the bread that is Christ's overwhelming love and care. And each one, over the wind and waves of countless terrors, can hear the voice of the one who says, "It is I; do not be afraid." Look and listen; the miracle has already begun!

# *Proper 13*

## *Sunday between July 31 and August 6 inclusive*

What is your reason for participating in a church choir? A part of each of us will likely answer, "for the sake of serving God and fellow Christians." We might also mention that our sense of commitment, gratitude, and evangelism keeps us regular in our attendance and energetic in our participation. But another part of us may acknowledge other reasons that are somewhat less benevolent in motive. We may participate simply for our personal joy, or for the spiritual high we feel, or for the camaraderie, or to keep up our musical skills, or to get us out of the house, or for the paycheck, or as an excuse to avoid the more tedious tasks of parish life. Maybe we shouldn't have taken that inventory after all!

In this Sunday's gospel Jesus questions the motives of those who have come looking for him. He tells them, "You are looking for me, not because you saw signs, but because you ate your fill of the loaves." That is a charge that stings sharply. Who could not have been impressed when, only the day before, Jesus had taken the five loaves and two fish, blessed them, and gave them to the five thousand present? They ate their fill, and twelve baskets were still left over. This miracle filled not only their imaginations; it filled their stomachs. This was a miracle that left a good taste in their mouths, and they wanted more.

Jesus saw the danger of that, and so he begins his discourse on bread. He speaks of the bread that endures, the bread that comes from God, the bread that represents and conveys God's love and care, the bread that is Christ. Christians of every era have recognized and treasured the eucharistic implications of this bread that is not just bread but so much more. Communion hymns particularly abound in this imagery, such as this one by an anonymous twentieth-century writer:

> *Jesus said: I am the bread kneaded long to give you life;*
> *you who will partake of me need not ever fear to die.*
> *I received the living God, and my heart is full of joy.*
> "I Received the Living God"

Our culture receives the same warning Christ gave his first followers. We, too, are often people who seek full bellies and tickled taste buds without a thought to nutrition. We pillage nature in exchange for more malls and entertainment complexes. We toss out masterpieces of music and poetry to make more room for songs that ask little or nothing of us. We detour around the rough roads of discipleship so we can spend more time in the green pastures. We teach what we like rather than search for what we need.

Maybe what we really need is for Jesus to spend even more time on this topic of bread. Search our motives, Lord; help us keep our priorities straight. Be so present for us and in us that we have no need to seek the bread that merely stuffs our stomachs. Let us be so filled with you that we cannot help but sing your praise and serve your world.

# Proper 14
## Sunday between August 7 and 13 inclusive

Have you ever been confused while watching a movie that contains flashback scenes? "Is this currently happening?" we might ask. "No," is the reply from those who never have trouble following the plot line of the most intricate stories. "This is a flashback to an earlier time, but not as far back as the last one when the main character was dreaming of the future, which still takes place before the previous flashback," they smugly conclude. "Come get me when it is over," we reply. "I will save my brain for a more important issue."

Then how about something theological? "The bread used in the Holy Eucharist remains bread, but it symbolizes the presence of Christ in our hearts," says one. "No," says another, "the bread remains bread but it also embodies the real presence of Christ." Yet another claims, "Once it is blessed, it is no longer bread at all, just the body of Christ." Still another argues, "All this talk of bread is too physical; Jesus was only speaking figuratively of food. He means it in a spiritual and emotional sense, I'm sure."

Such discussions take place in our seminaries, ecumenical organizations, classrooms, pulpits, and even in the privacy of our minds. And that is all right, for they take place in scripture, as well. This Sunday we hear some of Jesus' many sayings about bread, and they bring questions from believers and critics alike. "I am the bread of life," he claims. "Whoever comes to me will never be hungry, and whoever believes in me will never be thirsty." And he continues to tell of this bread that came down from heaven; this bread which, unlike the manna of their ancestors, shields from death; and this bread which, given for the life of the world, is his flesh.

This was confusing talk, to be sure. It blurred the lines between bread and flesh, heaven and earth, time and space, living and dying. We study and treasure the eucharistic theologies clarified by the biblical scholars and theologians over the centuries. They have sought to best understand and put into practice the will of Christ for the sake of his church.

But, as helpful as they are, even the most definitive and detailed doctrines fall short in discovering and expressing the vastness of this bread of life. It is indeed a new day as denominations draw their circles larger to embrace a richer, more inclusive eucharistic theology; it is indeed a hope-filled day as churches celebrate their points of unity more than they dwell on their disunity; it is a faith-filled day as Christians grow to discover and consider the many layers of tradition and practice. Our point of convergence is Christ and his promises. As we recall his claims to be the bread of life for us, as we accept his gifts and believe his promises, and as we see his promise granting life to the whole world, then we too encounter and proclaim the mysteries of this one who transcends all human limits of time and space, knowledge and belief. Hymnwriter Muus Jacobse writes:

*He became our bread; Jesus died to save us.*
*On him we are fed, eating what he gave us,*
*Rising from the dead.*

"We Who Once Were Dead"

John 6:35, 41-51

# *Proper 15*
## *Sunday between August 14 and 20 inclusive*

The music from Europe's Taizé Community has found its way into the songbooks and services of many denominations. One such piece, as composed by Jacques Berthier and fitted with text from John 6, begins like this:

> *Eat this bread, drink this cup,*
> *Come to me and never be hungry.*
> *Eat this bread, drink this cup,*
> *Trust in me and you will not thirst.*
>
> "Eat This Bread"

That is not just the beginning; it is also the ending and everything in between. For these short musical meditations are meant to be repeated over and over, even dozens of times, sometimes with an added text and other times just the simple refrain alone. When describing the Taizé chants it is hard to make them sound anything but tedious and boring. But, when sung with care and prayer, many Christians sense their deep spirituality. Placed alongside the great hymns of the ages, these chants modestly and devotionally tell of the richness of life, the simplicity of faith, and the joy and peace of community as found in the body of Christ.

There is repetition in this Sunday's gospel, too. Jesus continues to spin out his teachings on bread. He is the living bread from heaven, he says. Only those who eat his flesh and drink his blood have life in them; and those who have eternal life will be raised up on the last day. Why this obsession with bread? Why is it mentioned numerous times in this Sunday's gospel as well as next week, last week, and even before that in the miraculous feeding of five thousand?

Perhaps we should consider the difference between repetition and rhythm. Steady beats in music are necessary for drive, energy, and accuracy. Regular heartbeats and a steady pulse are signs of health. The patterns of days, months, and seasons orders our lives and our work. Repetition is tedious only if it is divorced from creativity and a sense of progression.

Each time Jesus speaks of bread, he has taught us one more time. Each time we receive the living bread in Holy Communion, he has fed and forgiven us one more time. Each time we worship, praise, and pray we have been comforted and empowered one more time. Jesus continues to make and keep his promises, and they grow stronger with each repetition.

And we are not quite the same person from one day to another, or even from one minute to the next. As we sing "Eat this bread, drink this cup," for the ninth time, we are older, perhaps wiser, perhaps more feeble, but surely closer to death than when we sang it for the eighth time. At each new moment we need to hear repeated the assurance of Christ's presence.

These steady Gospel beats give us the grounding we need in our often unsteady lives. Accompanied by that dependable rhythm, we are inspired and encouraged to live lives that are creative, responsive, and reflective of the Christ who faithfully feeds us the living bread, which is his very self.

# Proper 16

## Sunday between August 21 and 27 inclusive

Many choirs keep two membership lists. One contains that well-defined circle of folks who are, for the most part, reliable, regular, and ready to take on new tasks and challenges. The other list draws its circle a bit wider. It contains names of those who don't really fit the active category, but we don't really feel right about removing them either. They don't have the viable excuses of health, family, work, or travel that some do. We seem to remember their participation fading about the time changes were made with the hymnal, or the liturgy, or the robes, or the musical style, or the schedule, or the seating arrangement, or the director, or . . . Sadly, we cannot depend much on these folks, and their past contributions coupled with their sporadic present paint that larger circle a bland shade of ambiguous gray.

Jesus is cleaning out his membership roster too in this Sunday's gospel. Just as we have been doing over the last several weeks, his disciples are hearing the conclusion of Jesus' "bread of life" discourse. "Those who eat my flesh and drink my blood abide in me, and I in them," he states. This bread has come down from heaven, and those who eat it will live forever.

Scripture records that the disciples' response was similar perhaps to ours. "This teaching is difficult; who can accept it?" Jesus' follow-up comments do not help clarify the matter very much. St. John relates, "Because of this many of his disciples turned back and no longer went about with him." What were they feeling? Perhaps some were confused, having gotten lost somewhere around that first bread-and-body, flesh-and-blood statement. Perhaps some were disillusioned, hearing all this talk of giving up oneself and dying. Perhaps others understood his words all too well, and they knew they could not afford the cost of such discipleship.

Jesus finally asked the twelve a question, and in doing so he asks the same of us, "Do you also wish to go away?" We hope we can give the same answer as Simon Peter, "Lord, to whom can we go? You have the words of eternal life. We have come to believe and know that you are the Holy One of God."

What a definition of trust is expressed in Peter's response! Though we sometimes must follow in utter blindness, and other times in confusion or even protest, we still know deep down that Christ is the only one worth following. Nobody, not even ourselves, holds our best interest so highly. Nobody else has lived such a giving life, died such a tortured death, and yet came back to bring us through. We know in faith that Christ's is the only song worth singing.

Can we faithfully follow Christ's lead, keeping our enthusiasm high and our loyalty strong? Not by ourselves. Hymnwriter John W. Chadwick helps us pray for what we need:

> Oh, clothe us with your heavenly armor, Lord.
> Your trusty shield and sword of love endure;
> Our constant inspiration be your Word;
> We ask no victories that are not yours.
> Give or withhold, let pain or pleasure fall;
> To know that we are serving you is all.

"Eternal Ruler of the Ceaseless Round"

# Proper 17

## Sunday between August 28 and September 3 inclusive

Whenever the time comes in the liturgy to proclaim the holy gospel, Christians emphasize its importance in many ways. We usually stand, sing acclamations of praise and invocation, hear its announcement, and sing or shout, "Glory to you, O Lord!" These tributes are most appropriate, for we believe Christ is truly present as his gospel is proclaimed. We want to acknowledge and honor his holy presence, celebrate his great gift of grace, and prepare our selves to better receive his dynamic word. Many Christians embody still one more prayer. As they make small signs of the cross on their foreheads, mouths, and chests, they silently pray, "May your word be on my mind, on my lips, and in my heart."

What wealth of meaning lies in this prayer of few words! What deep faith is expressed by those who earnestly pray it! What power is unleashed as God answers it! And what a rich Gospel it professes! It tells of a Gospel that is not merely knowledge, not merely words, not merely emotion, but all three added together, multiplied, and still more.

Jesus is teaching about a thoroughly integrated faith in this Sunday's gospel. As the Pharisees criticize his disciples for not observing the Jewish rules of cleanliness, Jesus chastises them for their hypocrisy. They are so worried about following the human-made traditions that they barely even notice the many commandments that truly are from God. He goes on to point out the utter futility of any attempts to gain holiness by avoiding that which is deemed unclean. It is not the material things of this world that are our undoing—rather, we are our own worst enemy. We should acknowledge and seek to cleanse our own defiling natures, he says, and we should stop obsessing on self-righteous pseudocleanliness.

Jesus harsh pronouncement is a damning one, for who can hold their head high after such a sweeping indictment? But it is also a righteous pronouncement that ultimately frees us. We are freed from trying to win our own salvation, freed to accept the grace offered in Christ, freed for living lives of praise and service.

It is a constant battle for some of us—this battle that goes on deep inside involving our thoughts and actions, intentions and actualities, words and deeds. Like hymnwriter Johann F. Ruopp, we often plead:

> *Renew me, O eternal Light,*
> *And let my heart and soul be bright,*
> *Illumined with the light of grace*
> *That issues from your holy face.*
>
> "Renew Me, O Eternal Light"

The renewal for which we pray involves a clean sweep and some new connective tissues. We pray for a faith that unites all that we are and all that we do. Every time we sing we model the integration of mind and mouth and heart, and we pray that such a pattern would take over our whole life. Yes, Lord, give us that focused integrity and that harnessed energy that reveres, honors, and proclaims your holy gospel of grace.

# *Proper 18*
## *Sunday between September 4 and 10 inclusive*

Children have a hard time hiding their emotions. Whether excited or sad, they will usually behave in a manner that gives them away. Asking children to hide their emotions is like asking the sun to stop shining—it goes against their very nature. How about adults? Somewhere in adolescence a 180-degree turn often occurs. No longer can we count on childlike displays to tell us how a person feels. Relationships are often complicated by a lack of showing emotions, and many adults cannot even identify their own feelings.

In this Sunday's gospel we hear of many people with many emotions and many ways of expressing those emotions. First we will hear of a woman who pleads for her daughter's healing, and her request is indeed granted. Later, people brought to Jesus a deaf man with a speech impediment. The account says that they "begged him to lay his hand on him." Hymnwriter Anna Hoppe tells of this encounter:

> *The speechless tongue, the lifeless ear*
> *You can restore, O Lord,*
> *Your "Ephphatha" O Savior dear,*
> *Can instant help afford.*
> "O Son of God, in Galilee"

We are left only to imagine the emotions of those who were so wonderfully healed, for the account concentrates rather on the emotions of the crowd. Jesus orders them to tell no one. But, as Mark records, "the more he ordered them, the more zealously they proclaimed it." They could not help but proclaim what they had seen. It would have gone against their very natures to keep it in.

Why would Jesus try to suppress the enthusiasm of his followers? Probably he did not want the news of his supernatural powers to minimize the person he was and his many, less sensational teachings. The time was not yet right for this type of publicity. But, in spite of Jesus' plea, they proclaimed. They just couldn't help it.

What about us? Just as adults often do 180-degree turns, the modern-day church handles things quite differently from its infant counterpart. We seem to have a hard time proclaiming the good news—almost as if Jesus had told us to tell no one. This is perhaps our modern-day speech impediment. However, the time to keep quiet is past. Now is the age after Jesus' resurrection and after the sending of the Holy Spirit; now we have received the charge and the power to proclaim boldly.

Just what did these early followers proclaim with so much enthusiasm? Mark says their cry was, "He has done everything well; he even makes the deaf to hear and the mute to speak."

Surrounded by a culture with so much mediocrity and downright shoddiness, doing things well can really stand out in the crowd. As in Jesus' time, doing things well is its own witness. Let us then, in our music ministry as in all aspects of our lives, rededicate ourselves both to Christ's example of doing things well and to the disciples' example of joyful proclamation because "we just can't help it!"

Mark 7:24-37

# Proper 19
## Sunday between September 11 and 17 inclusive

Robert Louis Stevenson's Dr. Jeckyll and Mr. Hyde is a classic literary work. The title characters are, of course, one and the same person. The fine, decent Dr. Jeckyll transforms into the evil Mr. Hyde whenever a potion is drunk. The story has intrigued readers for generations, and many have made use of the psychological angle of the plot. Whenever someone displays great shifts in personality they might be called a "Jeckyll-Hyde" case. Many have felt that Stevenson has portrayed, in exaggeration for effect, the good and evil found in every person.

Peter is one who might be called a Jeckyll-Hyde character on account of his mixed responses. In this Sunday's gospel reading Jesus is asking his disciples, "Who do people say that I am?" After several incorrect answers, it is finally Peter who exclaims, "You are the Messiah." Jesus then goes on to relate what will happen to him. He tells of suffering, rejection, death, and resurrection to the followers whom he feels must now know more of the story. It is Peter who again reacts, rebuking Jesus for saying such things. Then Mark records some of the harshest words to come from Jesus, "Get behind me, Satan! For you are setting your mind not on divine things but on human things."

Will the true Peter please stand up? Was he the "rock" who was among the first to recognize and confess Jesus as the Messiah? Or was he the misguided, wicked one who attempted to attach a disclaimer to Jesus' words? Surely he was both. Just as humans of every age have had the ability to confess Jesus in one breath and deny him with the next, we find in Peter a true human, a man after our own heart—a "Jeckyll-Hyde" heart.

Many critics of the church like to use the old saw, "There are so many hypocrites in the church!" "There is always room for one more," goes the snappy reply. Or some might say, "The choir is filled with folks who get the message so right on Sunday and so wrong the rest of the week." "Yes," we reply, "and we have room for you, too, in this collection of characters who are simultaneously saints, sinners, and singers."

Christ has redeemed all parts of our lives—the parts that do good and the parts that do evil—the Jeckyll and the Hyde. In our striving to do good he blesses, encourages, and multiplies our humble efforts. In our failings, he stands ready to forgive, guide, grieve, and yet to love. Only Christ knows fully the Jeckyl and Hyde within us and only he can deal with it. Furthermore, only Jesus has the right to complain about hypocrites in the church or the choir, for only he is exempt. Bernard of Clairvaux penned quite a lofty goal for us:

> *May every heart confess your name,*
> *Forever you adore,*
> *And, seeking you, itself inflame*
> *To seek you more and more!*
>
> "O Jesus, King Most Wonderful"

But even such a task is not beyond Christ's ability. Even now, he takes those parts of us that do not yet acknowledge his rule and turns them into songs that proclaim, "You are the Messiah!"

# *Proper 20*
## *Sunday between September 18 and 24 inclusive*

In case you've never noticed, humans have a tough time keeping things straight. It may seem hard for anyone in this choir to imagine, but in some choirs it is actually necessary to remind singers to enunciate, to emphasize ending consonants, to de-emphasize R's and S's, to sing through the long notes, to listen for blend, and even to watch the director!

Jesus needed to keep reminding his followers important truths. In last Sunday's gospel we heard Jesus telling his disciples what was to happen to him. When Peter disagreed, he was harshly reprimanded. In this Sunday's reading, Jesus is trying again, giving warning of what to expect in the coming days. Surely they would understand this time. But, soon after, they are arguing with each other over who is really the greatest!

Time for another lesson. "He sat down," Mark records, "called the twelve, and said to them, 'Whoever wants to be first must be last of all and servant of all.'" Maybe this time it would finally sink in. To make sure, Jesus employed a technique with a long history of teaching success—a visual aid.

No, he didn't set up a flannel graph, or plug in a video, or make shadow puppets. Mark writes, "Then he took a little child and put it among them; and taking it in his arms, he said to them, 'Whoever welcomes one such child in my name welcomes me, and whoever welcomes me welcomes not me but the one who sent me.'" Jesus used a child to show his solidarity with the powerless, the least visible, the ones deemed to be of little value. Did his visual aid accomplish what he had hoped? It must have made some impact because the story was remembered, passed around, and finally preserved in written form. And it makes an impact today, for it is a story we never grow tired of hearing. We often sing of God's love for children, young and old, in hymns such as one by Caroline Sandell Berg:

> *Children of the heavenly Father,*
> *Safely in his bosom gather;*
> *Nestling bird or star in heaven*
> *Such a refuge ne'er was given.*
>
> "Children of the Heavenly Father"

This doesn't mean that Jesus' disciples then, as now, didn't continue to have some trouble living out his great lessons on servanthood. Our human tendency is to lose fervor and slip back into the standards of the culture around us. Constant reminders are, unfortunately, necessary when the message is both so important and so contrary to what the world tells us.

Will we ever fully understand and live Jesus' teachings on true greatness? On our own, we probably have a better chance of remembering all the choir director's advice and suddenly be rid of every bad vocal habit! But, through the work of the Holy Spirit, we can begin to glimpse the new world order Christ has planned for his children. And we pray for that Spirit to keep reminding, correcting, and forming us into the people whose only goal is to know and do God's will.

Mark 9:30-37

# *Proper 21*
## *Sunday between September 25 and October 1 inclusive*

Our gospel this Sunday sounds a bit like a catch-all, almost as if the gospel writer was remembering disjointed fragments of Jesus' teachings or that Jesus himself was in a miscellaneous mood. In a few short verses we hear him telling the disciples to not stop others who were casting out demons in his name, to regard those who are not against him as being for him, to give a cup of water in his name, and to avoid placing stumbling blocks. Then he begins the shocking charge to cut off whatever causes them to sin, using body parts as examples! After all this, he tells them they will be salted with fire, that salt is good but may need re-seasoning, to have salt in themselves, and finally, to be at peace with one another. Sounds like a good day to sing something from the "general" category of our choir files, doesn't it?

If there is a common theme to these sayings, it seems to be that of barriers, resisting the urge to put them in place, and removing them where they already exist. Jesus did his share of tearing down many of the barriers which society and religion had erected. His acceptance of children, women, sinners, the sick, and outcasts is an attribute we so fervently want to emulate. But the human tendency to build walls instead of bridges is, sadly, still with us. Even in the church, for example, we still cannot reach a consensus on the proper age children are "allowed" to receive holy communion, or on the need for accessible worship spaces, or on the importance of inclusive language. Even when we do act on such matters, we often are concerned with only those issues that affect us or those close to us. We must work for the breaking down of barriers simply for the sake of the gospel and for the vision of God that such actions proclaim.

And what of removing from our lives those things which tempt us to sin? Surely Jesus does not mean those words about bodily mutilation literally, for we should all be reduced to nothing. He reminds us elsewhere that sin comes from within. Our body parts do not have souls and wills of their own; they only carry out the sin that is a part of our weak will. His charge, then, is to get at the root of our actions. In choir, we would do a great injustice if we banished a singer who tended to sing flat. Rather, we hope we would diagnose a basic listening or breath support problem and fix it for the betterment of the singer and the whole group.

Literal interpretations or not, we are still not free from desperation over this dilemma until we acknowledge that, in matters of the heart, we cannot on our own become free of sin's hold. Jesus has once again told us the nasty truth so that we will be driven to fall onto the grace of God. But he has also told us the beautiful truth—of barriers that he has broken down in and for us, blessing us to be a blessing to others. Hymnwriter Frank Mason North vividly expresses this vision of Gospel grace:

> *Where cross the crowded ways of life,*
> *Where sound the cries of race and clan,*
> *Above the noise of selfish strife,*
> *We hear your voice, O Son of Man.*
> "Where Cross the Crowded Ways of Life"

# *Proper 22*

## *Sunday between October 2 and 8 inclusive*

Many folks believe that ours is a most complicated age in which to live. As in technical and bureaucratic fields, the intricacies of personal and family relationships often speak bewildering and ever-evolving languages of their own. The roles of single persons and spouses, parents and children seem to change every few years, causing some to yearn for the "good old days" when everyone unquestioningly "knew their place."

But our dilemma is not all that unique. Of all the eras where great changes have been preached and enacted, none has heard more radical claims or witnessed more radical deeds than the time when Jesus walked this earth. His disciples experienced the shocking new developments first-hand, hearing and seeing Jesus bring about his new world order. Each day there seemed to be yet another barrier he brought crashing to the ground.

In this Sunday's gospel we hear Jesus' teachings on marriage and divorce. In this new covenant, he says, men may not divorce their wives on a whim, as though they were selling property. He claims that wives and husbands are bound to each other, and neither has a claim stronger than the other. A wife's rights are equal to her responsibilities, a husband's responsibilities equal to his rights. How radical this must have sounded to their ears and, furthermore, to many ears ever since then. What could he be planning to take on next?

The next opportunity made its entrance right on cue. The disciples, trying to keep things orderly, speak sternly to some who were bringing children to Jesus. "Let the little children come to me," he calls, "do not stop them; for it is to such as these that the kingdom of God belongs." Not only does he speak his concern for them; he lifts them up physically and spiritually by praising their faith and blessing them.

After breaking down barriers to the sick, the poor, the foreigner, and now even the women and children, who is left? Precisely—nobody! There is much diversity among this collection of those whom he favors, but they do share one crucial thing—his acceptance. None are the same, yet all are equal.

Because of this Sunday's readings, many parishes will emphasize the family; and our families surely do need much in the way of thought and prayer. But we hope we will not paint our picture of the family on too small a canvas. If our definition of family excludes anyone of any age, condition, gender, origin, or marital status, then we have distorted Jesus' message. As a choir, we model a type of family. We embody the diversity of individuals and the unity of purpose found in all types of families. And we hope that the sounds we produce make manifest these truths of diversity, unity, and harmony. As in all healthy familial relationships, we find the affirmation, forgiveness, and love that frees us for abundant and benevolent living. F. Bland Tucker prays it so eloquently in a hymn for these modern days:

> *O Holy Spirit, bind our hearts in unity*
> *And teach us how to find the love from self set free;*
> *In all our hearts such love increase*
> *That every home, by this release,*
> *May be the dwelling place of peace.*
>
> "Our Father, by Whose Name"

Mark 10:2-16

# *Proper 23*

## *Sunday between October 9 and 15 inclusive*

This Sunday we will hear in the gospel reading that memorable but disturbing conversation between Jesus and his disciples about earthly and heavenly wealth. "It is easier for a camel to go through the eye of a needle than for someone who is rich to enter the kingdom of God," he states. His pronouncement stung then as it does now, and human beings have been looking for a loophole ever since! Is there any way out of this?

One possible area for hope lies in biblical scholarship. Some scholars believe the original text referred to a narrow crevice in the rocks, known locally as the "Needle's Eye." Others believe that "camel" is the mistranslated word. The metaphor would be more accurate if it spoke of a "rope" trying to go through a tiny hole. But, whether camel or rope, crevice or needle's eye, one thing is certain—this example was meant to impress upon us the extreme difficulty of the situation, if it is even a possibility at all.

Is this supposed to be good news? It sounds more like judgment. Even if we were to follow all the commandments, it would not be enough. "Then who can be saved?" is the question from Jesus' perplexed disciples, then and now.

Jesus responds with some very good news. "For mortals it is impossible, but not for God; for God all things are possible." His intent with these hard statements is to drive us in two directions. His judgment does drive us to despair as we come to grips with our complete inability to save ourselves. But his promise draws us into the open, loving, saving arms of a gracious God. For this God all things are possible, from making big things pass through small places to embracing and redeeming the whole, sinful human race. This, then, is a story of a God who meets us not halfway, but the whole way. This is a story of a God whom we can truly trust and love, praise and proclaim.

So we continue to examine, evaluate, and improve our lives based on the commands and expectations of God. But focusing on our own selves is not to be our primary activity. Rather, we place our attention on the source of our salvation—this God of great possibilities. Hymnwriter Robert L. Edwards helps us to express this truth:

> *Gifted by you, we turn to you,*
> *Offering up ourselves in praise;*
> *Thankful song shall rise forever,*
> *Gracious donor of our days.*
> "God, Whose Giving Knows No Ending"

Mark 10:17-31

# *Proper 24*
## *Sunday between October 16 and 22 inclusive*

How fortunate it is that God does not always grant what we request! Don't we often pray for things on a whim, or in a high or low emotional state, or without knowing full repercussions? When children ask for things their parents know would harm them, their reply is often, "You don't know what it is you're asking for!"

That same response is heard in this Sunday's gospel as James and John come to Jesus with the request, "Grant us to sit, one at your right hand and one at your left, in your glory." It does sound like a reasonable request. We all like to have friends in high places, and we feel our loyalty should count for something when the rewards are passed out.

But instead of a gold trophy Jesus shows them the tarnished, dented, sharp-edged cup that would be the reward for him and for any who would follow him. Only he knew the high cost of discipleship. They anticipated a crown; Jesus knew of a crown inseparable from a cross. "Whoever wishes to become great among you must be your servant," he warns, "and whoever wishes to be first among you must be slave of all." Martin Franzmann expressed some sharp edges of discipleship in his classic hymn, "Weary of All Trumpeting," which concludes:

> *To the triumph of your cross summon all the living;*
> *summon us to live by loss, gaining all by giving.*
> *Suffering all, that all may see triumph in surrender;*
> *leaving all, that we may be partners in your splendor.*
> "Weary of All Trumpeting"

Now, as then, Jesus is the ultimate model of determination and direction. He encountered daily temptations from foes and even friends to abandon the rocky path for the easy road. We often have a hard enough time discerning the right path, much less following it. And modern times seem to only complicate matters. The issues we encounter in worship and music are only a microcosm of what we face as struggling disciples. We have choices to make between contemporary or traditional styles, styles that blur the distinction between artistry and commercialism, and messages that proclaim a strong crown and a weak cross. They all compete for our loyalties and our dollars, and we cannot always determine the best direction to go.

Though many situations and solutions may be different now than in Jesus' day, they call for a similar struggle. The test of our quests must be in the shape of the cross—with a vertical connection between God and humanity, and with horizontal arms that reach out in service to others. At their intersection we find the Christ, the Son of Man who came not be served but to serve and to give his life as a ransom for all.

Mark 10:35-45

# *Proper 25*
## *Sunday between October 23 and 29 inclusive*

Has anyone ever said to you, "That piece the choir sang today expressed my thoughts and emotions so perfectly; it must have been written with me in mind." Or perhaps someone has said, "I felt as though God was speaking directly to me in that hymn today." Maybe it was the scripture reading, or the sermon, or the creed, or any other part of the liturgy. Perhaps we have had a similar experience ourselves. As Christians we believe that God speaks to us both as a community and as individuals. We are known and called by name, and the message is customized to fit us. It is only in the church that we can receive the benefits of a group encounter without giving up any of our individual attention. The God-to-person ratio is consistently and miraculously one-to-one.

A blind beggar named Bartimaeus received a customized miracle from Jesus, and we shall hear his story in this Sunday's gospel. A large crowd is following Jesus and his disciples out of Jericho. Trying to be heard over the rest, Bartimaeus shouts out, "Jesus, Son of David, have mercy on me!" Many try to stifle him, but his shouts are heard by the healer. Jesus did not answer him directly; instead, he tells the others to "call him here." The beggar did not even know his pleas were heard until the message reached him. "Take heart; get up, he is calling you." Those who had been merely observing the work of Jesus now got to play a part in it. How enthused they must have been as they brought the exciting news to the beggar that Jesus wanted to see him. They not only witnessed the power of God's grace—they experienced it themselves, having been chosen to be channels of the dynamic gospel.

Such is the awesome power Christ still grants to his church. Baptized and called to be ministers through music and numerous other ways, we are blessed to be the messengers that bring the exciting news to those who need it. We are the Spirit's tools.

Moreover, we are not merely passive transmitters. The good news we help convey blesses us as well; we are alternately and often even simultaneously bearers and recipients of God's call. It is yet another of God's many paradoxes. Giving and receiving, blessing and being blessed, and hearing our own name called amidst the crowd are only some of the rich mysteries of God's relationship with us. Marty Haugen has captured many of these amazing truths in a hymn which prays:

> *Gather us in, the lost and forsaken,*
> *gather us in, the blind and the lame;*
> *call to us now, and we shall awaken,*
> *we shall arise at the sound of our name.*
> "Gather Us In"

Like the messengers at Jericho, we are excited and honored to bear the Good News. And, like Bartimaeus, we hear the hopeful cry addressed to us, "Take heart; get up, he is calling you."

# Proper 26
## Sunday between October 30 and November 5 inclusive

Mention the terms "scribes, Sadducees, and Pharisees" and we instantly remember their antagonistic role in Jesus' earthly ministry. But we can learn much from them negatively, and the friction between them and Jesus was the source of energy that served as catalyst for many of Jesus' teachings, parables, and even miracles. Like sand in an oyster, their irritation brought about some great pearls for us to treasure.

In this Sunday's gospel we witness a rare, positive encounter between Jesus and a scribe. After observing Jesus in a dispute with the Sadducees, the scribe is impressed with his answers. So he asks him a question of utmost importance, "Which commandment is the first of all?" Jesus probably sensed immediately that this question was asked in a spirit of admiration and even camaraderie. This was quite a contrast from the motivation of others who tried only to trick him. Jesus boldly states this tenet of the faith, "Hear, O Israel: the Lord our God, the Lord is one; you shall love the Lord your God with all your heart, and with all your soul, and with all your mind, and with all your strength." And he goes right on to conclude, "The second is this, 'you shall love your neighbor as yourself.' There is no other commandment greater than these."

While other officials may have been disappointed to see Jesus earn an A-plus, our nameless scribe accepts Jesus' profession of faith and repeats it himself. It is a blessed moment when Jesus affirms their common ground. "You are not far from the kingdom of God," he says. We hope he made it!

We live in an age of many ecumenical dialogues, official agreements, and even mergers. Our zeal for unity is usually driven by an emphasis on common ground regarding the most important facets of the faith. Often, our biggest hurdle for unity is agreeing on which matters are the crucial ones and which are less important. But even our obsession with small details points to the importance we place on the integrity of the faith, our respect for our ancestors in the faith, and our concern for those who will follow us in the faith.

This encounter between Jesus and the scribe encourages us to treasure the truth wherever we find it. We need not deny differences in order to affirm common ground. It has often been in the church's music, poetry, and hymnody that much of the groundbreaking has taken place. Many Roman Catholic parishes sing with gusto Luther's "A Mighty Fortress Is Our God." Many African-American spirituals made their way into European-American hymnals long before we imagined that the races could worship together. Do you even know the denominational background of all the poets and composers represented in our choir folders? As long as their works effectively express the faith, does it really matter? Truly, as musicians we are often on the cutting edge of finding, affirming, and habitating common ground. Methodist hymn-giant Charles Wesley penned for us this universal plea:

> Jesus, thou art all compassion,
> Pure, unbounded love thou art;
> Visit us with thy salvation,
> Enter every trembling heart.

"Love Divine, All Loves Excelling"

Mark 12:28-34

# *Proper 27*
## *Sunday between November 6 and 12 inclusive*

It's back! We get to hear about humility again this Sunday. Oh, it's not that we don't need to hear it once in a while; but, as a choir, we have humbleness built right into our job description. Just consider the facts. Even if we wear flattering and fashionable clothes, we have to cover them up with vestments. And that choir loft might look like a place of honor, but it's always ten degrees more uncomfortable there than where the congregation sits. We have steps to maneuver, and there is nothing more humbling than tripping in front of everybody. We have pages and bulletins and books galore to handle, and seeing your octavo go sailing over the balcony rail gives you a slightly nauseous feeling. We do make some nice music, but we're always just one second away from a potential train wreck. And we do have some good soloists, but most of us have to settle for what is politely referred to as a "good ensemble voice." We come to church early and leave late, and, instead of getting holidays off, we work more than ever! Nearly every other group in the church has a plural title, but no matter how many individuals fill the chairs, we are still "the choir." Yes, we've been there and done that. Talking to us about humility is really like "preaching to the choir!"

Just what is the setting for the humility story this Sunday? The scene is the temple, and Jesus is teaching important lessons on the attitudes and possessions offered to God. First he points out the hypocrisy of the scribes, ridicules their public show of finery and piety, and exposes their dishonesty. A while later he is engaged in people-watching near the treasury. He notices the large sums dropped in by the rich people, but his excitement peaks as he observes a poor widow drop in a pittance. "This poor widow has put in more than all those who are contributing to the treasury," he proclaims.

We'll skip the stewardship implications for now, just in case there's a sermon on that coming up. So let us return to humility. Surely the poor widow receives Jesus' highest praise because she made her offering without fanfare, perhaps even secretively out of embarrassment. She gave of herself because it was a natural part of her life. Those who gave before her did help by giving large amounts, but it may not have had any impact on their lives or faith. Jesus' harshest condemnation falls on the scribes. Their actions are all for show, and they betray a spiritual vacuum, possessing neither humility nor benevolence.

We may not share the flagrant arrogance of the scribes, but we probably could not match the poor widow in humble intent either. Only God can cleanse our motives and inspire our generosity. We take our place in the choir, take note of our "singular" calling, and profess with hymnwriter Frances Ridley Havergal:

> *Take my voice and let me sing always, only for my king;*
> *Take myself, and I will be ever, only, all for thee.*
> "Take My Life, that I May Be"

# Proper 28
## Sunday between November 13 and 19 inclusive

Before and after the gospel reading each Sunday many Christians respond with the acclamations "Glory to you, O Lord" and "Praise to you, O Christ." It is fitting that we frame this high point in the liturgy with acts of praise. But occasionally we get one of those readings when our response might seem a bit out of place.

This Sunday will be one of those days. In the gospel, Jesus is telling his disciples about the end times, and he narrates quite a list! Stone walls will be torn down, false prophets will come and lead many astray, there will be wars and rumors of wars, nations will battle each other, earthquakes and famine will inflict their damage. And these are just the beginning, he warns. Glory to you, O Lord? Praise to you, O Christ?

Jesus did not spare his disciples the hard parts. Had he done so he would have surely drawn more disciples to himself, then and now. But to do so would have been brutally dishonest. During these last Sundays of the church year we also are asked to think on these things, for we would probably not do so on our own. We dare not claim to know when and how the end will come, but neither are we to live as though it will never happen.

At those times when we admit that we will someday die, we might say, "I hope I go fast, or even in my sleep." It not so much being dead that we fear as the process of dying. So it is with the death of this world as we know it. Jesus knows how we feel; he wants us to know about it but not to be obsessed with it. Just as he has given hope and encouragement for our individual deaths, there is much he can say for cosmic death.

Just where is the good news in this dismal passage? The final statement is pregnant with meaning. "This is but the beginning of the birth pangs," he says. Those last weeks of gestation are times of discomfort and even pain, but the anticipation is never far from our minds. The joy of new birth is exhilarating, and the promise of a bright future is energizing.

Just as Jesus could not help but tell the whole story, so must we. For if we tell only part of it we have failed to tell it at all. Integrity and faithfulness call us to cease our songs of naiveté and feel-good theology. Rather, we join in the song of the Savior, whose poetry and harmony expresses the deep richness of life and death and life again—his and ours. Bernhardt Ingemann speaks this language in a hymn:

> Onward, therefore, sisters, brothers;
> Onward, with the cross our aid.
> Bear its shame, and fight its battle
> Till we rest beneath its shade.
> Soon shall come the great awakening;
> Soon the rending of the tomb!
> Then the scattering of all shadows,
> And the end of toil and gloom.
> "Through the Night of Doubt and Sorrow"

Yes, by all means, "Glory to you, O Lord; praise to you, O Christ!"

Mark 13:1-8

# Christ the King
## Last Sunday after Pentecost
### Proper 29

Have you ever had or heard a bilingual discussion? The two participants, not able to communicate through a common language, can barely get across what they need to say. They try desperately to find a word or phrase shared by both languages, but that might lead to even more misunderstanding. In the end, they usually resort to gestures, giving up on words altogether.

Our gospel reading for this Sunday contains a conversation that sounds as if the participants are speaking different languages. Pilate calls Jesus to his headquarters for questioning. Their talk includes such words as "king" and "kingdom" as Pilate tries to understand the charges brought against Jesus. His answers sound vague and even evasive, but he cannot in all truthfulness agree to Pilate's definitions. "My kingdom is not from this world," he protests. That would explain his resistance to accept the world's definitions and expectations of a king. The conversation gets nowhere fast. Finally, Jesus too has to resort to gestures to explain himself. And the gesture that explained himself best was outstretched arms and bowed head.

On this final Sunday of the church year, we continue to call him "Christ the King." A part of us wants to celebrate with red carpets, pomp, and fanfares. And that is all right in one respect, for he truly deserves honor above that of any earthly monarch. But this king forever bears the marks of crucifixion; the cross is inseparable from his identity. Hymnwriter Caroline M. Noel speaks exuberantly of this crucified king:

> Humbled for a season, to receive a name
> From the lips of sinners unto whom he came,
> Faithfully he bore it spotless to the last;
> Brought it back victorious when from death he passed.
>
> "At the Name of Jesus"

The temptation for Jesus to bypass the cross and go right for the crown began just after his baptism. But Satan was not his only tempter. Even his closest followers had trouble understanding the sense of mission that drove him. The church, too, has not always held in balance and tension between the cross and the crown, and many of our current worship battles share the same struggle. Since kings and crowns are of this world, those are the terms and concepts on which we often fall back. It is precisely because the cross is so "unkingly" and so gruesome that we shy away from it. And so we are often impressed by music, poetry, and liturgy which are showy and pretentious, asking only that we like them and not look much deeper than their shallow surfaces.

We will probably never be fluent in "cross" talk; it is simply too contrary to human syntax. Our role as ministers is best fulfilled as we allow Christ to reveal himself in rich words, sounds, and gestures. In the proclamation of the word, in baptism and eucharist, in crucified and resurrected music, and in every deed of grace and mercy, we hear Christ speak his unique language of loving and sacrificing, dying and rising, ruling and saving.

John 18:33-37

# CYCLE C

# First Sunday in Advent

With the First Sunday in Advent the church embarks on a new year, one where we shall proclaim and hear the gospel primarily as told by St. Luke. As the other gospel writers have done, Luke has documented for us Jesus' warnings of the end time. He tells of signs in the sun and moon, distress among the nations, humans fainting with fear, and the vision of the Son of Man coming in great glory. "Now when these things begin to take place," he advises, "look up and raise your head, because your redemption is drawing near." A few verses later, he cautions us to be not weighed down with "cares of this life."

In both parts of the narration, Jesus is telling us to turn our attention and energies toward those things that are most important. It will not be easy, he wants us to know. Things that are most important are often hard to discern, often contrary to the culture around us, and usually require hard work. Hymnwriter Eleanor Farjeon captures this paradox in a superb Advent hymn:

> Furrows, be glad. Though earth is bare,
> One more seed is planted there.
> Give up your strength the seed to nourish,
> That in course the flower may flourish.
>
> "People, Look East"

Life has taught us similar lessons. Many of our greatest accomplishments have been wrought by patience, perseverance, prayer, thankless hard work, and by withstanding criticism from others and doubt from ourselves. These are often the ladder rungs to raising children, to overcoming addictions, to spiritual formation and self-discipline, and to being a part of the church in all its many aspects and activities. Surely we do not count salvation among our achievements, for only Christ in grace grants that. But in Advent we are called to be mindful of and responsive to the redemption which has already taken place in Christ's first coming and to anticipate its fulfillment when he comes again. The end time is described with such intensity precisely because it is so important.

The culture around us has once again spurned and already bypassed the Advent message as it tries to hype into us its commercial version of the "true spirit of the season." We in the church, however, pray to withstand the temptations to confuse busyness with preparation; temptations to give in to a cheap, sentimental peace rather than struggle to find God's deep peace; and temptations to be so weighed down with the cares of this life that we do not see them in proportion to the world-shattering occurrence which will be the return of Christ. As if rehearsing a cosmic choir for the great event, Jesus calls out, "Look up and raise your heads!" It promises to be quite a performance!

# Second Sunday in Advent

Have you heard that there is a special organization just for procrastinators? They have, however, no membership lists, officers, or meeting times because they never got around to doing them. There would probably be enough people to form many clubs just for the apathetic, but surely nobody would care enough to get the group going.

We live in a time filled with procrastination, apathy, and large quantities of other human foibles that cause us to fall down under their weight. Even the church can have a hard time motivating members and expressing goals and reasons for being.

To such a world comes the good news in this Sunday's gospel. It begins rather strangely, "In the fifteenth year of the reign of Tiberius Caesar, Pontius Pilate being governor of Judea, and Herod being tetrarch of Galilee, and his brother Philip tetrarch of the region of . . ." and so the list goes on until it concludes, ". . . the word of God came to John the son of Zechariah in the wilderness."

Why bother with such details that only a handful of historians could find interesting? The gospel writer took such pains to be precise so that we would know that God came into a particular place among particular people at a particular time in history. And just what happened to this particular person named John when he received this particular word from God? We sing it in a hymn by Charles Coffin:

> On Jordan's banks the Baptist's cry
> Announces that the Lord is nigh;
> Awake and hearken for he brings
> Glad tidings of the King of kings!
>
> "On Jordan's Banks the Baptist's Cry"

John proclaims that the entry of God's kingdom into the world will make mountains low, the crooked straight, the rough smooth, and that all flesh will see the salvation of God.

This is spine-tingling news, even to those hearing it 2,000 years later. But, we lament, how much greater it would be if God's word came to us as specifically, as forcefully, as convincingly as it came to John. He was at the right place at the right time.

Jesus did come at a specific time and place and to specific people—that's time with a capital "T." And he will come again, at another God-chosen time, also with a capital "T." But does that make our era less important? Is ours a time with a lower case "t?"

We may not share the times, lineage, food, or clothing of John the Baptist, but we do share the same command and the same God who gives the will, the power, the direction, and the energy to do what we should be doing until Christ comes. Now is capital "T" time!

# Third Sunday in Advent

Much of the world around us is well into its celebration of Christmas, and it is indeed hard to resist. Nearly everyone loves the sweet sounds, the vision of peace, the nostalgia for things the way we want to remember them. Maybe that's the problem—we love that part of it a little too much. We cannot always tell the difference between the cheap imitations of Christmas joy and the authentic joy that God and the church want for us.

Just how out of sync are the church and culture? John the Baptist returns in this Sunday's gospel to tell us. His opening greeting is not "Happy holidays!" Instead, he calls his audience a brood of vipers. He says nothing of gifts and greeting cards, but rather of the wrath to come, the ax that lies in readiness, of winnowing forks and unquenchable fires. He tells us to share, to be fair, and to repent.

If this is really what Christ's coming is all about, maybe we should do what some small sects do and not acknowledge the holiday at all. We may think that people resist Advent because they don't know what it is all about. Perhaps they know it too well!

Is there any joy in the advent of such a God? Ironically, this gospel reading concludes with the words, "So, with many other exhortations, he proclaimed the good news to the people." Yes, amidst the message of judgment is the message of hope, for God's word cannot seem to come without a promise. The gospel shines even more brightly when it stands surrounded by bleakness. It speaks of a joy that knows its salvation was borne out of tough love and costly grace. It acknowledges its source, as does the First Song of Isaiah, paraphrased by Carl P. Daw, Jr.:

> Surely it is God who saves me;
> I shall trust and have no fear.
> For the Lord defends and shields me
> and his saving help is near.
>
> "Surely It Is God Who Saves Me"

Those of us involved with the church's music know what preparation is like. Would we ever want to sightread our music on Sunday morning, thinking that preparation was unnecessary or that it somehow detracted from the performance? Rather, preparation and anticipation make it all the more meaningful, whether for a musical performance or for the celebration of our God's incarnation. We in the choir are really the lucky ones. While the rest of the congregation simply waits, we are refining the raw materials that will adorn and lead Christmas worship. But, even though our choir rooms may sound like Christmas is already here, we know it isn't quite yet and that's all right. We have much left to do—we are preparing for the future and, at the same time, living as though it is already here!

# Fourth Sunday in Advent

*Light four candles to watch for Messiah;*
*Let the light banish darkness.*
*He is coming, tell the glad tidings,*
*Let your lights be shining.*

"Light One Candle to Watch for Messiah"

This final stanza of a candle-lighting hymn by Wayne L. Wold finds us near the conclusion of this season. As we reach the Fourth Sunday in Advent we may feel we have absorbed just about all we can. The list of things we had hoped to accomplish by now has probably been revised if not tossed out altogether. What can yet inspire us and keep us going strong? This Sunday's gospel provides a much-needed boost. The entire reading can be summarized in just two words—"visitation" and "Magnificat"—but what great riches they bring to us!

The "visitation" part of the story recounts the visit of Mary to the house of her cousin Elizabeth. Without a word of prompting Elizabeth discerns Mary's condition and the importance of the baby she is carrying. Elizabeth's own baby, the yet-unborn John the Baptist, acknowledges the presence of Jesus and his mother by leaping, similar perhaps to the quickening we feel in our own bodies when we hear of such a profound encounter. Oh, what faith is able to perceive!

The "Magnificat" part of the reading is Mary's masterful song of praise to God for the child within her and for the work he will accomplish for the world. Besides thrilling us with its beautiful prose, the Magnificat proclaims the revolutionary work of God who turns around the ways of the world.

Within such pregnant readings are many special moments. One special gem is found at the end of Elizabeth's proclamation. She says of Mary, "Blessed is she who believed that there would be a fulfillment of what was spoken to her from the Lord." Amid all the other wonders of the season, this is indeed one of the greatest. Mary accepted what was asked of her and took a giant leap of faith. She discerned that the one making the request was her own faithful God of Israel. Though she could not see all that lay ahead, she had enough trust to say yes.

Oh, that we could let go and trust more fully! The God of Israel and Mary and Jesus is trustworthy beyond our imaginings, yet we often place greater faith in less-deserving powers—our culture, our leaders, our selves. Let us instead celebrate God being born for us, among us, and within us. Let our souls magnify the Lord, and let our spirits rejoice in God our Savior.

# The Nativity of Our Lord

*Silent night, holy night!*
*All is calm, all is bright*
"Silent Night, Holy Night!"

It is rather ironic that this hymn has become one of the most popular Christmas songs of all time. We hear it in churches, on television specials, and piped into the mall. It is everywhere! Yes, it does have a worthy text and a pleasant tune, and they do complement each other. The ironic part lies in its description of the night. We have a hard enough time picturing a Christmas night that is holy and bright, much less one that is calm. And silent? That hymn must be for those who lived in ages past, not for our modern, noisy days. Or maybe it still speaks to the "worship consumers," those folks in our congregation who just show up for a Christmas worship experience. Pastors, musicians, and other worship leaders are not meant to understand a silent, holy night, where all is calm and bright.

We have worked hard in our preparations for leading Christmas worship. We do it out of commitment and contracts, out of heart and habit. We give it as a gift to our God, to our congregation, and to ourselves. Celebrating and proclaiming the incarnation of our God is worth all we can give and so much more. We would probably feel guilty if we did experience a calm, restful, stress-free Christmas.

If that is the type of Christmas we think we want, we should think again. What was so calm about being in a strange town at the time a baby is to be born? What is so stress-free about trying to find a room in a sold-out town? What is so silent about animals? And, if the child Jesus was resting so quietly, why does so much of our Christmas music keep telling him to hush up and go to sleep?

The calm, the silence, the peace of Christmas is so noticeable because it is the exception; it stands in stark contrast to its surroundings, as much now as it did then. Peace is present, not in absence of its competition, but amidst it.

Joseph Mohr did not author "Silent Night, Holy Night" because he had nothing else to do or because he was so inspired by the sense of calm and peace around him. He created it frantically, on the very day it was needed, upon finding that the church's organ was broken and the scheduled music could not be used. The organist, Franz Gruber, was probably not thrilled when his pastor showed up with the news of the organ's condition and asked for a new tune on the spot. Christmas Eve was not the time to discuss job descriptions, unreasonable expectations, or staff relations. All was probably not calm nor bright as they rushed to write, prepare, and perform their new work that very evening. But, we hope that they were able to experience at least a small amount of the heavenly peace their creation has brought to the world. May our music be such a generous gift to all we will touch.

# First Sunday after Christmas

The scriptures record very few details about the childhood of Jesus. We would love to know more about those years. How was he different from the adolescents we know? How was he the same? Did any others besides Simeon and Anna recognize his divinity? Did he keep his room clean? Did he sing in a youth choir?

St. Luke recounts the story of the twelve-year-old Jesus who, along with his parents and a large entourage of relatives and friends, journeys to Jerusalem for the feast of Passover. On the way home they discover he is missing. They return to Jerusalem, searching for three days until they find him back in the temple, holding court with the teachers who are amazed at his understanding. His response to his distraught parents is one of gentle chiding, "Did you not know that I must be in my Father's house?" Maybe it was the strain of the journey or the stress of raising an adolescent, but, yes, they had overlooked that likely possibility.

Those of us who are active in our congregations often get asked if we live in church. It may seem that way to us, too, especially during the festival seasons. There is a special sense of "being home" when we are in our Father's house. There is a danger, however, if we become obsessively holed up behind the walls of our church buildings or houses. His Father's house was Jesus' source and center, his home-base, but it was not the arena for most of his work.

Where do we find Jesus? We find him in the manger, as a perfect and beautiful gift from God. We find him in his Father's house, at age twelve and regularly throughout his entire life. And we find him wherever there is the Father's business to be done. In a hymn by Marty Haugen we pray to Christ:

> As you lived to heal the broken,
> greet the outcast, free the bound,
> as you taught us love unspoken,
> teach us now where you are found.
>
> "Holy Child within the Manger"

Along with Jesus, may we, too, increase in wisdom and in stature, in favor with God and others.

# Second Sunday after Christmas

Some folks say they are in the home building or home improvement business, but what they really mean is that they work on houses. Calling them homes makes it more pleasant and warm because of what the title conveys. We might recall Guest's poem "It takes a heap of living to make a house a home."

An author writes hundreds of pages of a story with great action and suspense, but the editor says the main character does not seem real. "Put some flesh and blood on him," the editor advises.

A politician tries to run a campaign using only signs and media ads. Her advisor tells her she better get out, meet folks, and "press some flesh" if she hopes to gain a following.

In choir we say we have to keep track of our music, but what we are referring to are pieces of paper printed with words and symbols. With them we plan to make music.

Rather than bother with a real instrument or work with a real accompanist, a church opts for pre-recorded soundtracks. The notes are perfect, the technology impressive, but the final product lacks a sense of presence. It's hard to take seriously a musical offering created at another time, at another place, and by anonymous musicians.

What is missing from an empty house, a dry novel, a distant politician, a piece of paper with symbols, or canned music? The human touch, the genuine article.

Such is the world described by St. John in the opening paragraphs of his Gospel. The world came into being through the Word, but the world knew him not. What was the Father to do? In the words of a Bohemian carol:

> Into flesh is made the Word. Hallelujah!
> He, our refuge and our Lord. Hallelujah!
> On this day God gave us
> Christ, his Son, to save us.
> "Let Our Gladness Have No End"

In the incarnation of Christ, God made the ultimate leap. The Word Made Flesh makes all of human life the realm of God's presence. The divine has entered humanity's house and has made it a home.

# The Epiphany of Our Lord

A central symbol of the festival and season of Epiphany is the star. The vision of the Bethlehem star thrills those of every age. On this festival of Epiphany we will again hear of that brilliant glow which captured the attention of the Magi from the East. They came a long distance, from a foreign culture, not knowing exactly where they were going, but having enough trust in the holy sign to keep following it. That star did not disappoint them—it faithfully led them to the very doorway of the Christ they sought to worship and honor with precious gifts.

Stars are truly amazing things. From earliest history they have inspired astronomers and astrologers, navigators and nomads, poets and painters. To our eyes, stars are never static; they sparkle, change colors, and move with the passing of time and seasons. They seem alive. Science has taught us even more amazing things about stars. Those whose light we see now may not even be in existence anymore. Just like the saints, their legacy lives on. The imagery of stars enters into the church's hymnody, as well. The great Danish hymnwriter Nikolai Gruntvig wrote:

> As a star, God's holy Word
> Leads us to our King and Lord;
>> "Bright and Glorious Is the Sky"

German hymnwriter/composer Philipp Nicolai addresses Jesus:

> O Morning Star, how fair and bright!
> You shine with God's own truth and light,
> Aglow with grace and mercy!
>> "O Morning Star, How Fair and Bright!"

Contemporary American hymnwriter Kathleen Thomerson professes:

> God set the stars to give light to the world.
> The star of my life is Jesus.
>> "I Want to Walk as a Child of the Light"

Stars indeed are metaphors for Christ, for the gospel, for creation, and for our calling as Christians to let our lights shine in a dark world. The season when it is easy and even fashionable to shine has just passed. Many folks pack away their shine along with the tinsel and electric lights until next Christmas. But now, exactly when the rest of the world has hidden it all away, is the most important time for Christians to keep shining. Just how can we keep up our sparkle? We cannot do it on our own, for our light is not of our own making. Rather, we stay close to Christ, the true "star" of Christmas, for he is that life-giving presence which the world so desperately needs. And we stay close to each other in this church community, called to shine in work, worship, praise, song, and prayer to Christ, our light.

# The Baptism of Our Lord
## First Sunday after the Epiphany

Many of us can recall the decade-long news stories about the struggles of the working people in Poland. Their leaders' names became household words, and the name of their union gave new meaning to the word "solidarity." That word still brings to mind images of struggling, standing firm, banding together, working for just causes, and identifying with each other. The people came to trust in the union and join its cause not so much because of its name, as good as it was, but because of its actions. The people heard with their ears and saw with their eyes that this union was of them and for them.

This Sunday we will hear of an even greater pledge of solidarity. Once again we will proclaim and celebrate the beginning of Jesus' public ministry as he is baptized by John in the Jordan River. The Spirit descends like a dove, and a voice from heaven proclaims, "This is my Son, the Beloved, with whom I am well pleased." Jesus' baptism is the great sign that God is in solidarity with him.

Though he is God's beloved Son, Jesus still comes to be baptized. Who would have thought that Jesus would need to be baptized? Surely not John, who felt himself unworthy to even untie the thong of his sandal. Surely we would not have guessed it—we who are baptized for the forgiveness of sins and into the death and resurrection of this very Jesus. F. Pratt Green explores this paradox in a hymn:

> When Jesus came to Jordan to be baptized by John,
> He did not come for pardon but as the Sinless One.
> He came to share repentance with all who mourn their sins,
> To speak the vital sentence with which good news begins.

"When Jesus Came to Jordan"

Jesus' baptism is an example of what we are called to do. His and our baptisms are the source and sustenance of our ministries on this earth. His and our baptisms are the proclamation of God's solidarity with us in this life, in our deaths, and in the life to come. In our baptisms, God is well pleased; it is the assurance that God's promises are true. And that is a pledge of solidarity worth singing about!

Luke 3:15-17, 21-22

# Second Sunday after the Epiphany

We have all encountered persons whom we could call "minimalists." These folks do only what is required of them and no more. "Just enough to get by" is their motto. We cannot always pinpoint the reason why, but their attitude tends to drain enthusiasm and pleasure out of any activity they enter. If it is any consolation, these minimalists are the big losers, for they miss the opportunity to lift up, to inspire, to accomplish much, and to feel good about jobs well done. And they do make others try even harder, in a quest to fend off the dreariness of mediocrity.

Where do we turn for inspiration to be the generous, second mile people we would like to be? In this Sunday's gospel we will hear of the ultimate maximist. The setting is a wedding at Cana, and the occasion is Jesus' first recorded miracle. It still shocks some that Jesus was at a party, one where wine was flowing freely, no less! Even more shocking is when Jesus creates more wine, changing it from water. But the ultimate shocker has to be the wine itself. For it was of extraordinary quality. "You have kept the good wine until now," cry the guests as they chastise the host. And it was of immense quantity. John records, "Now standing there were six stone jars for the Jewish rites of purification, each holding twenty or thirty gallons." We can only hope that they were not all empty by the time the party was over!

Jesus could have made a few carafes of average wine, just enough to go around and save the host from embarrassment. But instead he gave an indulgent amount of superior quality wine. The Creator could have given the world a few pleasant views scattered around the earth, but instead we are given overwhelmingly beautiful sights at nearly every point on the globe. God could have provided a few good composers and a handful of harmonious sounds, but the expressive possibilities in music are truly inexhaustible.

Epiphany is the season when we proclaim and celebrate God among us in the person and ministry of Jesus Christ. Each revelation gives us a glimpse of what God is like. Gracious, generous to a fault, the ultimate maximist, God gives what we need and much more than we will ever comprehend. We can only dedicate our lives to telling, doing, and singing the story of such a God. We pray with the words of hymnwriter Christopher Idle:

> *Jesus, come! surprise our dullness,*
> *make us willing to receive*
> *more than we can yet imagine,*
> *all the best you have to give;*
> "Jesus, Come! For We Invite You"

# Third Sunday after the Epiphany

This Sunday we shall hear of more "firsts" in Jesus' earthly ministry. This time he is in the synagogue, and he stands up to read the holy scripture which has been handed to him. Yes, Jesus served as a lector in his local congregation! He reads from the prophet Isaiah of the Anointed One who will come, a prophecy well-known and revered by the Jewish people. Then he tells them that he is the very one in whom this scripture is fulfilled. Yes, the Word is out! (Pun intended.)

Many are the responses of those who, then and ever since, hear such a revolutionary claim—anger, joy, disbelief, confusion, faith. For believers, James Montgomery's classic hymn professes:

> Hail to the Lord's anointed, great David's greater Son!
> Hail, in the time appointed, his reign on earth begun!
> He comes to break oppression, to set the captives free,
> To take away transgression and rule in equity.
>
> "Hail to the Lord's Anointed"

This is, of course, the big message of Sunday's gospel reading. But, as in so much of holy scripture, there are little lessons tucked away between the big ones. How did Jesus happen to be in the synagogue that day? It says he went there "as was his custom." He went out of habit and commitment. What a great example for disciples of every age!

As singers in a choir, we know the necessity but also the joy of regular attendance and enthusiastic participation in worship. The knowledge that we are expected and needed gives us that extra boost that we might require at times. We know that we make a difference. Yet, even though we might at times come out of habit or personal need, we find that it is the encounter with God that is really the driving force in worship. The power of our commitments and habits are nothing compared to the power of the God who wants us in communion with the Holy Trinity and each other.

Perhaps that is something we can share with those around us—the joy of feeling needed, the satisfaction of good habits that are kept, the warmth of feeling at home in God's house, and, most importantly, the constant surprise of a relationship with the Anointed One.

# Fourth Sunday after the Epiphany

This Sunday's gospel is a continuation of last week's. Then, Jesus read from the prophecy of the coming Anointed One and proclaimed that he was its fulfillment. The scene ends with all eyes fixed on him in amazement.

The closing words of this week's reading are a bit different. St. Luke records, "And they rose up and put him out of the city, and led him to the brow of the hill on which their city was built, that they might throw him down headlong." Why the change in attitude? The intervening verses tell the story.

It seems that Jesus did not fit their picture of the Anointed One. Jesus was a hometown boy; surely a messiah must be more special than that. And Jesus reminds them, through stories of their own prophets Elijah and Elisha, that God has at other times bypassed the chosen in favor of those less deserving. That was more than enough to turn awe into wrath.

Humans cannot fathom, much less predict, the gracious works of God. We should have learned that lesson by now, but generations continue to make judgments as erroneous as those in Jesus' day. Even in issues regarding worship and music, we can see how what is disdained in one era is fully embraced in another. After a new innovation or sound is introduced, we wonder how we functioned without it. New light bulbs brighten as other ones dim.

Some see changes in liturgy and music as erosion; others see it as progress and as the work of the Spirit. Some see signs of both, with the challenge being to faithfully discern the true spirit of each trend. In choices tough to call, we are probably wisest when we are more accepting than rejecting, risking on the side of grace.

Jesus warns us once again of the mistakes we can make out of arrogance or pride when claiming to speak for God. Answers are discovered, not in isolationism or in settling for easy answers, but as we join in the struggle and maintain relationships with Christ and his people. Timothy Dudley-Smith addresses the issue masterfully in a contemporary hymn which begins, "He comes to us as one unknown." In its final stanza, he writes:

> He comes in truth when faith is grown;
> believed, obeyed, adored;
> the Christ in all the scriptures shown,
> as yet unseen, but not unknown,
> our Savior and our Lord.
>
> "He Comes to Us as One Unknown"

# Fifth Sunday after the Epiphany

A story is told of a man who desperately wanted to win the lottery. He prayed earnestly for hours every day that God would make this happen. Every day his pleadings became more frantic until, finally, God answered. What was God's response to him? "I've been trying to help, but the least you could do is buy a ticket!" Yes, he had such high hopes that God could make it happen that he never even bought a ticket. Silly, isn't it? Even if we believed that God did intervene in such matters, we know we would at least provide the vehicle for it to happen. At least we would like to believe that we would do just that.

Luke's Gospel tells of some fishermen who were getting discouraging results. Along comes Jesus who sits in the boat and teaches the crowd. When he tells the fishermen to cast out their nets, their reply is two-fold. First of all they protest, "Master, we toiled all night and took nothing!" This response is easy to understand; we often get discouraged if a few attempts fail to produce results. But their second response is what makes the story memorable. "But at your word I will let down the nets." We know the story from there. The nets are filled to breaking, and Jesus assures them, "From now on you will be catching people." Then they leave everything and follow him, becoming part of his chosen twelve and some of the earliest leaders and martyrs of the church.

Catching people is still a goal today, for so many have yet to come to know Christ. It is our calling in our daily lives and in our specific vocations, including music ministry. Our attempts at catching must be honest and authentic, proclaiming Christ and not ourselves. Frances Ridley Havergal's great discipleship hymn concludes with the prayer:

> Oh, fill us with your fullness, Lord,
> Until our very hearts o'erflow
> In kindling thought and glowing word,
> Your love to tell, your praise to show.
>
> "Lord, Speak to Us, that We May Speak"

What is the message to ourselves and each other? Invest in a ticket! Let down your nets! And along with them let down your selfish pride, your vanity, and your high walls. Let down your nets that God may fill them!

# Sixth Sunday after the Epiphany
## Proper 1

The Beatitudes are among the most famous sayings of Jesus. We find them in windows, banners, sermons, hymns, and choral music. They are indeed beautiful words—so beautiful, in fact, that we may fail to appreciate the revolutionary world they advocate.

This Sunday's gospel contains the Beatitudes as recorded by St. Luke. The differences between these and the ones from St. Matthew are noteworthy. Matthew's sound more refined; Luke's are more blunt. Matthew's address only those who are blessed; Luke's have a stinging pronouncement in counter-balance: For each blessing, Luke announces a woe.

The bluntness of Luke's version is evident from the very first statement. "Blessed are you who are poor, for yours is the kingdom of God," he records, giving it a bit more bite than Matthew's ". . . poor in spirit." And his "woe to you who are rich, for you have received your consolation" makes its point clearer and more keenly than we might like. The contrast between these two passages of scripture represent the struggle over ideologies and issues much beyond our present scope. But these issues do have practical impact—even on our worship and its music.

Is there a music of the poor? There is if we allow that label to describe authentic music of many immigrants, spirituals and genuine gospel, and the continuing influx of world music that is such an important new voice in many parishes.

For the poor, singing and hearing their music in new places gives them a sense of acceptance and affirmation. Their experiences have given them special insights into life that they can share with others. The established churches come to realize that the music of the poor need not be poor music. It can be a voice that speaks the gospel in radical new ways. For both the haves and the have-nots, sharing the same song exposes and addresses the deep poverty that exists in each one of us. We do have more in common that we might think. Has anyone led such a charmed life that they cannot sing with their soul the words of James W. Johnson?

> God of our weary years, God of our silent tears,
> Thou who hast brought us thus far on the way;
> Thou who hast by thy might led us into the light:
> Keep us forever in the path, we pray.
>
> "Lift Every Voice and Sing"

In many congregations today, the music of chants, polyphonic motets, cantatas, anthems, and hymns stand alongside the exuberant choruses and mournful laments of the world's poor. Sung together they proclaim a story of a people, simultaneously wealthy and impoverished, and of their God who makes them richly blessed and lovingly redeemed.

# Seventh Sunday after the Epiphany
## Proper 2

Jesus has some hard words for his followers this Sunday. He tells us to love our enemies, do good to those who hate us, bless and pray for our cursers and abusers, give a second cheek to those who strike the first one, give our shirts to those who take our coats, and give to everyone who begs. It may sound as if he wants a band of enablers and doormats to be his followers, except that we know from the rest of his ministry how much he wants wholeness for each and every individual. What is Jesus calling for in these statements? How do such irrational actions bring about anything beneficial?

Jesus calls for selfless love. Living in such a way is so hard for humans to even fathom, much less to do, that human hearts have always had great difficulty getting it right. Jesus finally had to show this truth, and it became fully manifest in his suffering and dying.

But, just as Jesus' story of selfless love does not end in the tomb, his call to us to exhibit such love does not end at sacrifice. Jesus tells us that whatever we give away will be ours in new, dramatic ways. If we do not judge or condemn others, neither will we receive judgment or condemnation. We forgive, and we are forgiven.

Does this sound as if our salvation is in our own hands? It does if we give and forgive in order to be given and forgiven. Christ works in the opposite direction—because we are forgiven we can risk forgiving others. Our actions and attitudes are not our contribution to the process of salvation; they are a natural response to the realization of what has already taken place in Christ. He wants that truth to be discovered by each of his disciples, and he sends his Spirit to make it known.

> In blazing light your cross reveals
> The truth we dimly knew:
> How trifling others' debts to us;
> How great our debt to you!
>
> "Forgive Our Sins as We Forgive"

confesses 20th-century hymnwriter Rosamond Herklots.

Jesus concludes, "For the measure you give will be the measure you get back." Why is it that those who are only minimally active in the parish often have more complaints than those who are fully active and who may know even more of its problems? Why is it that those who sit quietly and uninvolved in worship may leave untouched and wondering why they felt no spiritual presence, contrasting with those who participate fully with body, mind, ears, and eyes? It is a matter of investing the self, offering and receiving a greater measure.

Christ's claims of giving and receiving, living and dying, stand in stark contrast to the claims of the world. In all our thoughts and deeds, words and music, we can risk the giving of ourselves, for God's baptismal gift of salvation is already granted.

# Eighth Sunday after the Epiphany
## Proper 3

This Sunday's gospel is a continuation of Jesus' Sermon on the Plain as recorded by St. Luke. The proverbs and parables are numerous, and each one is a gem worth a lifetime of pondering. He teaches about the blind leading the blind, of teachers and students, of judging others and logs in eyes. Then he spends a bit more time talking about trees producing fruit. He tells of good trees and their good fruit, bad trees and their bad fruit, and their counterparts in human beings. "For it is out of the abundance of the heart that the mouth speaks," he summarizes.

We have often heard people speak exuberantly about their family, pets, jobs, vacations, hobbies, church, and, of course, their wonderful choir. You can tell from what they say and how they say it that they love and treasure the topic of conversation. It is as though they are bubbling over and would surely explode if they tried to hold in their enthusiasm.

It may not be as obvious, but this happens also with people who regularly spew out complaints and criticisms. It is as if their innards are pickled. Their words and actions are expressing the prevailing spirit that dwells in them, too.

Before we start to name names, we better return to that opening command to not stand in judgment of each other. For even positive people can have an occasional bad day, and even complainers are right sometimes! And nobody knows another's complete story. We best concentrate on ourselves, on the logs that are in our own eyes.

One of the ways we can respond to Jesus' words is to take a personal inventory. How do we think others really perceive us? More positive than negative? Do our unhelpful words, actions, or demeanor cancel out the good we may do in the choir or in our other ministries? How would we like to be remembered when we are gone?

Jesus is not encouraging a "put on a happy face" attitude; he wants honesty. But he does want our hearts to be full and our words to express it. We cannot by ourselves turn into such people; only the work of the Holy Spirit can do that.

Jesus chooses to end his sermon with the parable of the two houses, one built on a rock and the other on the ground. The picture is clear—hearing his words and acting on them is like building a strong foundation on the rock. With such a sure footing, we find that we are filled to overflowing with his presence. As Robert Lowry experienced it and expressed it in a hymn:

> No storm can shake my inmost calm
> while to that Rock I'm clinging.
> Since Christ is Lord of heaven and earth,
> how can I keep from singing?
> > "My Life Flows On in Endless Song"

# The Transfiguration of Our Lord
## Last Sunday after the Epiphany

The term "transfiguration" is not in the general vocabulary of most people. Even if we know that it means "to change the outward appearance of," we will not often find opportunities to use it in daily conversation.

We may give our house new shingles, shutters, paint, and shrubs, but we call it home improvement and not transfiguration. We may have plastic surgery to remove some wrinkles or tighten up some skin, but we call it a face lift and not transfiguration. We may watch Star Trek and hear the words, "Beam me up, Scotty," but that is called transmogrification and not transfiguration.

This Sunday's gospel does use this unique term. "And Jesus was transfigured before them, and his face shone like the sun, and his clothes became dazzling white." Brian Wren helps us sing of the awe and excitement in his hymn that begins:

> Jesus on the mountain peak
> stands alone in glory blazing;

"Jesus on the Mountain Peak"

Jesus, who always looked so fully human, was once again revealed to be more. He had one foot—no, rather he had both feet—in this world and both in another. He walks up the mountain with his human disciples, but there he speaks with the long-dead Moses and Elijah. To top it all, a voice from heaven says "This is my son, the Beloved; with him I am well pleased; listen to him!" Talk about special effects! Talk about a mountain top experience!

So, the Epiphany season comes to a close as it began, with a heavenly voice confirming that this Jesus truly is the Son of God and commanding us to listen to him. The festivals of Baptism of Our Lord and the Transfiguration are the "bookends" of the Epiphany season. Both are mountain top experiences and both pack enough energy to carry us through the "ordinary" times of life.

Christ is ever present for us in our own high and low points—as present in our times of joy and assuredness as in our times of pain and doubt, in spite of our perceptions otherwise. Life, like a landscape, is not all peaks nor all valleys. And, as in music, the highs and lows define each other and need each other to express the heights and depths and richness of life.

This will be a Sunday for joyous praise and glorious alleluias. But be assured that Lent is just around the corner, and the story of salvation travels a route straight through the streets of Jerusalem on its journey to Easter.

# Ash Wednesday

*Savior, when in dust to you*
*Low we bow in homage due:*
*When, repentant, to the skies*
*Scarce we lift our weeping eyes;*
*Oh, by all your pains and woe*
*Suffered once for us below,*
*Bending from your throne on high,*
*Hear our penitential cry!*

"Savior, When in Dust to You"

In this hymn by Robert Grant we sing of such things as dust, repentance, weeping, pains, woe, suffering, and penitential cries. It can mean only one thing—Lent is upon us!

What will we give up for Lent? Even in traditions that do not emphasize a special Lenten discipline of denial, we are likely to be giving up something. Communally, it might be boisterous music and elaborate arrangements, descants and alleluias that we give up. Individually, we might hope that the spirit of the season will inspire us in our attempts to crush some old, destructive habits or start some new, beneficial ones. We pray once again that this Lenten season will have an effect on us as individuals and as a community so that we can gather all creation together at the foot of the cross. What a great reward that would be for our Lenten season.

The term "reward" will be heard extensively in the gospel for Ash Wednesday. Jesus tells of many who parade their piety by praying, fasting, or giving offerings in public, just for the sake of showing off. They already have their reward, Jesus declares, and we can imagine it is a reward that is rather empty and short-lived.

In contrast to them, Jesus tells of those who secretly give offerings and do good deeds, who pray in private, and who fast for its spiritual benefits alone. Their reward is not in earthly trinkets but rather in heavenly treasure.

There are some folks who seem to give up choir and even worship for Lent. Perhaps it is the icy cold weather that hits during this time period in many parts of the northern hemisphere. Perhaps it is the icy coldness of the pronouncement "Remember that you are dust, and to dust you shall return." That statement should give us the shivers. But they can be shivers of warm excitement rather than cold dread. For the ashes that mark our foreheads are not just dust, they are the cleansing crosses of our Baptisms. This is not to be a season for going away; it is one for coming home.

Let us enter this season awake to its rich symbolism, immersed in its purple harmonies and scarlet poetry, and treasuring the deep rewards of walking the road with Christ.

# First Sunday in Lent

It is fitting that we should come head to head with the devil this First Sunday in Lent, for that is exactly who Jesus had waiting for him as he began his ministry. Still wet from his baptism in the Jordan, no time was wasted in getting Jesus and his adversary to clash. Their encounter sets the pattern for the rest of Jesus' earthly life, as Satan would prove to be a constant thorn in his side and, ultimately, his fiercest enemy.

Though the gospel writers differ on the number and content of specific details, even the laconic Mark tells us that the encounter with the devil took place at the very beginning of Jesus' public ministry. The holy signs that convinced the disciples of his messiahship must have confirmed the fact for Satan as well, for he appears in full force. And Satan is no slouch, either, as Matthew and Luke relate. He quotes scripture like a pro, and he has a bunch of special effects in his repertoire which he uses to enhance his sales pitch.

The good news is that Jesus won this first battle. The bad news is how much even he had to endure to do it. Temptation and the power of evil are no small force, Jesus wants us to know. Martin Luther, as hymnwriter, wrote:

> The old satanic foe
> Has sworn to work us woe!
> With craft and dreadful might
> He arms himself to fight.
> On earth he has no equal.

> "A Mighty Fortress Is Our God"

The devil has been imagined in many ways throughout history. Even in music there is a tradition of avoiding an augmented fourth because it is the "devil's interval," and Tartini composed a piece for violin that contains the "devil's trill." And we all find passages in music that we find "devilishly" hard, and occasionally we skip a rehearsal or service because "the devil made us do it." And so we see how easy it becomes to domesticate and trivialize a power so strong that even Jesus had to ferociously fight it.

Our focus for this Sunday, as for our entire lives, should be on realizing the immense proportions of sin and evil, our utter impotence to overcome them, and, most importantly, the grace won for us by the battle-scarred Christ, who holds the field victorious.

# Second Sunday in Lent

This Sunday's gospel contains images that we might expect to find more in a fable than in scripture. When Jesus receives word that Herod wants to find and kill him, his response begins with the words, "Go and tell that fox for me . . ." Soon after, he turns to those around him and grieves for Jerusalem who kills the prophets sent to it. Then he yearningly laments, "How often have I desired to gather your children together as a hen gathers her brood under her wings, and you were not willing!"

The fox and the hen! Jesus has chosen two very convincing images in this short passage. The image of a fox helps us picture Herod as sly and sneaky. The vision of Jesus as a mother hen is equally convincing, as we picture the desperate, determined drive to provide protection, warmth, and security. We can only wonder if Jesus meant for us to take the allegory one step further, for we all know what usually happens when a fox catches a hen!

The scriptures and the church are storehouses of divine images, and new ones are constantly being added. Many have wondered if we should be using earthly images at all in our attempts to describe and understand God. Images surely have their limitations; but, as humans, what else can we use? Since no single image can express it all, we heap them up by the thousands, hoping that some truth will emerge from the energy of their friction.

Artists use paints and canvases, chisels and stones, needles and fabric, pencil and paper to give us new ways to comprehend God. Writers use prose and poetry, rhythms and rhymes, similes and metaphors to give us new ways to experience God. And we, as musicians, use voices and instruments, harmony and counterpoint, consonance and dissonance to praise God and minister to those we lead in worship.

We need not be suspicious of strong, meaningful, earthly images. The scriptures are full of them, and many come from Jesus' own lips. Christ as mother hen, from this Sunday's gospel, is still a startling picture to some because of its feminine imagery. Philippine hymnwriter Moises Andrade was inspired by the image to write:

> When twilight comes and the sun sets,
>     mother hen prepares for night's rest.
> As her brood shelters under her wings
>     she gives the love of God to her nest.
>
> "When Twilight Comes"

May we never stifle the Spirit's gift of imagination as we strive to understand, experience, and proclaim the God who birthed and redeemed us, and who continues to nurture and brood over us.

# Third Sunday in Lent

One of the harder parts of leading a Christian life is finding that proper balance between self-evaluation, self-judgment, and self-aggrandizement. We hear the call from Christ and the church to search our souls to discover what is bad and purge it, and to discover what is good and amplify it. Yet, we know what happens when we become so judgmental of ourselves that we fear we might be beyond even God's reach. Conversely, we risk becoming so proud that it leaves no room for God. We might even become so preoccupied with the process of evaluation that we accomplish little else. None of these extremes is healthful for our well-being or for our relationship with God. It is surely a hard balance to keep.

But we are not alone! In this Sunday's gospel we will hear Jesus' disciples telling of some Galileans who had met with particularly violent deaths. They must have related the incident with some degree of smugness to receive the response they got from Jesus. "Do you think that because these Galileans suffered in this way they were worse sinners than other Galileans?" Then he answers his own question, "No, I tell you. But unless you repent, you will all perish just as they did." Jesus' message is quick and clear. We humans are all in the same boat, and that boat is up the creek without a paddle! Our self-evaluations mean nothing in the long run—only God's evaluation counts.

The reading also contains a parable. Jesus tells of a fig tree which has not produced fruit for three years; its removal has been ordered to provide space for one that will produce. The gardener intervenes, promising to loosen the soil and apply fertilizer, and asking for just one more year to produce. "Whatever happened to that tree?" we may ask. We can only hope that it took advantage of its grace period, for it is such a clear metaphor for each one of us and our gracious God. Hymnwriter Carl P. Daw, Jr. has provided a prayer for us "fig-tree" people:

> O Spirit, wake in us the wonder of your power;
> from fruitless fear unfurl our lives like springtime bud and flower.
> "Restore in Us, O God"

No gardener can force a tree to produce, even though that term is often used in the profession. What they do is to provide optimal conditions for it to flourish. We, too, have been given such opportunities. Through the church's ministry of word and sacraments, God's Holy Spirit loosens the packed soil of sin, applies the nutrients of forgiveness, and radiates the energy for productive lives. As our ministry of music is blessed by the Spirit, we are simultaneously workers and recipients of each other's ministry. Just as we are all in that same boat, we truly are in the same garden with each other—equally undeserving of God's grace, but equally the recipients of God's nurturing care and call to produce fruitful lives.

# Fourth Sunday in Lent

Jesus' parable of the prodigal son is a familiar favorite of many Christians. It is a story so believable that we can surely find at least one character to whom we can relate. This Sunday we will hear again of the son who leaves the family nest, squanders his money in loose living, comes home in shame, and whose highest hopes are dramatically exceeded when his father forgives and rejoices over him. Many have said that this parable should be named after the loving father, for that title puts the focus on the grace that is manifest. Others have tried to imagine the story from the viewpoints of the mother or the older brother.

Which viewpoint is most meaningful? It will change from person to person and even from time to time in the same person. Maybe we will experience it in a new way this Sunday. Not all of us will have the chance to be a forgiving parent. But, if we do, what an example is set out here for us! Not all of us have led lives that set us straying far from our families or from responsible living. But, in our spiritual lives, it may be a different matter. Regardless of our family histories, we all do share the human tendency to stray. Kevin Nichol's hymn puts us right in the middle of this parable when we sing:

> Our Father, we have wandered and hidden from your face;
> in foolishness have squandered your legacy of grace.
>
> "Our Father, We Have Wandered"

Yes, there are many possible perspectives from which to experience this multifaceted parable. But which, we may ask, did Jesus have especially in mind? We best look at the context. St. Luke records that the tax collectors and sinners were coming to listen to Jesus, and the scribes and Pharisees were grumbling and saying, "This fellow welcomes sinners and eats with them." The concluding verse, "So he told this parable . . ." sets the stage for several parables, all about the joy over finding what was lost. Only the parable of the prodigal son contains a character who protests the rejoicing. It is the older brother, the one who was loyal all along, the one who never left or squandered the riches, the one who resented the attention paid to the errant younger brother.

Jesus must feel that smug self-righteousness is as much an enemy of a relationship with God as is being a delinquent. His parable paints the older brother as the "heavy" who has no capacity for joy because of all the room taken up by resentment. We hope that we are free from any of his characteristics. Do we ever feel that our loyal faithfulness to our church or choir grants special favors? Do we feel that new members have to prove themselves before they are let into the inner circle? Do we ever resent the special attention paid to new or returning members and wonder when something will be done to honor us pillars? If we do, then we are like that older brother whose attitude was surely reasonable but had its priorities all wrong. May we always be so caught up in rejoicing over our sisters and brothers that we forget to worry about ourselves. And let's let them rejoice over us!

# Fifth Sunday in Lent

Many congregations experience difficulties when it comes to making decisions. There will often be trustworthy people with noble goals on both sides of many issues, making it all the more difficult to determine who are the good guys and who are the bad guys. If it is any comfort, we can consider three points about such tensions. First, they have a long history; our ancestors in the church can testify that our generation didn't create something new. Second, the presence of tension indicates that the subject matter is important; it shows we care enough to risk the consequences of conflict. Third, friction produces heat; stirring the fire occasionally ignites and energizes those embers and members on the verge of going out completely.

Many tension-filled issues revolve around the setting of priorities. Into which causes and projects do we put the most time, energy, and money? Should we heat and cool our buildings so we can be comfortable and thereby focus on doing the Lord's work? Or should we stoically accept any temperature out of solidarity with those who have little protection from the elements and use the money saved to assist them? Is God proclaimed more rightly in richly-decorated opulence or in stark simplicity? Does excellent music assist in worshipping God and edifying the people? Or is the incarnation better expressed in popular, earthy, or commercial sounds? Is Christ given more honor in heart-felt outpourings of adoration or in simple acts of charity?

If we can solve these questions, we should let the rest of the church know. For it is the same type of issue that is set forth in this Sunday's gospel. It is the story of a woman, identified as one of the Mary's in some biblical accounts and unnamed in others, who extravagantly anoints the feet of the Anointed One. Some who are present condemn her wastefulness. Judas even plays that well-worn trump-card of the pious—the admonition to help the poor instead. As noble as it sounds, it is an argument often put forth if we oppose an issue at hand and handily omitted when we favor it. Jesus has a quick response for Judas. Knowing of Judas's record with benevolence, Jesus reminds him that the poor will always be there for him to assist. But he praises the woman's selfless motive and her act of pure worship.

Jesus is telling us that our actions are visible signs of our inner spirit. Even such a noble act as feeding the poor is made less noble by flawed motives. And even extravagance, coming from an overflowing heart, praises and proclaims the lavish grace of God. Isaac Watts captures this profound truth in his great hymn of the cross:

> *Were the whole realm of nature mine,*
> *That were an offering far too small;*
> *Love so amazing, so divine,*
> *Demands my soul, my life, my all!*
> "When I Survey the Wondrous Cross"

John 12:1-8

# Sunday of the Passion/Palm Sunday

For most Sundays of the church year we strive for thematic unity. Worship planners spend time and use their expertise organizing services where the preaching, scriptures, prayers, music, art, and all other parts of the liturgy unite in proclaiming some facet of the good news of God.

This Sunday stands at a unique place in the rhythm of the church's life. Even its name, Sunday of the Passion/Palm Sunday, exposes the specialness of the day. It is a day of dualities when we will hear two gospel readings—that of Jesus' triumphal entry into Jerusalem, and by contrast, that lengthiest of all Gospel pericopes—the Passion of our Lord. We gather for a palm procession; we depart, immersed in the heaviness of Holy Week.

The people of Jerusalem knew only the festivity of the day as they expected Jesus to be ushering in the triumph of Israel. Jesus obviously had a different scenario on his mind, for he knew this was only the beginning of the end. "Ignorance is bliss," goes the saying. Anyone can praise a victor, but even the disciples departed once they realized what was happening in the days that followed. Sadly, the same is true for many in our congregation and even in our choirs. "Let me know when the big, happy festivals are coming up," some say. "I don't want to ruin my good mood by going on a somber day," they might as well add. Those who worship faithfully know the risks of coming on a day when we will be confronted with the crimson details of the passion story. But it is worth the risk, for we trade in a superficial, feel-good experience for a deeper, richer encounter with the Christ who has himself gone through it all.

The function of our worship this Sunday will be, as always, to praise the triune God, proclaim the gospel, pray together, offer ourselves in service, and be fed by Christ's communion with us and by our communion with each other. But we will not merely remember that first Palm Sunday; we will experience it anew. For Christ continues to be praised and lauded, continues to display his scars, continues to come to us and feed us, continues to save and redeem us.

Our music will be a part of that experience. With voices and instruments united we will relive the festivity of Christ's coming and ponder the depths of his suffering and death. Hymnwriter Samuel Crossman allows us to eloquently profess:

> *Here might I stay and sing*
> *No story so divine!*
> *Never was love, dear King,*
> *Never was grief like thine.*
> "My Song Is Love Unknown"

As Holy Week is ushered in once again, we pray that our minds and hearts will be open and ready to ponder and receive such a high and deep declaration of love.

# Holy Week/The Three Days

Christians do some amazing things this week. Some will make a pilgrimage to their church every single day, whether to worship, pray, rehearse, decorate, clean, or even to help with all the extra worship bulletins. Our daily routines of work, school, or family care will go on much as usual, but on top of these we still add additional tasks. We also anticipate Easter Sunday by planning for meals, company, clothing, and even decorating the eggs. But, rather than ignoring or working straight through these intervening weekdays, we plan to savor and struggle with them.

Thousands of words will be spoken and heard in the course of these days, for there is so much to tell and express. But such wondrous things are encapsulated best in poetry from the church's hymnwriters. The gospel readings for Monday, Tuesday, and Wednesday in Holy Week bring Jesus and us ever closer to the time and place of sacrifice. James Montgomery bids us:

> *Go to dark Gethsemane,*
> *All who feel the tempter's power;*
> *Your Redeemer's conflict see.*
> *Watch with him one bitter hour;*
> *Turn not from his griefs away;*
> *Learn from Jesus Christ to pray.*
>
> "Go to Dark Gethsemane"

On Maundy Thursday (or Holy Thursday) we receive Jesus' command to love each other, and he seals that command with his own gifts of bread and wine, water and towel. An ancient Latin hymn expresses our unity with the church in all times and places:

> *Where true charity and love abide, God is dwelling there.*
> *Ubi caritas et amor, Deus ibi est.*
>
> "Ubi Caritas et Amor/Where True Charity and Love Abide"

On a Friday that Christians dare to call "good," we contemplate the ultimate sacrifice, pray for ourselves and each other in the shadow of the cross, and adore the one crucified for the salvation of the world. Bernard of Clairvaux, along with Paul Gerhardt and other translators, asks with us:

> *What language shall I borrow To thank thee, dearest friend,*
> *For this thy dying sorrow, Thy pity without end?*
>
> "O Sacred Head, Now Wounded"

Finally, on the Vigil of Easter, the climax is reached. The risen Christ is proclaimed as new light in the darkness, the history of God's salvation is recounted, new members are incorporated into the death and resurrection of Jesus, baptisms are renewed, and we eat and drink in the presence of the Risen Lord. Surrounded by such richness, we can only rise up and proclaim in the splendid poetry of John Geyer:

> *We know that Christ is raised and dies no more.*
> *Embraced by death, he broke its fearful hold,*
> *And our despair he turned to blazing joy. Hallelujah!*
>
> "We Know that Christ Is Raised"

# The Resurrection of Our Lord

There's light at the end of the tunnel! Though we are still in the midst of Holy Week, we can count down the days and hours rather than the weeks of the Lent behind us. Though we have some music to still polish and much to still deliver, we can already taste that post-Easter peace we have come to savor. Church musicians, especially at the final worship service on Easter Day, can sing with great conviction (and with a little chuckle at its double meaning) the ancient Easter hymn:

> The strife is o'er, the battle done;
> Now is the victor's triumph won!
> Now be the song of praise begun. Alleluia!
>
> "The Strife Is O'er, the Battle Done"

As long as we have done our best, we need not feel ashamed of the relief we may feel once Lent is over. Our alleluias will sound more joyous because of their sabbatical. The whites and golds will sparkle more brightly because the purples and scarlets have told us their story. The sunlight streaming through the windows will carry more intensity because of the times we met in darkness. The organ and other instruments will sound more jubilant after the deep, rich sonorities of Lent. We will treasure more our rejoicing because we have grieved.

Jesus probably experienced some relief, too, as he saw the light at the opening of the tomb. Salvation's song had reached the highest notes of its intense climax; it was time for the coda and the cadence. What great joy must have been his as he shared the jubilant news of his resurrection with those he loved the most! Their fright must have given way quickly to joy and peace, made all the more intense because of the deep of sorrow they had experienced. That was Jesus' special gift to those who had known him the best. It is a gift he continues to give to us as we walk with him on the passion path to Jerusalem and as we invite him to walk with us on our rocky roads.

Just as Jesus reveled in the satisfaction of a tough job well done, the relief we feel as another Holy Week and Easter are reached surely goes beyond our creaturely comforts. For all is made new. We have caught a glimpse of the Paschal candle piercing the darkness, and we recognize it as the light of Christ which he has planted within us. We have seen the first rays of daylight illuminating the far corners of the cave, and we know that tomb is ours. And we have visited the garden, expecting only to grieve, but instead we are surprised and comforted by his living presence.

There is indeed light at the end of the tunnel—it is the rest of our lives! Christ has fought and won a tremendous battle for the sake of that light which blesses our baptisms, guides our living, hallows our dying, and promises our resurrections. We cannot help but sing praises and proclaim such good news.

# Second Sunday of Easter

**M**uch of the culture around us has already packed Easter away until next year—or at least it has been marked down to half price! But the church has the audacity to keep celebrating Easter for 50 days! In spite of this Sunday's nickname of "Low Sunday," we continue to sing our alleluias and proclaim that Christ is risen to all who will hear. This season is a time to rejoice and reflect on the meaning of the resurrection and to try to fashion our lives to be the Easter people that Christ has made us.

This Sunday we will hear the wonderful story from John's Gospel that tells of the resurrected Jesus appearing to his disciples. It might make for a good test question—when Jesus suddenly appears to his fearful disciples meeting behind locked doors, what are his first words to them? Perhaps "surprise" or "cheer up" or "it's me" might be understandable responses. But Jesus surprises us almost as much as he must have surprised his disciples when he says, "Peace be with you." Many hymnwriters, including Jean Tisserand, have made note of this:

> That night the apostles met in fear;
> Among them came their master dear,
> And said, "My peace be with you here."
> Alleluia!
>
> "O Sons and Daughters of the King"

Peace is a hard concept to define. We usually describe it as the absence of strife whether between nations, families, or individuals. As important as such arenas are for peace, these are not the same as the peace Jesus gives.

Sometimes we feel peace through some outside stimulus. Drugs or manipulative words or music can cause us to ignore the reality of life around us. This is likewise not the peace that Jesus gives.

Some have objected to the sharing of the peace in worship, arguing that well-wishing and personal greetings are not appropriate for something as important as the worship time. If that was all that was taking place, then the critics would be correct. But the peace we give and receive is not merely an expression of good wishes. It is the peace of Christ that we give, and he has given us the opportunity and responsibility to be channels of this peace to each other. Christ's peace is deep in meaning, rich in scope, and full of the power that only a dying and rising Savior can give. It is a release from real forces and a rescue from ourselves. Christ's words do not merely wish us peace—they grant it.

That is the peace we mean to share in worship—in the word, in the sacraments, in the fellowship, in the holy surroundings, and in the music whether it be jubilant or meditative. May the peace of Christ dwell in us richly this Easter season as we are called to be channels and recipients of the peace Christ has won for us.

John 20:19-31

# Third Sunday of Easter

This Sunday we celebrate the Third Sunday of Easter, and our gospel reading from St. John tells us of the "third time that Jesus appeared to his disciples after he was raised from the dead." It is a story of actions and emotions, told with marvelous details only those who experienced it could have remembered and treasured. And it is a fish story, for many of the disciples have returned to that which was their vocation before hearing and heeding the call to follow Jesus. Their all-night fishing trip has produced no catch, but a stranger from the shore calls to them, "Children, you have no fish, have you?" It is not a taunting or teasing question; rather, it is filled with care and concern. Perhaps that is why they obeyed this stranger's strange command to cast out on the other side of the boat. Soon the nets are full beyond belief, and they are stretching beyond their capacity. "It is the Lord!" John cries, and they immediately hurry to shore.

Once again, Jesus has been revealed through his generosity. It is Cana revisited as he gives way beyond human comprehension. And, as before his death and resurrection, Jesus continues to not merely tell but to show the extravagant grace of God.

The story does not stop here. Once the disciples get to shore they discover that this Son of God has built a fire and is preparing breakfast. Soon they are eating fish and bread, served to them by nail-scarred hands. Such a memory they would surely hold for the rest of their lives, and we can be sure that mealtimes would never again be the same for them.

This gracious story contains yet one more scene. Three times Jesus asks Peter "Do you love me?" Three times Peter responds, "Yes, Lord." And three times Jesus responds to the response. "Feed my lambs . . . tend my sheep . . . follow me." Once again, Jesus has given his own unique definition of love. That which we humans keep trying to contain as a nice emotion, Jesus keeps insisting is an action. It is action rooted in his love for us, energized by our love for him, and empowered by his promise to work with and through us. In a provocative social ministry hymn of the 20th-century, F. Pratt Green writes:

> For he alone, whose blood was shed,
> Can cure the fever in our blood,
> And teach us how to share our bread
> And feed the starving multitude.
>
> "The Church of Christ, in Every Age"

Then what are we doing here? Why do we spend time, energy, and money on church buildings, choirs, organs, and worship? Because all these things provide opportunities for the word to be proclaimed and the sacraments administered, offering channels of praise and prayer, building up the body, and equipping the saints to become strong in their love of God, both in emotion and in action. Yes, Lord, we love you. Fill us and stretch us beyond our human capacities so we can feed your sheep.

John 21:1-19

# Fourth Sunday of Easter

Good Shepherd Sunday gives us many helpful lessons. We resonate with the images of Jesus as the shepherd, ourselves as the sheep, and the forces of evil as thieves, wolves, and impostors. Yes, each sheep can know the personal care of the Shepherd, so why does he keep talking of many sheep? What is so important about being in a crowd, a member of the flock?

Christ is teaching us about community. We share in his goal when we support the church, participate in local congregations, and work to widen the embrace to include those yet outside the family of faith. In partnership with work are our prayers, and we may earnestly pray with William H. Turton's hymn:

> And hear our prayer for wanderers from your fold;
> Restore them, too, Good Shepherd of the sheep,
> Back to the faith your saints confessed of old,
> And to the Church still pledged that faith to keep.
> "Lord, Who the Night You Were Betrayed"

Does that sound a bit idealistic? What is so crucial about the church anyway? Does it go beyond camaraderie, companionship, and support? Can't we sheep belong to the Shepherd without belonging to each other? Must we "baaa" in chorus?

Amidst all the sheep and shepherd talk in this Sunday's gospel is a discussion between Jesus and those who want to know if he really is the Messiah. "Tell us plainly," they ask. "The works that I do in my Father's name testify to me," he responds. He sees no reason to attempt further measures to convince them, for they are, in reality, a hopeless case. "You do not believe, because you do not belong to my sheep," he bluntly states.

That's a loaded statement. It implies the reverse as well—that they do not belong to his sheep because they do not believe. And we can flip it around a bit more, too. Is he saying that those who believe do so because they belong to his sheep, and that those who belong to his sheep do so because they believe? Like some Bach fugue in retrograde and inversion, the themes and counter-subjects of this statement weave a texture that is complex and clever, yet expressive and profound.

Many of us are afraid to admit that our faith seems strongest when we are at worship, or in a choir rehearsal, or in a Bible study, or in any other group of believers. Put us in a group of non-believers or, God forbid, by ourselves, and we wonder why our faith seems dim. We may fear this is a sign that we are faithless.

In baptism, Jesus strongly calls us into Christian community, for this is the place where faith is planted, nurtured, challenged, expressed, and even expected to grow. It is a circular pattern—we belong to each other in Christ because we believe, and we believe because we belong to each other in Christ. Let us not be too sheepish to admit our dependence on one another, and let us flock in faith around the Great and Good Shepherd.

John 10:22-30

# Fifth Sunday of Easter

These Sundays of Easter are filled with stories of Jesus appearing to the disciples after his resurrection. That these appearances were important to them is certain, for they remembered and recorded them with such vivid detail. Jesus must have felt them to be important, too. Through these appearances he reinforced their faith in him, and he got one more shot at teaching them what he most wanted them to remember. With renewed eyes and ears they considered all the deeds and words of his years of ministry. Things spoken by the resurrected Christ seemed to carry even more weight.

This Sunday we shall hear Jesus say, "I give you a new commandment, that you love one another. Just as I have loved you, you should love one another. By this everyone will know that you are my disciples, if you have love for one another." Yes, we reflect, what a wonderful summary of Jesus' life and teachings. What a helpful thing to be telling his disciples just as he is about to leave them.

But, wait; there is something amiss here. Maybe you have already caught the anachronism, but these are not the words of the risen and soon-to-be-ascended Jesus. Though the church proclaims this gospel reading in the Easter season, this passage comes from John's account of the Last Supper, on the eve of Jesus' death!

Surely, as they first heard these words, the disciples had already seen and heard much of this side of Jesus; their minds were already filled with images of his radical type of love. But they had much yet to witness—specifically a love that would love to the grave and even beyond. What they had grasped before his death would pale by comparison to their post-resurrection view of Jesus' love. Hymnwriter Brian Wren expresses such jubilance:

> Christ is alive! Let Christians sing.
> His cross stands empty to the sky.
> Let streets and homes with praises ring.
> In death his love shall never die.
>
> "Christ Is Alive! Let Christians Sing"

So it is with us. We may not have the disciples' advantage of first-hand, eye-witness experience. But we do have the advantage of viewing all aspects of life from this side of Jesus' resurrection. We can sing with more gusto, serve with more vigor, live with more love, and love with more life, all because Christ has told us and shown us how it's done.

# Sixth Sunday of Easter

The lectionary gives a choice of two gospel readings for this Sixth Sunday of Easter. In one, Jesus comes across a man who has been ill for thirty-eight years. He has been trying to reach the healing waters of the pool by which he lies. Jesus asks only if he wants to be made well, but, instead of giving a straight answer, the man relates his difficulty in getting to the water while it is stirred up. He seems to be hoping Jesus will merely help him into the water. Instead, Jesus simply heals him where he is, in a way that seems to be saying, "You set your sights too low. I can do more than you ever imagined!"

In the other suggested reading, Jesus is telling of the connection between loving him and keeping his word and of our promised futures with him and the Father. He has spoken so much good news like this in his ministry—news that can surely give strength and hope when we need it the most. But how will we remember it all? Jesus knows our every weakness, so he promises that the Holy Spirit will be sent for the very purposes of teaching us everything and reminding us of all Jesus has said. What good news to hear that our salvation does not depend on our often poor capacity to remember God's many promises!

We will probably not hear both of these readings proclaimed or preached this Sunday, but each one packs a punch. And they do have some special messages for us when considered together.

In both episodes it is the relationship and encounter with Christ that counts the most. He gives beyond our expectation and imagination. He steps in when our faith is weak to keep us mindful of his presence and promises. He is on our side. It is our lack of vision and faith that is our own worst enemy. Our concept of God is too small; we often ask and expect too little.

One of the greatest gifts of being in community is the support we can give one another. Just as singing is made easier when we are surrounded by others joining on the same song, believing is made easier when we are surrounded by fellow believers in a common faith. We can be lifted by our shared stories, carried by our shared songs, and strengthened by our common faith in the one who grants grace in spite of doubt, faith in spite of weakness. John Newton was inspired by this God of amazing grace to write:

> See, the streams of living waters,
> Springing from eternal love,
> Well supply your sons and daughters,
> And all fear of want remove.
> Who can faint, while such a river
> Ever will their thirst assuage?
> Grace which, like the Lord, the giver,
> Never fails from age to age.
> 
> "Glories of Your Name Are Spoken"

Let us set our sights high—on the one resurrected and reigning for us.

John 14:23-29 or John 5:1-9

# The Ascension of Our Lord

The symbolically strong number of forty is held up once again as we celebrate the Ascension of Our Lord forty days after his day of resurrection. These have been forty days of rejoicing, learning, and eating with the Risen One and, through him, with his disciples throughout history. The summaries of the faith he gives are so helpful; the peace he grants is so comforting; the promises he makes are so uplifting. It is with high but mixed emotions that we see him carried up into heaven. Though he has promised to still be with us in new and even better ways, we know things will never be quite the same. And although we cannot understand why he must go in order to be present, we are willing to believe his promise. William Chatterton Dix addresses this mystery in a great hymn;

> *Alleluia! Not as orphans are we left in sorrow now;*
> *Alleluia! He is near us; faith believes, nor questions how.*
> "Alleluia! Sing to Jesus"

There are many who have trouble with some aspects of the Ascension story. Talk of monarchs and enthronements does not hold as much positive meaning as in earlier times. Perhaps our greatest difficulty lies in the concept of heaven as up in the sky, someplace above the clouds, somewhere over the rainbow. Having traveled millions of miles into space, we have a less literal belief in the location of heaven, if indeed it is a location at all. But if we feel we can no longer look toward heaven, do we instead cast our eyes downward or even close them altogether?

Looking upward is still our best bet. Looking upward is how navigators steer their course. Looking upward is how we stay together when singing in a choir. Looking upward gives us new perspectives, new vistas, new comrades, new opportunities, and new energies. Looking upward moves our focus beyond ourselves. The disciples looked upward on that day of Jesus' ascension. Yes, they saw his departure with bittersweet emotions. But as they looked upward they received his blessing, his promise to send power from on high, and his great energy that sent them rejoicing back to Jerusalem. St. Luke records that they worshipped him and were continually in the temple blessing God.

Does it not seem strange that they returned and went to the temple? Did not Jesus call them his witnesses and did he not charge them to proclaim all they had seen and heard? Were their priorities misplaced already?

Hardly! Their worship of the Ascended One began right there at Bethany, in response to his glorious and gracious presence. It continued on their journey back to Jerusalem, and they were drawn magnetically to the house of worship. From there, they were energized by his Spirit to live lives of proclamation and service—even to the point of martyrdom. Such is the power of Christ's promises, of vibrant worship, and of lifting our eyes to the Ascended One. Look up! The time for singing has come!

Luke 24:44-53

# Seventh Sunday of Easter

Anyone involved in research knows the importance of primary sources. Crime investigators want eye-witnesses, archaeologists want genuine artifacts, musicologists want original manuscripts and instruments. Their goal is to gain insights and reach conclusions that are more accurate than those taken from copies, transcriptions, or second-hand opinions. The more we are removed from the original source, the more we fear we have missed important details or even the essence itself.

The church shares similar concerns, and different branches of Christianity have developed certain ways of trying to keep the faith pure. The gospel has passed through so many generations and over so many cultures and languages, that it is a most realistic concern. Though the arguments and schisms that occur over such matters are unfortunate, they do point out the importance we place on these issues. At their best, disagreements keep interest high and senses sharp.

It is assuring to hear in this Sunday's gospel that Jesus shared the same concerns. In his "high priestly prayer," he is praying for his disciples' protection and unity. He continues in his closing petitions, "I ask not only on behalf of these, but also on behalf of those who will believe in me through their word, that they may all be one." Alongside the care he is showing his disciples, he expresses concern for all future believers and, for their sake, the truths of the gospel.

We owe a debt of gratitude to all our ancestors in the faith—the great church leaders from all ages, the saints and reformers, our teachers and families. Their hymns and catechisms, literature and liturgies, teachings and values are the arks that honor, preserve, and convey the treasures of the faith. What they pass on to us is not just the faith itself; their gifts also include the responsibility and opportunity to be links in the chain for all those who will come after us. Hymnwriter Somerset Lowry gives us a similar call to stewardship:

> Yours the gold and yours the silver,
> Yours the wealth of land and sea;
> We but stewards of your bounty
> Held in solemn trust will be.

"Son of God, Eternal Savior"

Before we leave the Easter season, we should be reminded what this has been all about. Why all the concern over proclaiming Jesus' resurrection? Why the intense concern over unity of the messengers and purity of his message?

It is all for the sake of love—loving relationships, loving feelings, and loving actions, all of which are rooted in divine love. Jesus closes his lengthy prayer with his own summary, "I made your name known to them, and I will make it known, so that the love with which you have loved me may be in them, and I in them." To such a prayer, let all the people shout, "Amen!" And may our music truly be a love song!

John 17:20-26

# The Day of Pentecost

The gospel reading for Pentecost is filled with Jesus' promises regarding the Holy Spirit who is to come. This spirit will be an advocate for us who will be with us forever, he says. This will be the Spirit of truth, one whom we will know intimately because he will dwell with us and in us.

In this and other passages Jesus paints such an irresistible picture of this Spirit. We can hardly help but yearn for this Spirit to be present with and in us. Surely we can resonate with Christians of every generation in the ancient Latin hymn:

> *Veni, Sancte Spiritus.*
> *Come from the four winds, O Spirit,*
> *come, Breath of God;*
> *disperse the shadows over us,*
> *renew and strengthen your people.*
> *Veni, Sancte Spiritus.*
>
> "Veni Sancte Spiritus"

But, wait a minute! Were not these promises of Jesus fulfilled shortly after giving them? And won't the account of that first Pentecost be proclaimed in worship even before we hear these promises of Jesus? Is it a sign of faithlessness to keep praying "Come, Holy Spirit" in light of such news?

No, it is not faithlessness that cries "Veni, Sancte Spiritus" but rather deep faith. Just as we can earnestly pray "Veni, Emmanuel" after the incarnation, we can plead for the Spirit's presence even after that first Pentecost. Yes, Christ's incarnation, crucifixion, resurrection, and sending of the Spirit took place at certain times in history. But such earth-shattering events shattered also the distinctions between time and space.

Pleas of "Veni, Emmanuel" and "Veni, Sancte Spiritus" are cries of earnest faith in the midst of struggle and doubt. They are uttered out of a faith that does not doubt divine presence so much as it doubts its own worthiness, receptiveness, and ability to respond. They are cries that do not forget that the Savior and the Spirit have come so much as they are a cry that God will keep coming, keep knocking, keep comforting, keep loving.

Since Pentecost, time and place are not barriers anymore. In word and sacrament, prayer and praise, music and meditation, a timeless God comes to us, surrounding us with divine presence and with a cloud of witnesses from all times and places. Called into community with and by the Holy Spirit, we offer our breath in praise and prayer to the one who dwells with and in us. Veni, Sancte Spiritus. Alleluia!

# The Holy Trinity
## First Sunday after Pentecost

The gospel reading for this Trinity Sunday is short but pithy. Jesus is summarizing how things will be when the Spirit of truth comes. This Spirit's message will be trustworthy, he says, because it will contain only what has been heard from Jesus himself. And Jesus' authority is equally impeccable. "All that the Father has is mine," he states, completing the circle. In this short passage Jesus also summarizes the important reason for trinitarian unity—it is for the purposes of glorifying and declaring the great truths of God.

The self-revelation of God as Holy Trinity is a most critical truth. How distant and impersonal is a faith that acknowledges only a powerful father-figure God! How flat and earth-bound is a faith that lives only by the moral teachings of an ancient rabbi! How fleeting and sectarian is a faith that relies only on inner voices and feelings! But how strong and unified is a faith that is rooted in the God revealed as Father, Son, and Holy Spirit!

We see the importance of a strong and unified message in many arenas—including worship. How flat and out-of-balance is any service of worship that tries to rely only on the spoken word, or only on musical performance, or only on gesture, or only on feelings. But, when brought together, their diversity and unity praise and proclaim with a stronger voice.

Our goals in worship—as in all of life—are praise and proclamation. Cooperation, humility, hard work, knowledge, skill, and passion are all important attributes for those who would assume leadership roles in worship. As each leader effectively carries out his or her own role, and as each person acknowledges the ministries of other competent leaders, a strong bond of unity and respect is created which better praises and proclaims the mystery.

As the festival portion of the church year gives way to the more "ordinary" part, we stand in awe of the God revealed and continuously reaffirmed as Father, Son, and Holy Spirit. We join our voices with Christians of every generation in one of the classic hymns to the Trinity:

> *Lord God, Almighty, unto thee be glory,*
> *One in three persons, over all exalted!*
> *Glory we offer, praise thee and adore thee,*
> *Now and forever.*
>
> "Father, Most Holy"

John 16:12-15

# *Proper 3*

## *Sunday between May 24 and 28 inclusive*
### *(if after Trinity Sunday)*

This Sunday's gospel is a continuation of Jesus' Sermon on the Plain as recorded by St. Luke. The proverbs and parables are numerous, and each one is a gem worth a lifetime of pondering. He teaches about the blind leading the blind, of teachers and students, of judging others and logs in eyes. Then he spends a bit more time talking about trees producing fruit. He tells of good trees and their good fruit, bad trees and their bad fruit, and their counterparts in human beings. "For it is out of the abundance of the heart that the mouth speaks," he summarizes.

We have often heard people speak exuberantly about their family, pets, jobs, vacations, hobbies, church, and, of course, their wonderful choir. You can tell from what they say and how they say it that they love and treasure the topic of conversation. It is as though they are bubbling over and would surely explode if they tried to hold in their enthusiasm.

It may not be as obvious, but this happens also with people who regularly spew out complaints and criticisms. It is as if their innards are pickled. Their words and actions are expressing the prevailing spirit that dwells in them, too.

Before we start to name names, we better return to that opening command to not stand in judgment of each other. For even positive people can have an occasional bad day, and even complainers are right sometimes! And nobody knows another's complete story. We best concentrate on ourselves, on the logs that are in our own eyes.

One of the ways we can respond to Jesus' words is to take a personal inventory. How do we think others really perceive us? More positive than negative? Do our unhelpful words, actions, or demeanor cancel out the good we may do in the choir or in our other ministries? How would we like to be remembered when we are gone?

Jesus is not encouraging a "put on a happy face" attitude; he wants honesty. But he does want our hearts to be full and our words to express it. We cannot by ourselves turn into such people; only the work of the Holy Spirit can do that.

Jesus chooses to end his sermon with the parable of the two houses, one built on a rock and the other on the ground. The picture is clear—hearing his words and acting on them is like building a strong foundation on the rock. With such a sure footing, we find that we are filled to overflowing with his presence. As Robert Lowry experienced it and expressed it in a hymn:

> *No storm can shake my inmost calm*
> *while to that Rock I'm clinging.*
> *Since Christ is Lord of heaven and earth,*
> *how can I keep from singing?*
> "My Life Flows On in Endless Song"

# Proper 4

## Sunday between May 29 and June 4
### (if after Trinity Sunday)

We humans get awfully caught up in rewards. If somebody receives something good, we may size up the situation and say, "I am so glad something good came to her, she is so deserving." Or we might just as likely think, "She sure got something better than she deserved." Conversely, when tragedy strikes, we are likely to offer our evaluations based on whether we feel the subjects deserved their fates or not. And mixed in with our evaluation of others is the tendency to keep track of our own records, to make sure we get what we feel is due us or even to deny ourselves rewards out of low self-evaluation. In light of such confusion, we can only be grateful that we are ultimately not in charge of evaluations and their resulting rewards and punishments.

Jesus tells us who really is in charge of such important matters. This Sunday we shall hear of a centurion who seeks healing from Jesus for one of his slaves. As a Roman, he is not deemed worthy to make the request on his own. Instead, Jewish elders go on his behalf to plead, "He is worthy of having you do this for him, for he loves our people, and it is he who built our synagogue for us." Those are quite impressive credentials, we must admit. Jesus must be intrigued, too, for he sets out for the centurion's house. But a surprising scene awaits his arrival. Friends are delivering the centurion's message which begins, "Lord, do not trouble yourself, for I am not worthy to have you come under my roof; therefore I did not presume to come to you. But only speak the word and let my servant be healed."

What a contrast between the picture painted by the elders and the centurion's self-portrait! Yet, both are based entirely on feelings of worthiness. Jesus cuts through the tangled webs of human evaluation and heals the slave. And instead of responding to anyone's "worthiness," he praises the centurion's radical faith.

Acknowledging Christ and his power to work wonders is more important than any scale of human worthiness we might invent. Only Christ is worthy—worthy of all praise and worship—and only he makes us worthy to stand in his presence and receive from his loving hands. As he has overlooked our own, self-made unworthiness, we strive to see others through the eyes of Christ. Hymnwriter Thomas H. Troeger puts such a prayer on our lips:

> Oh, praise inclusive love, encircling every race,
> oblivious to gender, wealth, to social rank or place:
> We praise you, Christ! Your cross has made us one!
> "Oh, Praise the Gracious Powers"

Luke 7:1-10

# Proper 5

## Sunday between June 5 and 11 inclusive
### (if after Trinity Sunday)

They don't get much better than this one! This Sunday's gospel has it all. There is a funeral procession, a weeping mother, a compassionate savior, a life-giving touch, a joyful reunion, and an active crowd who sees it all, responds to each step of the action, and spreads the word about what has taken place. All this in seven short verses!

If there were to be a stage or movie enactment of this miracle at Nain, we can be sure the action would center on Jesus, the widow, and her son. The crowd would surely take a role secondary to the main players. But are they present just for effect?

This crowd plays a major role in this story. Though they themselves are not at one moment dead and at the next alive, and though it is not they themselves that are childless at one moment and a parent again the next, they do experience the drama and see what this all means. Luke records their shouts. "A great prophet has risen among us!" and "God has looked favorably on his people!" are their cries. And they carry this story all around Judea and the surrounding country. The crowd could very well be responsible for this story being remembered and recorded.

Why is it that we can get so involved in a story that is not ours? How can even fictional characters involve us in their joys and sorrows? Because every story of life and death is about the human family and, consequently, about us. The crowd's cry was not just for the widow and her son and their happy ending. It was for themselves, for the sign of hope that God was breaking through to them and for them.

As a choir, we often get assigned the same role as that crowd. We are at times the narrator of the story, or the actor of a part, or the prompter of responses, or the director of the action, or the interpreter of the deeper levels of meaning. Sometimes we are just the stage and the scenery for others. But, whatever our secondary roles, we are primarily the subject of the dramas set forth in the great gospel scripts. We are those who grieve, those who rejoice, those who die, those who encounter Jesus, those who are resurrected. And, when we lift our voices, we sing as much to each other as we sing to the depths of our own souls the hymn of F. Bland Tucker:

> Awake, O sleeper, rise from death,
> and Christ shall give you light;
> so learn his love, its length and breadth
> its fullness, depth, and height.
>
> "Awake, O Sleeper"

Let us go about our supporting roles with the same vigor and passion we give our starring roles, proclaiming a God who breaks through time and space, acting with and for us.

# Proper 6

## Sunday between June 12 and 18 inclusive
### (if after Trinity Sunday)

Jesus had a radical way of dealing with women—he treated them with dignity and respect. His encounters with women seem revolutionary even today; we can only imagine how scandalous his words and actions were to those of his day and culture. This Sunday's gospel recounts some of these episodes, and included are some briefly described and one told in great detail.

Several women are accompanying Jesus and the twelve as they travel to villages and cities, proclaiming and bringing the good news of the kingdom of God. These women have something in common with each other, Luke says, for they have been cured of evil spirits and infirmities by Jesus. They cannot help but follow and serve this one who restored their lives to them.

An even greater story of healing and devotion is enacted in the first portion of this gospel passage. A woman comes to Jesus as he is eating, bathes his feet with her tears, dries them with her hair, kisses them, and anoints them with an expensive ointment. The host is appalled at this, for he knows this woman is a sinner. Jesus defends her presence and her extravagant tribute. She feels great gratitude to Jesus because he forgave her great sin. The others cannot understand, he says, for their lesser gratitude is in direct proportion to their lesser perceived sin.

The devotion of these women seems extravagant, careless, and even foolish to observers. But their response, too, is in proportion to the gratitude they feel. We can only imagine the magnitude of the changes Jesus must have wrought for them.

Jesus has some dramatic changes in store for us as well. We, too, can be forgiven much and see our lives change for the better. We, too, are capable of living lives of praise, proclamation, and service. We can know Christ's love and care in as real and radical a way as did these women of the gospel. We long for the eyes to see the great things Jesus does for us and for the faith to respond in boldness. A hymn by Marty Haugen is our prayer:

> *Healer of our every ill,*
> *light of each tomorrow,*
> *give us peace beyond our fear,*
> *and hope beyond our sorrow.*
>
> "Healer of Our Every Ill"

# Proper 7

## Sunday between June 19 and 25 inclusive
### (if after Trinity Sunday)

What is the measure of discipleship? Is it how much time we spend at our church, or how many roles we take in the parish? Is it being well-known for what we do? Is it official certification, consecration, or ordination? Is it simply a desire to be in the presence of Jesus? The closing verses of this Sunday's gospel tell of a man who begs that he might join up with Jesus, but Jesus sends him away! Who was this amazing man and how could he get such a response from the Savior?

This nameless man is known only by his affliction; he is a demoniac—one possessed by demons. His story is exotic, colorful, and full of excitement. He has been insane and has lived among the tombs for a very long time, and he wears no clothes. As he meets Jesus, the demons recognize the divine presence and fear their banishment. At Jesus' permission, the demons leave the man and enter a herd of swine, sending them over a cliff and into a lake. The crowds are amazed and frightened over such upsetting incidents, and they ask Jesus to leave.

At the quiet center of the chaos is the man, formerly possessed, now clothed and in full possession of his mind, sitting at the feet of Jesus. After such a rescue from such a tortured past, Jesus could have had in him a most ardent follower. Yet, this is the very man whom he sends away. How does he justify that?

"Return to your home, and declare how much God has done for you," Jesus tells him. There was no need for him to stay with Jesus—he had learned firsthand the powerful essence of the good news. His work was to be a disciple, all right, but his assignment was to be deployed into the community where his witness could do the most good. Luke records that he did go away, proclaiming throughout the city how much Jesus had done for him.

Worship and witness are once again tied together into one entity; telling the story and bringing the glory are simply not separable. A hymn by Ronald A. Klug shares this conviction:

> Come, celebrate; your banners high unfurling,
> Your songs and prayers against the darkness hurling.
> To all the world go out and tell the story
> Of Jesus' glory.
>
> "Rise, Shine, You People"

What is the measure of discipleship? Disciples are those who worship in their witness and witness in their worship, rising and shining with the light of Christ who still works wonders.

# *Proper 8*
## *Sunday between June 26 and July 2 inclusive*

D on't let your little mistakes turn into big ones," is a warning we may hear in choir rehearsal. "If something goes wrong just recover quickly and go on," the advice continues. Can we imagine what chaos would arise in a worship setting if, upon missing an interval, singers stopped to analyze what went wrong before continuing? Or what if we stopped and gave ourselves a reprimand for singing "through" when it should have been "though?" Our message would be quickly jumbled and our ministry interrupted. There is a time for drawing attention to mistakes, analyzing them, and working to eradicate them—it is called rehearsal. And there is a time for putting mistakes quickly behind us, overcoming them, and staying focused on the task at hand—it is called worship. To behave in such a way is not denying mistakes; it is putting them into perspective.

Jesus is giving some important lessons on perspective in this Sunday's gospel. As he and his disciples are traveling between villages, someone on the side of the road says, "I will follow you wherever you go." What a magnificent outpouring of loyalty! Yet, Jesus challenges what he sees as a "fair-weather" promise. Though even birds and foxes have places to call home, Jesus says he himself does not. Those who pledge their loyalty may not have a full perspective of what it entails. To others Jesus does issue the call, "Follow me." One says he will follow as soon as he buries his father; another needs only to go home first and say farewell. Jesus' response is shocking. "No one who puts a hand to the plow and looks back is fit for the kingdom of God," he states. What could he be saying in such harsh pronouncements?

Jesus is not teaching family values here; this is a message about discipleship. He is not just saying that working in God's kingdom is more important than minor things. He is saying that working for God's kingdom is even more important than major things— even more than those things which are in themselves good, such as honoring a loved one or showing care to those left behind. Following Christ means more than turning away from things that are bad or indifferent. We must be willing to place our loyalty above even our highest ideals.

Life is not something we get to rehearse before attempting the real performance, and the same is true of discipleship. Looking back can keep us from being fully functional for the present and fully focused for the future. Fortunately, we can rely on disciples around us to help us find our place in the score. And, most importantly, we have a Savior who is directing and cueing us in the glorious song which proclaims the loving kingdom of God. We pledge and pray with hymnwriter John E. Bode:

> *O Jesus, you have promised to all who follow you*
> *That where you are in glory your servant shall be too.*
> *And Jesus, I have promised to serve you to the end;*
> *Oh, give me grace to follow, my master and my friend.*
> "O Jesus, I Have Promised"

# Proper 9
## Sunday between July 3 and 9 inclusive

This Sunday's gospel is the exhilarating story of the seventy who are sent out at Jesus' command. He utters the poetic charge, "The harvest is plentiful, but the laborers are few; therefore ask the Lord of the harvest to send laborers into his harvest." The message is clear: There is much to do, there are not enough to do it all, it is God who does the sending, and it is surely God's harvest, not our own, into which we are called. Hymnwriter Erik Routley versified this call of Jesus:

> In your days of wealth and plenty,
> Wasted work and wasted play,
> Call to mind the word of Jesus,
> "Work ye yet while it is day."
> "All Who Love and Serve Your City"

Jesus' words not only call his disciples to action, they give instructions regarding luggage, sharing the peace, eating and drinking, curing the sick, proclaiming the kingdom, and responding to rejection. Furthermore, Jesus identifies their message with himself. Rejecting his messengers rejects Christ and ultimately the one who sent him.

Disciples ever since have felt these words true for them. We, too, see the magnitude of the harvest, feel the power of God's call for laborers, and sense the blessing on our ministry as we take part in God's harvest. Luke records that the seventy returned full of joy and pride in their accomplishments. Jesus shared their joy and congratulated the work successfully done in his name. But he gives one final bit of advice. "Nevertheless," he says, "do not rejoice at this, that the spirits submit to you, but rejoice that your names are written in heaven."

Does Jesus wish to take away the joy in ministering and the satisfaction we feel when our efforts achieve success? Not at all. But he knows more than anyone else that ministry is not always filled with joy and that efforts do not always produce measurable results. With his advice, Jesus is in reality paving the way for even deeper joy and greater satisfaction. Conditional joy, based on success, pales in comparison to the joy founded on God's unconditional acceptance of us. And that is a joy that can motivate us for ministry and get us through some otherwise joyless times.

It is much the same in our ministry of music. A commitment based on enjoyment will likely be short-lived. A commitment that is a response to God's loving call to us will be able to weather the seasons because it is based on something deep and unchanging. That is the kind of labor relations Christ wants for his workers. Let us rejoice in our call to be a part of his plentiful harvest.

# Proper 10
## Sunday between July 10 and 16 inclusive

Did you hear the one about the lawyer and the loophole? She promised her client she would work until she found one. And she kept her word; unfortunately the only loophole she ever found was at the end of a noose! Any lawyers who started to leave the choir room can come back now; it was only a joke and it is over. And we must confess that all humans have a tendency to look for loopholes, especially ones that help us escape from our nooses.

Jesus had an important conversation with a lawyer, and we shall hear about it this Sunday. Jesus is summarizing the law by holding up its two pillars: love of God and love of neighbor. The lawyer wants to justify himself, writes Luke, so he interrogates Jesus by asking, "And who is my neighbor?" Jesus must have suspected this question's intent was to find a loophole by narrowing the definition of neighbor. No such luck with Jesus! He responds with a story known to many as the parable of the Good Samaritan who takes care of a wounded stranger. The case is clear, beyond a reasonable doubt: Our neighbor is anyone who has a need.

The lawyer, along with everyone else who heard this parable at its premiere performance, must have felt a bit uneasy after hearing this verdict. There are some questions for which we would rather not know the answer. They probably saw people in need every day of their lives. How much more can we, through modern communications, be overwhelmed as we are faced every minute with the immense, aching needs all around the world. A hymn from Ghana addresses our global neighborhood:

> Neighbors are wealthy and poor,
> varied in color and race,
> neighbors are nearby and far away.
>
> "Jesu, Jesu, Fill Us with Your Love"

And, if that is not enough of a challenging call to action, what are we doing spending more time, energy, and money on choirs and rehearsals? Why worship at all when our call is so clearly to serve those in need? We may not be very good at it; we may need all our resources and more to be effective. How can we keep from becoming overwhelmed and frustrated?

There are more wise words in our hymn from Ghana. Its refrain keeps praying:

> Jesu, Jesu, fill us with your love,
> show us how to serve the neighbors we have from you.

And there are more wise words in the parable. By portraying the Samaritan as the merciful one, Jesus was choosing an unlikely hero in the eyes of his audience. But, by doing so, he has erased any reason for us to feel inadequate to the task. "Everyone can be great because everyone can serve," preached the Reverend Martin Luther King Jr. And everyone can serve because Christ shows us, frees us, energizes us, and empowers us through word, sacrament, prayer, song, and the companionship of fellow neighbors on our journey together.

# *Proper 11*
## *Sunday between July 17 and 23 inclusive*

If your choir is like most others, you have some individuals who can be counted on to look after the little details such as pencils, robes, attendance, lining up, filing music, and unplugging the coffee pot. You no doubt also have those who consistently work to improve their musical abilities, keep up on current trends in worship and music, help evaluate our effectiveness, and constantly forget to unplug the coffee pot! Many people have taken tests to help identify and label their styles and habits. Understanding our own drives helps us be more tolerant of others. Amidst all the different styles and habits among us, we do tend to get the task done. And, surely, understanding and tolerating others is a worthy, Christian attribute, isn't it?

Jesus puts a bit of a twist on this topic in Sunday's gospel. He is paying a visit to Mary and Martha. But, despite being sisters and carrying twin-like names, their dispositions are vastly different. Mary, basking in the presence of Jesus and learning much from his words, is reprimanded by Martha who has been stuck with all the work. When Jesus praises Mary for "choosing the better part which will not be taken away from her," he is delivering important advice. Surely all would agree that time spent with Jesus is far superior to time spent on frivolous matters. The "Marys" among us can feel vindicated by Jesus' pronouncement.

But the "Marthas" among us may feel a bit uneasy with such a slick answer. How do we know that Martha was doing trivial things? Perhaps Jesus and Mary ate heartily of the meal that she prepared. Perhaps the lamps that Martha filled illuminated the room so their discussion could continue past dark. Where would the dreamers be without the caretakers? How can we continue to improve our worship and music abilities if nobody remembers to unplug the coffee pot?

We "Marthas" hope Jesus did not mean to discredit our honest busyness or our attention to detail. We hope he was only putting priorities in order of importance and in sequence. For nobody is completely a "Martha" any more than anyone is exclusively a "Mary." Perhaps both Mary and Martha should have prepared ahead of time so they could both kneel at the feet of the master. Perhaps we all need to look after details and do our homework so that quality time and space is created for worship and meditation. Perhaps we all need to be "Marthas" in the choir room so we can be "Marys" in the pew. And perhaps we need to be reminded of the master's presence in both our busyness and our quietness. The ancient Irish hymn prays for us:

> *Be thou my vision, O Lord of my heart;*
> *naught be all else to me, save that thou art:*
> *thou my best thought by day and by night,*
> *waking or sleeping, thy presence my light.*
>
> "Be Thou My Vision"

(And, will somebody please remember to unplug the coffee pot?!)

# Proper 12
## Sunday between July 24 and 30 inclusive

Have you ever counted the number of times your congregation prays during a worship service? If you did, your count would probably vary widely from many others—even from those at the same service. Some would just tally the number of times we say "Amen." "Don't forget how many of our anthems and motets are prayers," vocalizes a choir member. "I offer the prelude as a prayer," the organist pipes up. "The tolling bells are the voice of prayer," chimes an usher. "Many passages of scripture are prayers," articulates a lector. "Look at all the prayers I lead," intones an assisting minister while previewing the service bulletin. "It is ordained that I lead the prayer of confession, collect, eucharistic prayer, and closing blessing," comments the presiding minister. Do each of these prayers count as one, or can they be multiplied by the number of all those present? How about the countless individual prayers made in silence? Does the number of prayers matter at all? Are we somehow more holy for praying more times?

If we look at worship as just a series of specific prayers interspersed with other non-prayer things, we are selling short both prayer and worship. We need to widen our definition of prayer beyond just those things that are called prayers and end with an amen. If prayer is open communication between God and us, then the entire worship service can be considered prayer and treated prayerfully. *The Book of Common Prayer* is the title of the major worship resource for churches in the Anglican fold, and many other traditions also use the terms "morning prayer" and "evening prayer." With such a vision of worship, our music preparation, singing of hymns, giving of offerings, receiving communion, and being sent forth can be as prayerful as those things that are called prayers and end with an amen. It is a vision we must learn, just as we must learn to utter our very first words of prayer.

Jesus' disciples had to learn to pray. Being in the holy presence of Jesus, they came to acknowledge the "God-shaped hole" in each of their lives. In this Sunday's gospel they utter an earnest plea that is a prayer in itself, "Lord, teach us to pray." And teach them he does, for after delivering the treasured words of the "Our Father" he goes on to tell parables of good friends and loving parents who give when they are asked.

James Montgomery penned many prayer-filled hymns. In one he gives us potent words to call on God:

> We perish if we cease from prayer;
> Oh, grant us power to pray.
> And when to meet you we prepare,
> Lord, meet us on our way.
>
> "Lord, Teach Us How to Pray Aright"

Let us learn to keep praying and pray to keep learning, taking up our part in the ongoing prayer of the church at worship, where only two or three are gathered, and in our solitude. The possibilities are countless!

# Proper 13
## Sunday between July 31 and August 6 inclusive

A member of one choir says to a member of another, "We have so many singers now that we have outgrown the choir loft, and we don't know what we are going to do!" "That's a nice problem to have," is the dry reply. "My choir has improved so much that I cannot find enough challenging music for them," one choir director brags to another. "My heart bleeds for you," is the sarcastic response. "I've spent much of the week meeting with financial consultants, and we still can't decide the best way to invest our endowment," complains one pastor. "I'd love to exchange problems with you for even one week," sighs the pastor of a struggling congregation. Empathy is surely hard to convey when what we feel is more akin to envy or even resentment.

In this Sunday's gospel Jesus tells of someone whose problems are ones we might like to have. A landowner has had such bountiful crops that he has no room to store the harvest. He plans to solve his dilemma by tearing down existing barns so he can build larger ones. Then he will be able to relax and make merry, knowing that his fortune and future are secure. Jesus calls the man a fool. But his fault does not lie in being too successful a farmer, or too wise a steward, or even too careful a planner. His fatal flaw is his preoccupation with his wealth, his anxiety over keeping it, and his presumption that life will be long and carefree as long as his fortune is secure. The man can neither predict nor prevent his imminent death, and his storehouses will do him no good. "So it is with those who store up treasures for themselves but are not rich toward God," Jesus concludes.

Measuring the richness we build up toward God is a much more complicated matter than keeping inventory of crops and cash. Many throughout Christian history have tried to put price tags on our acts of charity, prayers, offerings, and devotions, hoping thereby to keep track of deposits into our heavenly bank account. But our preoccupation with numbers is as futile in measuring heavenly treasures as it is counterproductive in hoarding earthly goods. Only God can grant riches; our wealth lies in becoming more and more aware of the grace God keeps applying to our treasure. Our acts toward God do not win our salvation; but our absorption with earthly matters can hinder our relationships with God, fellow Christians, and those whom God would have us serve. Harry Emerson Fosdick has expressed this teaching of Jesus in a prayerful hymn:

> Shame our wanton, selfish gladness,
> Rich in things and poor in soul.
> Grant us wisdom, grant us courage,
> Lest we miss your kingdom's goal.
>
> "God of Grace and God of Glory"

Let us not dwell on the number of our occupied choir chairs or on our level of achievement. Let us instead sing of Christ, who gifts us with treasure we cannot measure or even begin to comprehend. But that's a nice problem to have!

# Proper 14
## Sunday between August 7 and 13 inclusive

Ricky Ricardo, of the classic television show "I Love Lucy," was a master of the mixed metaphor. Whether he was burning his bridges before they hatched or counting his chickens behind him, he was usually able to make his point. His listeners had to struggle a bit to sort and realign the skewed images, but they enjoyed the wordplay, took delight in the unlikely combinations, and rose to the challenge of discovering his intended message. Words do indeed carry huge loads of potential meaning— they can confuse or enlighten, intrigue or bore, relieve or burden, delight or depress.

Our gospel reading for this Sunday is told, of course, in words; and the images they convey are numerous and concise. Jesus, addressing the people as his "little flock," tells them to make purses that do not wear out, that the unfailing treasure is in heaven, that no thief or moth can touch this treasure, and that our treasure and our heart dwell together. And these are just from the first few verses! The remainder of the lection continues to pile on the images in rapid-fire succession, barely giving us time to visualize one before another is presented. Maybe this reading is one we will especially want to revisit throughout the week, pondering each image individually and carefully.

One scene receives a bit more coverage than the rest. It is of slaves who are waiting in readiness for the return of their master. They are dressed for action, they have their lamps lit, and they are ready to open the door when he knocks. This part of the story we recognize from other places in the scriptures, and its message bears repetition. But the master in this story plans to do some amazing things when he arrives. "Truly I tell you," narrates Jesus, "he will fasten his belt and have them sit down to eat, and he will come and serve them." Even for a parable, this is no ordinary master. This master scandalizes society's protocol by becoming a slave to his very own slaves, elevating them to master status. His slaves must have had greater things to anticipate than those who were waiting for just a status-quo master. Their readiness would be more out of love than mere obligation, more out of hope than fear.

The parable is a beautiful one. It sheds new light on this radical God and on the nature of God's relationship with us. The hope and love we feel for such a master will shape our words, our songs, and our prayers. A hymn by Joseph R. Renville, drawing on Native American images, breathes the spirit of such a master-servant:

> Grant unto us communion with you, O Star-abiding One.
> Come unto us and dwell with us;
> with you are found the gifts of life.
> Bless us with life that has no end,
> eternal life with you.
> "Many and Great, O God, Are Your Works"

The story of Christ is in itself a very special mixed metaphor. How else can we even attempt to express a master serving his slaves, a people crucifying their king, a God dying and rising?

Luke 12:32-40

# *Proper 15*

## *Sunday between August 14 and 20 inclusive*

The music sung by most church choirs comes from many different traditions and many different eras. It is a practice that honors our ancestors in the faith, displays our rich heritage, celebrates God's work throughout history, embraces the larger family of faith, and, most importantly, proclaims anew a gospel that transcends culture, time, and place. Especially when singing music of the Western tradition, we usually like to know its era. Knowing that different styles call for different vocal and conducting techniques, we can render with greater conviction the flowing restraint of a Medieval chant, the refined reverence of a Renaissance motet, the contrapuntal vigor of a Baroque cantata, the buoyant clarity of a Classical mass, the emotional sensuality of a Romantic anthem, and the . . . and the . . . Just what is it that we can say about 20th-century music? Why do we have such a hard time trying to define our very own era?

There are at least two reasons for that. For starters, ours is an age of diversity and plurality, and we are intrigued by the past. We use music of all other eras, write new pieces in the styles of past eras, freely borrow from numerous sources outside the standard traditions, and still have room for some genuinely new sounds. A second reason why we cannot clearly label our era is that we are too close. We haven't the emotional and analytical distance that impartial judgment needs. We will just have to wait for another generation to evaluate us and give us a label that is accurate and, we hope, complimentary.

Jesus has some things to say about interpreting the times in this Sunday's gospel. He points out to the crowd how they easily predict rain when they see a cloud in the west and how they confidently brace for heat when they feel the wind from the south. What is wrong with them, then, that they cannot interpret the present time? His accusations are as scorching as the heat to which he alludes, and the blast crosses the centuries to singe us as well.

How does the present generation score in this matter of discerning the present and predicting the future? We have weather channels, election polls, economic indicators, computer projections, and psychic hotlines. We have data beyond our ancestors' wildest imagination, but we probably have made little gain in that commodity called "wisdom." It is hard to identify our packages' contents and even harder to judge them trivial or crucial when they are all wrapped up in shiny wrappings and glittery bows. We often evaluate our activities by the feelings they give us, our hymns by their popularity, our anthems by their covers.

Jesus left no easy answers to this dilemma, just the charge to strive for wisdom, to struggle for truth , and to stay close to the One who holds the answers. We confess and profess with the words of hymnwriter Martin Franzmann:

> *Weary of all trumpeting, weary of all killing,*
> *weary of all songs that sing promise, nonfulfilling,*
> *We would raise, O Christ, one song: we would join in singing*
> *that great music pure and strong,*
> *wherewith heaven is ringing.*
> "Weary of All Trumpeting"

# *Proper 16*
## *Sunday between August 21 and 27 inclusive*

Each and every time we assemble for worship there is a spirit of anticipation in the air. We gather in response to the divine command and call, out of our need to be surrounded by the presence of the Holy Trinity and all the saints, and in expectation that we will depart as changed, healed, forgiven, empowered people. A hymn by Isaac Watts, sometimes sung with additions by Robert Lowry, calls us together for such an encounter:

> *Come, we that love the Lord,*
> *and let our joys be known;*
> *join in a song with sweet accord,*
> *and thus surround the throne.*
>
> "Come, We that Love the Lord"

Yes, what a great gift is the Lord's day! May we always give it our best efforts, take advantage of its power, and protect its integrity.

Jesus had many things to say about the Sabbath and the practices he found in place. By word and example he affirmed its importance, but he had some changes to make and some priorities to adjust. Of all the laws that were in place at the time, the restriction against healing on the Sabbath was the greatest source of friction between Jesus and the religious leaders. It was one he openly and repeatedly defied; for this was one rule that was not merely bothersome. It stood in complete opposition to divine intent, stifling the witness of God.

The recipient of Jesus' Sabbath healing in this Sunday's gospel is a woman, crippled and bent over for eighteen years. At Jesus' touch she is healed, stands up straight, and praises God. The synagogue's leader immediately criticizes the incident and points to the other six days when it would have been lawful. Jesus' response is short but pointed. Even animals may be untied and led to water on the Sabbath, he reasons. "Ought not this woman . . . be set free from this bondage on the Sabbath day?" His argument was convincing then and it still resonates today. What could be a more noble blessing or a higher calling for our day of worship? In the word and sacraments, absolutions and intercessions, songs and assembly, we proclaim, pray, and embody that freedom from bondage which Christ grants.

How blest we are to be channels, witnesses, and even recipients of the freeing acts of God! But are there times when we could be better disciples? Might we at times be hindrances to freedom, defenders or even builders of barriers?

For many, our worship spaces may be sending a message that only the physically fit are expected to attend regularly, hear and see clearly, or commune easily. For many, our leadership roles and language style may be sending a message that one gender represents the reign of God better than the other—or even exclusively of the other. For many, our musical styles may be sending a message that an educated aesthetic—or the complete lack of it—is the preferred language of the gospel.

May God forgive us for the bondage we tolerate, heal us of our own crippling afflictions, and empower us to live and proclaim God's Sabbath of grace and freedom.

Luke 13:10-17

# *Proper 17*

## *Sunday between August 28 and September 3 inclusive*

There is an awful lot of eating going on in Luke's Gospel. Even when Jesus' parables, miracles, or discussions did not specifically pertain to a meal, Luke faithfully pointed out when they took place in such a setting. What's the big deal? How can we stay on our diets if we keep hearing about banquets? Didn't we come to church to resist temptation? What's in a meal, anyway?

Perhaps many of our meals are eaten alone, or in a hurry, or surrounded by strangers, or while we work, walk, or drive. Such meals serve only to fend off hunger and to fuel us up for the rest of the day. But, even if they are no longer commonplace in our lives, we all know of a different type of meal. These special meals are events in themselves, usually to celebrate or commemorate. For this type of meal the expectations are highly detailed and extremely important. The menu must be creative and unique, the food plentiful and exquisite, the guest list customized and scrutinized, and the seating plan intentional and symbolic. One other thing hasn't changed much over eras and across cultures—eating together implies acceptance, and it sets a seal on those who participate.

Jesus' mealtime discourse, as told in this Sunday's gospel, sounds more like a lecture on etiquette. "Do not sit down at the place of honor," he advises, but "go and sit down at the lowest place." It is an honor to be invited to a place of higher honor, but a disgrace to be told to move lower, he says. It is yet another reminder of the servant attitude he wants for his disciples, and it points to the reversal of roles between God's kingdom and the world's ways.

Then he goes on to address the host and, in reality, each of us. "Do not invite your friends or your brothers or your relatives or rich neighbors," he says. If they can afford to repay you, then you haven't really given of yourself. Instead, invite those who have no possible hope of ever repaying. Only then is generosity noble and selfless.

Following Jesus' command would accomplish many beneficial things. For starters, the outcast would literally be fed and there would be less hunger in the world for one night. But that much can be accomplished anonymously and from a safe distance, without any real impact on the giver or any promise for the future. We must put this teaching back in its setting at the banquet hall, complete with expensive food and drink, the best china and silver, seats of honor, and the presence of a gracious host who invites and welcomes, honors and serves.

Jesus is surely teaching about actions in this lesson, but he is also asking us to discern our motives. Do we ever do good things in the hope that good will proportionately come our way? Do we come to worship in order to get a warm feeling rather than to glorify God and edify our neighbor? Are we in choir for the recreation of singing and might we leave if it no longer fits our needs? We pray for pure motives and clear actions in a hymn by Marty Haugen:

> *Give us to drink the wine of compassion,*
> *give us to eat the bread that is you;*
> *nourish us well, and teach us to fashion*
> *lives that are holy and hearts that are true.*

"Here in This Place"

# Proper 18

## Sunday between September 4 and 10 inclusive

Are there any among us who cannot recount a time when we began a project, discovered there was more to it than we anticipated, and then abandoned it? If you are like most folks, you too have your unfinished scrapbooks, unused kitchen organizers, piles of unspread mulch, even uncompleted rooms and garages. Such unfinished projects, especially if visible to the neighbors, tend to embarrass us. Sometimes we may wish we had never started the project at all.

Jesus tells us in this Sunday's gospel to consider two persons who risk a similar predicament. First, there is one who wishes to build a tower. He estimates the cost of the project so he can avoid any ridicule should he be unable to finish it. Secondly, there is a king who, before going to war, makes sure he can follow through lest he have to surrender in shame. Is Jesus just giving good advice on saving money, saving time, and saving face? Hardly! For these examples are wedged between some of his hardest sayings on discipleship. "Whoever comes to me and does not hate father and mother, spouse and children, brothers and sisters, yes, and even life itself, cannot be my disciple," he warns.

Count the cost, Jesus is telling us. Discipleship is not a casual diversion or even a major commitment. It is total. Few of us can truthfully sing the hymn by Frances Ridley Havergal that begins:

> Take my life, that I may be
> Consecrated, Lord, to thee;
>> "Take My Life, that I May Be"

other than as an ardent prayer for the way we would like to be.

> Take my silver and my gold,
> Not a mite would I withhold . . .

doesn't sound like a very glamorous way of life. So we settle into a degree of comfort and commitment that seems to match those around us. Being lukewarm may not be hot, but isn't it better than all those outright cold people we see every day? Isn't occasional worship attendance better than none? Isn't halfhearted choir participation better than never coming at all?

Jesus' answer might surprise us. Let's get back to those characters he spoke about in his story, and let us consider the neighbors of the tower-builder and the enemy of the war-wager. Avoiding their ridicule was a major concern in the decisions to proceed or abort their respective projects. Are they not like the unchurched with whom we come into contact every day? When asked about their decision to remain unchurched, their reason is often that the Christians they see are rather lukewarm and unconvincing. The minute those around us know of our church membership or our involvement with a Bible study or a choir, we become to them a picture of the church. What a marvelous opportunity to share the infectious joy of commitment! What a crushing blow if the faith they witness through us is bland, halfhearted, or even objectionable. This view of Christianity may keep them from ever digging deeper.

Count the cost, Jesus says. I want you as my disciples; and I want you to know the fulfillment of total commitment, not only for yourselves, but for the sake of the whole world I have redeemed.

# *Proper 19*

## *Sunday between September 11 and 17 inclusive*

In this Sunday's gospel we hear the Pharisees and scribes murmuring because Jesus "welcomes sinners and eats with them." They mean it as an insult; Jesus takes it as a compliment and says so in several parables. The first is about a man who cannot find one of his hundred sheep, and the second is about a woman who loses one of her ten coins. In both instances, the owner searches diligently for what is lost, finds it, and rejoices. Thus, says Jesus, there is great joy in heaven over one sinner who is found—even more than over those who were never lost.

Though this hardly seems like a fair response, we can see once again how Jesus has used a very realistic example to make a point about the kingdom. Does not the turning around of a wayward child cause even more joy than one who never left the fold? In the church and even in our music programs, do we not tend to shower our greatest attention on those members who are new or newly activated?

But there is a flip side to these examples. What about those 99 good sheep, those nine coins that never left the purse, the faithful child, the committed choir members? Along with the prodigal son's brother we may feel a bit bent out of shape for the oversight. Is the silent majority to be taken for granted?

There is yet one more message we can glean from these parables. In both the sheep and the coin episode, the owners call together their friends once they find that which was lost. "Rejoice with me, I've found the lost!" is their cry. It is hard, if not impossible, to celebrate alone. We want to be surrounded by our friends, knowing that sharing joy does not divide it—it multiplies it. Jesus reminds us that rejoicing is a community function. We in the church need to think, act, and rejoice as the one body that we are—the body of Christ.

Before we get too self-righteous about being the "in" crowd, we should note that we may be playing more than one character in these stories. What is found is not just someone else—often it is us. We place great trust in the hymnic words of Erdmann Neumeister:

> *Jesus sinners will receive.*
> *Even me he has forgiven;*
> *And when I this earth must leave,*
> *I shall find an open heaven.*
> *Dying, still to him I cleave—*
> *Jesus sinners will receive.*
>
> "Jesus Sinners Will Receive"

Yes, Jesus welcomes sinners and eats with them. Let our joy at finding and being found erupt in the continuous and endless song that fills the dwellings of God.

# *Proper 20*
## *Sunday between September 18 and 24 inclusive*

In the business world we often hear of those who are called "detail people." They are the ones counted on to find and fix all the loose ends, the little details, those things not usually even noticed unless they are amiss. Companies like to find a happy balance of workers where some dream big and some dwell on the little, for such a combination will surely complete excellent work.

In a choir there are those who are leaders and those who are happy to be followers, but one thing is very different here. All must be detail people in a choir; even a small voice can be heard if it enters too early or releases too late, if it dwells too long on that ending consonant or sings through a rest. Little details can't make up for poor singing, but they sure cause a lot of distraction when they are not in order.

So it is with faith, Jesus says in this Sunday's gospel. Tucked in between his complicated parable about the dishonest steward and that memorable pronouncement, "You cannot serve both God and wealth," is a short but weighty proverb. "Whoever is faithful in a very little is faithful also in much; and whoever is honest in a very little is dishonest also in much," he states.

Isn't Jesus being a bit too picky? Even in the church doesn't much get accomplished because some are the prime movers and some are the detail people? As long as the work gets done can't we let a few details slide for others to pick up? In choir we can stagger our breathing on those long phrases. Can't we fill in another's shortcomings as they do ours?

Jesus calls for integrity in each and every individual, not just in a community average. He calls us to live justly toward others and faithfully toward God. Yet, these words may be more than just a command. He seems to be stating as a fact that those who are faithful in a very little are faithful also in much, and that those who are dishonest in a very little are dishonest also in much. Truly, dishonesty infects even the little details of life; likewise, faithfulness grows until it permeates the entire being. There is little room for dishonesty where faith resides, even in its far corners.

To produce a good choral sound is not within the capability of any one singer. We each do our part, surround ourselves with others who share the same goals and calling, and follow the lead of one who is trustworthy. Likewise, it is not within human ability to produce a life of perfect faithfulness. Certainly, we work and pray for faith to fill our every cell, but it is ultimately only through the grace of Christ that faith matures and grows to consume ever more of us. In every detail of our lives we strive to know God more clearly and serve God more fully. We give thanks for the gracious gifts of faith in a hymn translated by Catherine Winkworth:

> *All depends on our possessing*
> *God's free grace and constant blessing,*
> *Though all earthly wealth depart.*
> *They who trust with faith unshaken*
> *By their God are not forsaken*
> *And will keep a dauntless heart.*
>
> "All depends on Our Possessing"

# *Proper 21*
## *Sunday between September 25 and October 1 inclusive*

Have you ever heard people telling of their religious experiences? God's presence was made so vivid to them that it has had an impact on the rest of their lives. "How lucky," comments those who feel their spiritual lives have taken a more level and pedestrian path. "It must be a real boost to have a sign that is so convincing and inspiring. If we had that kind of experience we would surely get more involved in the church and the world. With that kind of assurance we would definitely turn our lives around and give of ourselves more freely." And so we wait and watch for revelation to come, comfortable in the conviction that our Christian response seems to be pretty much in proportion to the inspiration we feel we have been given. That same attitude can affect us in our church choir, too. The big festivals thrill and energize us, but tepidness may set in when we realize not every day can be Christmas, Easter, or Pentecost.

To this Jesus speaks in this Sunday's gospel. We will hear the parable of a rich man, traditionally named Divies but unnamed in Luke's account, who lived a sumptuous life. He was oblivious of the poor man, Lazarus, who begged at his gate. After their deaths, their stations were switched. Lazarus finds himself in the bosom of Abraham, Divies in the torments of hell. Only then does Divies show some concern for others, asking if someone could go to his still-living brothers to warn them of the fate that awaits them unless they repent. "If someone should go to them from the dead," he reasons, "they will surely believe them."

Abraham's response? "If they do not hear Moses and the prophets, neither will they be convinced if someone should rise from the dead." Surprising? Certainly! Sad? Yes! True? Regrettably so! It is a human tendency to be oblivious of the obvious, to overlook the daily reminders of God's power and Christ's presence while we wait and watch for some extraordinary revelation which may or may not come.

The Body of Christ is clearly present here and now. In the annual rhythm of the church year; in the daily and weekly assemblies of word, sacrament, song, and prayer; and in every gathering of Christ's people; we have the opportunity to celebrate and learn from One who has come back from the dead. Perhaps the divine presence is so predictable that we take it for granted. Perhaps we are too occupied with ourselves to notice. Perhaps we come expecting so little that we ask for nothing. At these times we must admonish ourselves, "If God seems far away, guess who moved!"

Christ is the constant giver, the constant presence, the one who awakens our awareness and awaits our response. With hymnwriter Martin Schalling, and with poor man Lazarus, we pray:

> *And then from death awaken me,*
> *that these mine eyes with joy may see,*
> *O Son of God, thy glorious face,*
> *My Savior and my fount of grace*
> *Lord Jesus Christ, my prayer attend, my prayer attend,*
> *And I will praise thee without end.*
>
> "Lord, Thee I Love with All My Heart"

Luke 16:19-31

# *Proper 22*

## *Sunday between October 2 and 8 inclusive*

Don't many of our frustrations come as a result of someone else's behavior? Children may not behave as we wish, spouses may not do their share of household projects, colleagues at work may not contribute as much creativity as they could, members of a choir may be sporadic in attendance, overly talkative, or inattentive. Perhaps an even greater frustration sets in when we realize that we are often powerless to control others. We do our best to influence, coerce, and even manipulate others—and on occasion these tactics may even work—but we must admit that we can never completely control another person. We may wish we could rig these folks up on strings and we could be the puppet-masters. Or we may wish we could replace them all with robots and put ourselves in charge of the control panel!

Do we ever feel that way about ourselves? We knowingly sigh with St. Paul as he laments, "I do not do what I would like to do, but instead I do what I hate" (Romans 7:15). At some of our deepest soul-searching times have we ever wished that God would take complete control of all our actions and even our thoughts? We could surely please God more if we were not in control. We wistfully sing John E. Bode's hymn:

> *Now speak to reassure me, to hasten or control;*
> *Now speak and make me listen, O Guardian of my soul.*
> "O Jesus, I Have Promised"

One of the most precious, yet most painful, gifts we can give to a child, a spouse, or a close friend is freedom. Freedom demands a willingness to risk pain and even loss, but it is borne ultimately out of love—a love so strong that it wants in return only a love which is offered willingly. A love that loves out of freedom is the only love worth having.

So it is with God—that supreme parent, spouse, and colleague—who has made us neither robots nor puppets, but individual beings capable of thinking, responding, and loving. God knows that not all will return that love and serve the kingdom, but those who do love and serve out of their freedom are worth the price.

Jesus tells us about free, loving response in this Sunday's gospel. In this parable the servants do the job of serving their master just as a matter of course. No "thank you's" are even expected because, as one servant puts it, "we are only doing what is our duty."

Each day is full of choices of varying size and importance. In all our freedom, may we be ever mindful, appreciative, and responsive to the God who loves freely and sets us free to serve and adore.

# *Proper 23*
## *Sunday between October 9 and 15 inclusive*

This Sunday we will hear the gospel account of ten men who suffered with leprosy. After Jesus healed them, only one returned to thank him. How selfish of the other nine, we may conclude. We would surely have made the extra effort to go back and thank the one who gave such a great gift. But, before we criticize the other nine, we might want to consider their situation. After years of disease and ostracism, they were granted a new lease on life. All thoughts surely turned to celebration and enthusiasm for the possibilities that suddenly lay ahead. The story doesn't tell us where the other nine went in such haste, but we can imagine that they ran to their homes, families, and friends—people and places from which they had been severed with no hope of reunion. Their failure to stop and thank Jesus was not necessarily selfish or thoughtless; it was just not as respectful as Jesus and we might have wished.

Gratitude is an amazing commodity. Attitudes can completely turn around when a proper "thank you" is given. After doing something for someone, the absence of gratitude can sour the atmosphere, turning a favor into a grudge or even a debt. Yet, if we receive a simple "thank you," we are transformed. "Don't mention it; it was nothing." What a change of attitude, just because of two words!

Jesus told the grateful man, "Rise up and go your way, your faith has made you well." Does this imply that the other nine did not have faith, or that they might even regain their disease due to their ingratitude? Certainly not! God does not work that way, we sigh in relief, or we'd all be stricken. Jesus' pronouncement was a reminder to the thankful one. His simple act of returning to Jesus had brought him many blessings. His conscience was cleansed, his humility was encouraged, his faith was praised, and his future was blessed. His thankful spirit was the catalyst for meeting the Christ, and now this one who had freed him from his physical and social prisons freed his conscience as well. There was no debt to remunerate, no required paybacks to perform—just the grace-filled command, "Rise and go your way." He could return to this moment and draw from its power for the rest of his life. After he uttered his gratitude in words, he no doubt lived it in attitude and action.

So it is with the rest of us. The healing granted to us in baptism is not dependent upon our show of gratitude, but, how richly we are blessed and empowered as we return to our baptisms in confession and profession, in singing and signing, in attitude and gratitude. As it is expressed, thankfulness blesses both the giver and the receiver. Hymnwriter Michael Saward expresses this for us:

> *Baptized in water, sealed by the Spirit . . .*
> *thankfully now God's praise we sing.*
> "Baptized in Water"

One more thing before we move on: for your ministry of music in this place and for your presence here at this time—a very big thank you!

# *Proper 24*
## *Sunday between October 16 and 22 inclusive*

This Sunday we shall hear and consider the parable of a persistent woman and a judge. The woman continuously and insistently appealed to the judge until he finally ruled in her favor. It was not for the sake of compassion or justice that he ultimately acted; he granted vindication merely for his own peace of mind.

Pesky people with pesky problems can do that to us. Children learn early that persistence always wears down and often pays off. And Dagwood Bumstead isn't the only one who tries to fight with but eventually buys needless items from door-to-door salesmen just to get rid of them. How about in choir? The things the director keeps harping about might be quirky or extremely important, but we often conform just so we can move on. "Get rid of that "R" sound! Hang up your robes! Be quiet during the prelude! Watch for cutoffs! Smile!"

As strange as Jesus' parable may seem at first, he has again chosen a convincing image that transfers well across cultures and centuries. It may be disappointing to hear that pesky people with pesky problems will always be with us, but there is much more to appreciate in this vignette.

First of all, the woman was well aware that she did not hold the power or authority to obtain her vindication. She carried no delusions of her own abilities. But she was just as solidly aware of the identity of the one who did hold such power, and she wisely invested her time and energy into a passionate campaign. Jesus has made his point, and he closes the story by asking, "And will not God grant justice to his chosen ones who cry to him day and night?"

Even though we may be able to see the realism in this parable and be encouraged in our prayer, it still bothers many that Jesus was comparing God to an unrighteous judge. Does God eventually answer prayer just to get some peace and quiet? That makes God seem a bit more human than we'd like.

In many of his parables which compare the human and the divine, Jesus made declarations which began, "How much more . . ." and that dynamic is at work in this scene as well. If persistence to an unrighteous judge paid off, how much more will our prayers and pleas be heard and granted by the God of perfect righteousness. Keep praying for justice and do not lose heart, Jesus tells us. How and when God will answer is not for us to predict. But that God *will* answer is a conviction worth the investment of our time, energy, trust, and our very lives. Carolina Sandell Berg wrote poetically of such a faith in a hymn:

> *Oh, what joy to know that you are near me*
> *when my burdens grow too great to bear;*
> *oh, what joy to know that you will hear me*
> *when I come, O Lord, to you in prayer.*
> *Day by day, no matter what betide me,*
> *you will hold me ever in your hand.*
> *Savior, with your presence here to guide me,*
> *I will reach at last the promised land.*
>
> "Day by Day"

And don't forget to smile, put away your music, and watch the pesky director!

Luke 18:1-8

# *Proper 25*
## *Sunday between October 23 and 29 inclusive*

A question to ponder: Is membership in a church choir a blessing or a burden? Before you answer, consider some facts. Choir members get to wear special vestments, have reserved seating, and get to command the congregation's attention during the worship service. Yet, choir members are usually asked to make many extra trips to the church, spend even more time at the busiest seasons of the year, seldom get individual praise, and are usually the last to reach the refreshments. Our question again: Is membership in a church choir a blessing or a burden?

The answer is likely to be "yes," for choir membership calls us to both an exalted and a humble state. Exalted because we adorn and help to lead the worship of Almighty God; humble because we are often reminded that we are less than perfect in the presence of this God. Exalted because we explore and keep alive the church's vast treasury of liturgy, poetry, and song; humble because our own individual contribution is rather small by itself. Exalted because our visible participation encourages others to commit more deeply in their particular ministries; humble because our own motivation may not be as pure as we would like, and our idiosyncrasies may actually be hindrances to some. To make matters even more complicated, we sometimes exalt ourselves for being so good at humility!

Which attribute does Jesus want for his disciples? This Sunday's gospel contains an answer in parable form. It is about a tax collector and a Pharisee who went to pray. "I thank you that I am not like the others," gloats the Pharisee. "God be merciful to me, a sinner!" prays the tax collector. Jesus has painted a rather clear picture of the situation. Though the Pharisee may indeed have led a life more holy than the other, and though the tax collector may indeed have had more sins separating himself from God, it was their level of honesty which Jesus wanted us to notice. Delusion contaminates; coming clean is a crucial step toward becoming clean.

Jesus is not calling us to deny our gifts or hide our worthy accomplishments; false modesty and inferiority complexes are not humility. His type of humility was so hard to explain because it was so opposite of the ways of the world. Finally, he had no other recourse but to show us through his life of humble service, through his death of selfless love, and, only after all that, through the resurrection and exaltation granted to him by the Father. A hymn from Japanese Christian Koh Yuki contemplates the humble Christ:

> *Visiting the lone and lost, steadying the tempest-tossed,*
> *Giving of himself in love, calling minds to things above.*
> *Sinners gladly hear his call; publicans before him fall,*
> *For in him new life began; this is he. Behold the man!*
>
> "In a Lowly Manger Born"

Neither humility nor exaltation are within our own grasp; both are gracious, costly, intertwined gifts from the one who lived the purest form of humility and won the highest state of exaltation. But his humble nature is still intact, and he still dwells among us to caringly bless our burdens and to lovingly burden us with blessings.

# Proper 26

## Sunday between October 30 and November 5 inclusive

Short people of the world, rejoice! For this Sunday is our high holy day. In this Sunday's gospel we will hear proclaimed the encounter between Jesus and the vertically challenged Zacchaeus. And it's a great day for fans of sycamore trees, too, for one of them was honored to assist Zacchaeus to see and meet his Savior. Those who are less passionate about trees, along with those who breathe the air of the higher stratospheres, are still welcome to come and celebrate with us gnomes on our special feast day.

Of all the interesting aspects of this charming story about Zacchaeus, the charisma and power of Jesus stands out. What force drove Zacchaeus to run ahead and climb a tree? Did he not know that his dishonest nature might clash head-on with the righteousness of the Savior? Was his desire to see Jesus a statement in itself of confession? Regardless, his life is changed from their encounter, and Jesus has used the opportunity to make visible his divine work of discerning souls, forgiving sins, and renewing lives. As the crowd grumbled, "He has gone to be the guest of one who is a sinner," Jesus must have rejoiced. Hallelujah! They noticed!

Hymnwriter Johann Horn put us up in the tree with Zacchaeus with short, six-syllable phrases:

> Once he came in blessing,
> All our ills redressing;
> Came in likeness lowly,
> Son of God most holy;
> Bore the cross to save us;
> Hope and freedom gave us.
>
> "Once He Came in Blessing"

Great things often come by way of small words, small deeds, and small messengers. Is this devotion over already? Yes, it was a short one!

# Proper 27
## Sunday between November 6 and 12 inclusive

We are near the halfway point between last Easter and next Easter. For church musicians, that's a good place to be. We are long-recovered from the extra demands of that feast of seasons, and we have a while yet before we need to finalize details for next year's celebration. Even though we understand how each Sunday is a "little Easter," the big spring festival is still pretty much packed away these autumn days. These last Sundays of the church year are dealing much more with death, destruction, and the end of time. Yes, we're quite a far distance from Easter.

The Sadducees do have "resurrection" on their lips in this Sunday's gospel, but they are voicing it only in an attempt to trick Jesus into disproving it. He dismisses their shallow questions, affirms the faith of those who do believe in the resurrection, and goes on to tell even more. Those who have died in faith he calls angels, children of God, and even children of the resurrection. To God, they are not even considered as dead but rather as alive. "Now he is God not of the dead, but of the living," is his memorable synopsis.

"God of the living"—what a great title! And how central to our faith to know that this God dwells with us in our earthly lives, struggles with us when we face death, and stays with us even when the world considers us dead and forgotten. This is the jubilant faith we sing in Samuel Medley's hymn:

> He lives and grants me daily breath;
> He lives, and I shall conquer death;
> He lives my mansion to prepare;
> He lives to bring me safely there.
> "I Know that My Redeemer Lives!"

Yes, these November Sundays deal plentifully with death, destruction, and the end of the world. And that is precisely why the Easter theme is making a comeback. Easter may spend its springtime planting crops and flowers, but it returns full force in the autumn to tend to the ripening fruits and dying leaves.

Our worship and its music these Sundays must rise to the occasion. Those facing their own deaths must hear gospel promises from the victorious God of the living. Those who have lost someone must hear the gospel consolation from the God who considers the dead alive. Those who are yet untouched by death or decay must hear the gospel warnings from the God who knows and holds our future. And all those who are under the rule of Christ must proclaim the great gospel truths that render all else worthless.

We are indeed between Easters. We inhabit a point somewhere on the time line between that first resurrection day and the final, cosmic Easter. For children of the resurrection, it's a great place to be!

# Proper 28

## *Sunday between November 13 and 19 inclusive*

Many musicians are terrified at the prospect of improvising, especially on short notice. Organists will long remember the terror they felt when a draft blew their music shut while they were playing, or when their assistant turned a page too early! Singers get a bit nauseous when they remember the time the inner page of their octavo went sailing over the balcony rail. Soloists still shudder to think of that time when they forgot the text of a song they thought they had memorized. What were those strange words they made up, again? We try to predict and prepare for things that might happen; it's the truly unimaginable moments that leave us grasping for lost chords and creating new languages.

The church is hearing and proclaiming some special teachings of Jesus these latter days in the church year. He is describing the final days of the earth as we know it, and the sights and sounds he describes are beyond our comprehension and imagination. "All will be thrown down," he says, and he tells of impostors, wars, earthquakes, famines, plagues, portents, and some great signs even from heaven. Then he gets personal, and says that we will be arrested, persecuted, and handed over to rulers. Then we will get the opportunity to testify, Jesus says.

Hold the phone! What is this he slipped in about testifying in defense of ourselves and the faith? Even the earthquakes, wars, and impostors don't sound so bad compared to this potential disaster.

Jesus knows how we handle pressure and how we fear going on stage without a script. "I will give you words and a wisdom that none of your opponents will be able to withstand or contradict," he assures us.

Choir members know what it is like to have others put words into their mouths. They receive their scripts every time they pick up their hymnals and choir folders. And choir directors need not create every word they provide for the choirs and congregation. We sing the very words of holy scripture, the prose and poetry of God's people from every age and place, and new creations that manifest the continuing inspiration of the Holy Spirit. Their words do not replace ours; their voices become our voice as we discover and bear witness with them to the great truths of God. Even now we have a foretaste of the great things we are privileged to utter in the name of Christ. For that future time, we need not worry about our eloquence, our improvisational skills, or our effectiveness under pressure. Christ knows the score intimately, and he promises to conduct us from introduction to coda, cueing every note and rest. We can sing with confidence the hymn by Dietrich Bonhöffer:

> *By gracious powers so faithfully protected,*
> *so quietly, so wonderfully near,*
> *I'll live each day in hope with you beside me,*
> *and go with you through every coming year.*
> "By Gracious Powers"

Luke 21:5-19

# Christ the King
## Last Sunday after Pentecost
### Proper 29

The long Pentecost season comes to a close this Sunday when we will celebrate the festival of Christ the King. We have been hearing these many weeks about Jesus' ministry of preaching, teaching, and healing, and he has been equipping his disciples to do the same. He seems to have been quite at home on this earth, and we have come to appreciate his humanity. It has been awhile since we heard even passing references to the more dramatic events and divine aspects of Jesus' life. In spite of some difficulty with the royal and patriarchal metaphors, it will be good to celebrate Christ as king so we can, figuratively, put him back on his throne.

We will hear this Sunday of the kingdom and of its king who rules the earth and will come again to sit in judgment and glory. We will, no doubt, also sing of this king, perhaps in the words of hymnwriter Edward Perronet:

> Let every kindred, every tribe
> On this terrestrial ball
> To him all majesty ascribe
> And crown him lord of all.

"All Hail the Power of Jesus' Name!"

But we will be unfaithful if we do not let the gospel reading define the day. Divorced from any trappings of hierarchy, royal protocol, or gender is this king who hears soldiers saying, "If you are the King of the Jews, save yourself!" This king is offered sour wine and is heckled by the crowd. The makeshift sign over this king only mockingly reads, "This is the king of the Jews." The royal attendants of this king are two criminals, and to one of them he promises, "Today you will be with me in paradise." This king is being executed on a cross, wearing a crown of thorns.

The church in different times and in different places has emphasized the cross and the crown of Jesus in different proportions and configurations. Truly, both concepts are necessary to speak faithfully of Christ, and both help us understand the human experience and condition. Only a faith that confesses a Savior who is both crucified and exalted is worth proclaiming and living. Christ has not merely told us of crosses and crowns, he has shown us.

And so we end one church year and begin another in the name of this king who has made his home with us so that we may find our homes in his grace-filled presence.

# LESSER FESTIVALS
# & OCCASIONS

# SEASONAL PRAYERS

# Of Saints and Angels, Apostles and Martyrs

*Ye watchers and ye holy ones,*
*Bright seraphs, cherubim, and thrones,*
*Raise the glad strain: "Alleluia!"*
*Cry out, dominions, princedoms, powers,*
*Archangels, virtues, angel choirs: "Alleluia!"*

"Ye Watchers and Ye Holy Ones"

How vast is that cloud of witnesses who escort us through our lives, encourage us through our deaths, and stand ready to welcome us when we take our place among them. The church keeps their witness present to us on both a weekly basis and in a yearly cycle. At each eucharist we unite in prayer ". . . with the church on earth and the hosts of heaven," praising God's name and joining their unending hymn of "Holy, Holy, Holy Lord." And we honor many of these faithful messengers also on their special day each year. Their diversity is enriching; their stories are inspiring; their witness is empowering.

Just who are some of these who make up the cloud? Many are Jesus' disciples, apostles, and evangelists. As Jesus' call touched Andrew, Thomas, Peter, Matthias, Philip, both Jameses, Barnabas, Bartholomew, Matthew, Simon, Jude, and even Paul, Mark, and Luke, their lives were changed, and our hope is revived as their stories are told. We cringe at the tales of their martyrdom and of the high cost of discipleship to them and also to Stephen, John the Baptist, and the anonymous Holy Innocents of Herod's day and all innocent victims ever since. We envy the tender relationships Jesus shared with John, Mary Magdalene, Joseph, and his mother Mary, and we crave that closeness. We are intrigued by St. Michael and all the angels, long to know more about their exotic world, and sharpen our eyes to recognize God's messengers among us.

Yet, in spite of the magnitude of this cloud of witnesses, there is a special place for each of us. It is not merely a reserved seat for the future, it is for us here and now. We take our place in the cloud whenever we profess the faith for which they struggled, echo their proclamation, and lose ourselves with them in praise and prayer.

That cloud of witnesses is, essentially, a choir. Yes, they offer grand choruses that reflect God's great glory, and they sing songs that more modestly proclaim the incarnation. But, just as our choir serves in various roles, so does that grand group of cloud singers. They, like us, are prompters. By their example and through their leadership, others are encouraged to join the song. By their witness we know we are not alone, and we are humbled and honored to share the choir loft with them.

That hymn stanza by J. Athelstan Riley calls on all the angels to raise the glad strain. He goes on to invoke Mary, the "bearer of the eternal Word" to lead us in her Magnificat. Then the patriarchs, prophets, martyrs, saints triumphant, and the holy twelve are encouraged to raise the strain. Finally, all God's friends are invited to join the song. Just what does a cloud of witnesses sing when we get together? It goes like this:

*To God the Father, God the Son,*
*And God the Spirit, Three in One:*
*"Alleluia! Alleluia! Alleluia! Alleluia! Alleluia!"*

# The Presentation of Our Lord

Much of the church year follows a chronological order. It gives a sense of continuity and progression to tell the story of Jesus' life in the order it happened. We follow him from conception to birth, from childhood to baptism, from the first joyful moments of his ministry to his bitter end, from his resurrection to his ascension, from the sending of his Spirit to his promise to come again.

But in addition to this chronology, we treasure another order of days that sometimes determines what we will proclaim and ponder in our worship. Since the earliest days of the church, these special days have been faithfully and rhythmically punctuating the year; and many observances go back further than the seasonal pattern itself. That is why, after three weeks of considering Jesus' baptism and early ministry, we might feel in a time warp as we return this week to a scene only 40 days after his birth. The setting is the temple at Jerusalem;. the occasion is the Presentation of Our Lord.

Mary and Joseph are fulfilling the laws of their faith as they bring their firstborn son to the temple. They are there to make sacrifices and present their child to the Lord. But other faithful eyes and welcoming arms are there that day, too. Anna, the 84-year-old prophet, and Simeon, a righteous and devout man, have not given up on God's promise to send the Messiah. They instinctively know the identity of this infant, exclaim the news to all present, offer thanks to God, and prophesy the destinies of this child and his parents. Simeon's emotional song is beautifully recorded by St. Luke. Christians ever since have treasured the "Nunc Dimittis" both as a liturgical canticle and in numerous hymn versions. One by Ernest E. Ryden sings:

> O Lord, now let your servant depart in heavenly peace,
> For I have seen the glory of your redeeming grace:
> A light to lead the Gentiles unto your holy hill,
> The glory of your people, your chosen Israel.
>
> "O Lord, Now Let Your Servant"

The account of the presentation is so effectively related by Luke that we feel as if we are there. In a way, that is the powerful message of the presentation 2,000 years later. For we, too, have seen the Lord's salvation. We, too, praise God for the gift of salvation, for opening our eyes to recognize the divine presence, and for placing in our mouths the beautiful and powerful words and music to proclaim God's work among us. Now we, like Anna and Simeon, can peacefully leave behind our lives, for all else pales in the bright light of God's generous gift of salvation.

# Corpus Christi

Most Christian festivals celebrate important events in the life of Christ, of those near to him, or of his church. The Holy Trinity is the most universal of another type of festival which celebrates instead an important tenet of the Christian faith. It is not merely a theology or a doctrine that is explained these days, however; these are times to lift up truths that are so ubiquitous that we take them for granted, so rich in scope that we often slight them, so mysterious that we fear to address them. It takes a special people with a special faith in a special God to come together and celebrate Corpus Christi—the body of Christ. The faith traditions which celebrate this unique festival hold one important thing in common—the conviction that Christ is truly present in the bread and wine of the Eucharist.

What could be simpler than bread and wine, yet what could be more complex than the eucharistic theologies and practices that spring from them? What could be more unifying than eating and drinking together in the presence of the Lord; yet what could be more divisive than the bitter disagreements that have plagued and divided the church for generations? Our willingness to fight over the issue points out its extreme importance to us; our failure to overcome our schisms points out our desperate need for the forgiveness it brings. Yes, we need the eucharistic presence of Christ frequently and continuously. And we need a eucharistic festival to lift up our minds in awareness, our eyes in recognition, our voices in praise, our hands in acceptance, and our lives in witness.

Each of the three gospel readings for the Corpus Christi cycle is a rich source for contemplation and proclamation. We hear one time of living bread and the eternal life that is granted to all who eat. At another time we hear Jesus' words instituting his holy meal. At still another time we hear of the miraculous feeding of 5,000, the meagerness of the provisions, and the magnitude of the leftovers. Each speaks of something extraordinary that happened at Jesus' command, and each speaks of a miracle that continues, at his bidding, to bless us.

As the bread and wine are brought to the assembly and prayed over, they are treated with great reverence. For they will be for us the presence of Christ. Oh, that we would seek that same integrity in all that we offer—our actions, our language, our music, our art. For the incarnate God has taken the things of this world, blessed them in dignity, broken them for service, and given them in love.

It is no mere coincidence that the eucharistic bread and the assembly who eats it carry the same title—the body of Christ. For we are what we eat, and we ask only that we too be taken, blessed, broken, and given for the glory of God and in service to others. We embody the prayer from the second-century *Didache*:

> As grain, once scattered on the hillsides,
> was in this broken bread made one,
> so from all lands your Church be gathered
> into your kingdom by your Son.

"Father, We Thank You"

Keep coming, Lord, and keep blessing, loving, forgiving and feeding us—your body.

# Holy Cross Day

Fort McHenry in Baltimore, Maryland was the setting for Francis Scott Key's "Star-Spangled Banner." Every year on June 14 one can witness there an especially impressive event. By the hundreds, people of all ages meet, are given their assigned color of red, white, or blue, and go to stand in a specific place on the rectangular field. The gigantic, living U.S. flag which they form is impressive to all who view it from afar or see the aerial shots that appear on television and in the papers. Though they themselves cannot even see the symbol they helped to form, the participants say it is a most meaningful experience. By coming together and focusing their attention and energy on the same goal, great things are accomplished. How treasured is the flag and all it represents, and how special it is to actually be the symbol! They cannot become such a flag on their own, so the cooperation of the community is of extreme importance. And they keep coming back, year after year, to the "Living Flag Day."

In millions of churches, Christians gather regularly to experience that which is greater than themselves. And they often assemble in a configuration that shapes them and expresses the central symbol of their faith. How meaningful it is to not only see the cross, but to actually be the cross! As they assemble, they are made more aware of their role as the body of Christ. They need each other to help form the symbol, for none can do it by themselves. And it bears repeating.

Though the cross is seen, signed, sung, and spoken numerous times at every Christian gathering, a special day called "Holy Cross Day" is observed by the church each September 14. We need to be reminded of all the complex truths that are contained in this simple geometric shape. Crosses are literally everywhere. Some are intentional—such as the cruciform shape of many churches, religious decorations, and jewelry. But what about those "unintentional" crosses—utility poles that bring us energy and communications, the white jet streaks that intersect and bless the sky, alto and soprano melodies that travel into each other's territory and surprise us with their bold, unexpected timbre? Crosses are indeed plentiful; if we fail to get the message it is surely not from lack of exposure. Perhaps the problem is just the opposite—we have domesticated an instrument of execution and atonement into a pretty decoration.

How can we keep the cross plentiful in its representation yet potent in its message? By staying close to Christ's story and his own cross-talk. In the gospel for Holy Cross Day we hear his prophecy, "Just as Moses lifted up the serpent in the wilderness, so must the Son of Man be lifted up." We proclaim Jesus to be the Crucified One as well as the Glorified One, for they are inseparable in his life, mission, and identity. As we strive to be faithful messengers we lift up the cross and crown to proclaim the Christ who bore them. George Kitchin and Michael Newbolt gave the church a hymn to strongly proclaim:

> O Lord, once lifted on the glorious tree,
> As thou hast promised, draw us all to thee.
> Lift high the cross, the love of Christ proclaim
> Till all the world adore his sacred name.

"Lift High the Cross"

# Reformation Day

Well, here it is, time to once again celebrate the Reformation. Time to dust off the red paraments, tune the organ, and strain a few vocal chords singing Martin Luther's hymn:

> A mighty fortress is our God,
> A sword and shield victorious.
> He breaks the cruel oppressor's rod
> And wins salvation glorious.
>
> "A Mighty Fortress"

As glorious as that hymn is, its reputation as the "battle cry of the Reformation" has to be modified a bit now that it has entered the hymnbooks of most Christians denominations—even those against whom it was originally sung! Does that change this hymn's impact on us? Has the battle cry become a canticle of peace? Has the festival of the Reformation outlived its usefulness, as some have suggested?

It has if it is the occasion for any type of triumphalism or any elevating of self by putting others down. It has not if we treasure the Reformation as a precious gift and a challenge to realize that those who celebrate it the most are called to live it the most. Maybe in addition to the rousing Reformation hymns we should be singing "Let there be reform on earth, and let it begin with me."

The Reformation brought God's word and sacraments more fully to the people. The church was not to be simply the storehouse and occasional dispenser of God's grace; it was to be the ever-open channel through which God reached each and every individual soul.

Of all the verbs used in the scriptures to define the action of God's word—such as hearing, receiving, or listening—none is as dramatic as that in John's Gospel. This Sunday we will hear the words of Jesus, "If you continue in my word, you are truly my disciples." Not just hearing or reading, not just for occasional stretches even if intense, but to be continuing in God's word is our call.

It is said that the Reformation's hymnody sang God's word directly and forcefully into the very hearts and minds of the people. What a great testimony to the power of hymnody! What an awesome responsibility! Christians place high expectations on hymns, music, liturgy, preaching, praying, and the sacraments because we have witnessed their power to bring the gospel to the hearts and minds of the people.

A faith that both the heart and the mind can accept is one that, with the work of the Holy Spirit, will become an integral part of each believer. When gifted with that kind of faith, we come closer to being continually in God's word. That is the kind of faith that keeps us singing and believing, renewing and reforming, steadfast in the conviction that the kingdom is ours forever.

# All Saints Day

What a special day it is when we celebrate the Festival of All Saints! We thrill to the strains of Vaughan Williams' strong tune "Sine Nomine" and William W. How's colorful text as we sing:

*For all the saints who from their labors rest,*
*All who by faith before the world confessed,*
*Your name, O Jesus, be forever blest. Alleluia!*

"For All the Saints"

We picture the saints of days gone by—those who lived in Old Testament times, those who knew Jesus when he lived on earth, the early church leaders, those who brought about reforms. They answered the call and God made them great and famous examples for all generations. Nathan Söderblom once said, "Saints are those who make it easier for others to believe in God."

In worship, and especially in the Eucharist, the limits of time and space are transcended and we are made one with Christ's church of all times and in all places. We experience a foretaste of the feast to come when all the saints will gather with God. Our jubilant music assists in experiencing the festivity of the day; and our gentler sounds help to recall those now gone, console those still feeling the pain of separation, express longing for the hereafter, and ponder the mysteries of life and death. Such richness we hope to convey to others and to experience ourselves this All Saints Day.

In some years, the gospel reading for All Saints is the dramatic story of Lazarus. We receive the news of his death, witness a Savior who mourns and weeps, lament with Mary and Martha over their brother, hear Jesus' command to "Come out!", witness the bound figure walking toward us, and rejoice over life restored. Lazarus and his sisters did not experience the resurrection that day, for they eventually had to face death once again. But how differently they must have viewed death from that point on! They had been treated to a glimpse of glory, a foretaste of the feast to come.

In other years, we will hear Jesus call many persons "blessed." Are they the giants in the faith? The ones he chooses to point out instead are the poor, the mournful, the meek, the hungry and thirsty, the merciful, the pure in heart, the peacemakers, the persecuted. Once again Jesus has taken our limited perspectives and turned them upside-down.

In God's heart there is a special place for the "little people," the least of our sisters and brothers. Jesus has told and shown us that over and over, yet we often get it wrong. How often does not even the church say or imply that the children, the elderly, the single, the childless, or anyone "different" are somehow the exception to the norm? We may need to look deeper into the eyes of the least of these saints to see and believe in God, but God is truly there, nonetheless, crucified and risen.

In all aspects of our church life—in education, fellowship, outreach, worship, and music—let us keep God's pronouncement in clear view. The blessed are surely those whom we revere as saints of God. But the blessed are no less the little people, known sometimes only to the God who weeps for them. Through them we can see and believe.

# Concert Time

**M**any church musicians avoid using the term "performance" to describe what we do at worship. We fear that it places too much attention on the messenger when it should be focused on the message. A performance mentality in worship shifts our priorities from ministering to entertaining, our expectations from faithfulness to flashiness, our roles from channels of grace to "putting on a happy face."

But there are times when we should accept and even embrace our vocation of performing. For God's great gifts of prose and poetry, melody and harmony, and voices and instruments are too abundant to keep behind church doors. Though always rooted in the church's worship, their wealth of energy, joy, and exuberance cannot help but spill over beyond our times of worship into our times of concerts and, yes, "performances."

"What works will you perform?" is a question often asked of us when we are preparing for a concert. The listeners may want to prepare themselves to receive our offerings as we prepare ourselves to give them. Jesus was asked the same question. John records that a crowd called out, "What signs are you going to give us, then, so that we might see it and believe in you? What work are you performing?" (John 6:30). They had witnessed Jesus performing many works of healing and other miracles, and they had come to expect it of him. In this instance he tells them of the bread of life, of the life that it will give, and of himself, blessed, broken, and given for the life of the world.

Our performances give praise to the Lord of Life, honor those musical messengers of past days, bear witness to the creative Spirit who ever inspires new creativity, and declares to the world the power, grace, and peace of God. We add our voice to the song that began at creation and will continue into eternity. A hymn by Wayne L. Wold:

1. *God is praised in music ancient; liturgies and chants and hymns*
   *show a God beyond our culture, greater than our passing whims.*

2. *God is praised in music modern; new, creative textures, sounds*
   *show a God beyond our limits, broader than our human bounds.*

3. *God is praised in music humble; simple, honest melodies*
   *show a God who dwells among us, sharing joys and miseries.*

4. *God is praised in music mighty; organs, choirs, and instruments*
   *show a God beyond our knowing, larger than our measurements.*

Refrain  *Let us then make music boldly, as an offering true and strong.*
*God is praised, proclaimed, and honored as we join the eternal song.*

# Seasonal Prayers

## Advent

Stir up our hearts, O God,
to prepare the way for the Savior of the world.
Let our song be the voice of a herald
announcing the coming of the dawn,
that your people may abound in hope
while awaiting the day of Jesus Christ, your Son, our Lord.
**Amen**

## Christmas

Glory in the highest be to you, O God,
for you have come among us bringing peace.
Make your home in our hearts,
and let our songs be bearers of the Word,
that your people on earth may join the angels in adoring you,
with your Son and the Holy Spirit, one God forever.
Amen

## Epiphany

Blessed are you, O God,
for the gift of music that crowns our joy in your never-ending love.
Reveal your presence in our hearts,
and teach us to sing with all the peoples of the earth
the glory of your just and holy reign;
through Jesus Christ, who is Light from Light forever.
**Amen**

## Lent

Merciful God, in your great compassion
you forgive our sin and sustain us with your bountiful Spirit.
By the grace given to us in baptism,
renew your image in our hearts,
that our mouths may proclaim your praise;
through Jesus Christ, our healer and redeemer.
**Amen**

## Holy Week/Three Days

In the midst of the congregation we will praise you, O God,
for you bring us with Christ through the flood of death into an endless life.
Fill our hearts with love for you and for one another,
that in our song we may tell the victory of the cross
and bear the light of Christ,
who is our salvation, our life, and our resurrection.
**Amen**

## Easter

Mighty and gracious God, you are our strength and our song;
you have raised us with Christ to become a new creation.
Be known to us in the breaking of the bread,
and by your Holy Spirit ignite our hearts with joy,
that we may join with saints and angels to make the vault of heaven resound;
through Jesus Christ, who lives with you and the Holy Spirit forever and ever.
**Amen**

## Season after Pentecost I (Summer)

God of all creation,
you visit the earth and provide for the needs of every living thing.
Nourish our hearts that we may grow in faithfulness,
and let our voices echo the hills and meadows that shout for joy and sing.
We pray in the name of Jesus Christ, the Bread of life.
**Amen**

## Season after Pentecost II (Autumn)

O God, you gather us into one from our scattered places;
you send us into our labors to bring forth good fruit.
With grateful hearts we offer to you the gift of music that is your blessing first to us.
Use us to sound your living word,
that your people may go out gladly to reap the fullness of justice and mercy;
through the Lord of the harvest, your Son, Jesus Christ.
**Amen**

## Season after Pentecost III (November)

Holy God, you are the end and the beginning;
you are fount of every blessing and our eternal home.
In life and in death, refresh our souls with the music of Jesus' name.
Tune our hearts to sing with all the saints
the wonder of your grace and the hope of endless glory;
through the same Jesus Christ, who rules in love
with you and the Holy Spirit, one God, now and forever.
**Amen**

## Church Musicians and Artists

God of majesty, whom saints and angels delight to worship in heaven:
Be with your servants who make art and music for your people,
that with joy we on earth may glimpse your beauty,
and bring us to the fulfillment of that hope of perfection
which will be ours as we stand before your unveiled glory.
We pray in the name of Jesus Christ our Lord.
**Amen**